SHADOW OF THE DICTATORS

TimeFrame AD 1925-1950

EUROPE

TimeFrame AD 1925-1950

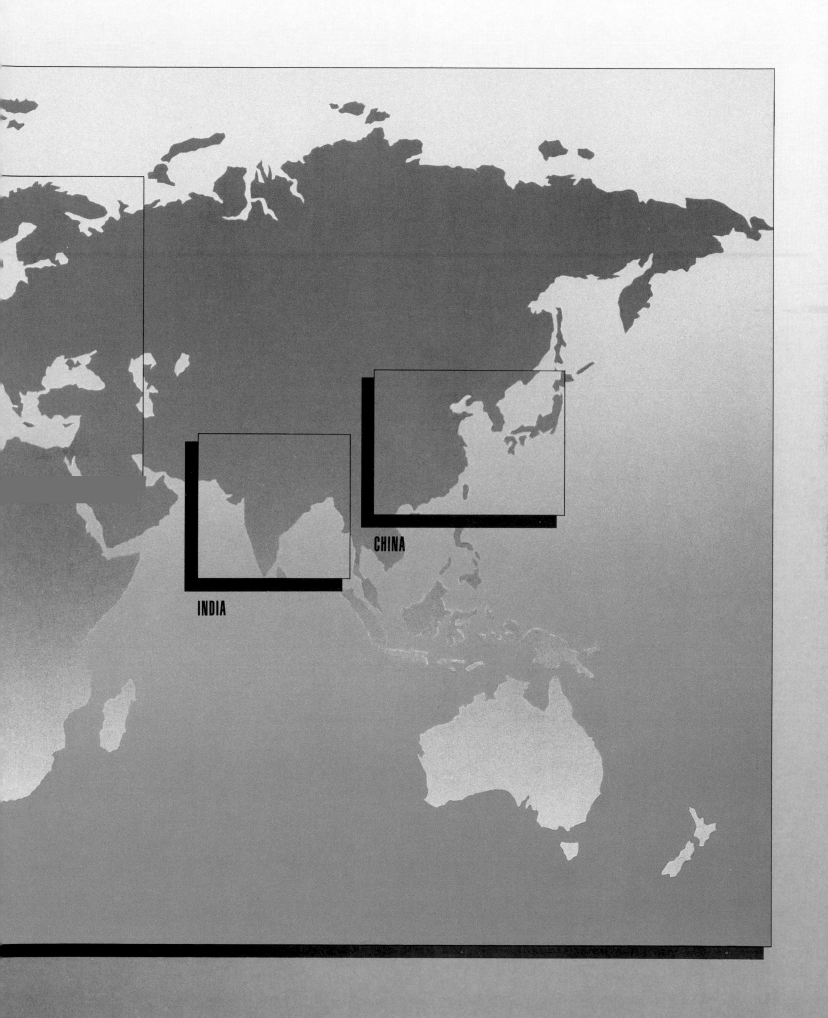

INDIA

CHINA

This volume is one in a series that tells the story
of humankind. Other books in the series include:
The Age of God-Kings
Barbarian Tides
A Soaring Spirit
Empires Ascendant
Empires Besieged
The March of Islam
Fury of the Northmen
Light in the East
The Divine Campaigns
The Mongol Conquests
The Age of Calamity
Voyages of Discovery

SHADOW OF THE DICTATORS

TimeFrame AD 1925-1950

BY THE EDITORS OF TIME-LIFE BOOKS

TIME-LIFE BOOKS, ALEXANDRIA, VIRGINIA

Time-Life Books Inc.
is a wholly owned subsidiary of
TIME INCORPORATED

Editor-in-Chief: Jason McManus
Chairman and Chief Executive Officer:
J. Richard Munro
President and Chief Operating Officer:
N. J. Nicholas, Jr.
Editorial Director: Richard B. Stolley

THE TIME INC. BOOK COMPANY

President and Chief Executive Officer:
Kelso F. Sutton
President, Time Inc. Books Direct:
Christopher T. Linen

TIME-LIFE BOOKS INC.

EDITOR: George Constable
Executive Editor: Ellen Phillips
Director of Design: Louis Klein
Director of Editorial Resources:
Phyllis K. Wise
Editorial Board: Russell B. Adams, Jr.,
Dale M. Brown, Roberta Conlan,
Thomas H. Flaherty, Lee Hassig, Donia
Ann Steele, Rosalind Stubenberg
Director of Photography and Research:
John Conrad Weiser
Assistant Director of Editorial Resources:
Elise Ritter Gibson

EUROPEAN EDITOR: Sue Joiner
Executive Editor: Gillian Moore
Design Director: Ed Skyner
Assistant Design Director: Mary Staples
Chief of Research: Vanessa Kramer
Chief Sub-Editor: Ilse Gray

PRESIDENT: John M. Fahey, Jr.
Senior Vice Presidents: Robert M.
DeSena, James L. Mercer, Paul R.
Stewart, Joseph J. Ward
Vice Presidents: Stephen L. Bair, Stephen
L. Goldstein, Juanita T. James, Andrew
P. Kaplan, Carol Kaplan, Susan J.
Maruyama, Robert H. Smith
Supervisor of Quality Control: James
King

Correspondents: Elisabeth Kraemer-Singh
(Bonn); Christina Lieberman (New York);
Maria Vincenza Aloisi (Paris); Ann
Natanson (Rome). Valuable assistance
was also provided by: Betty H.
Weatherley, Robert H. Wooldridge, Jr.
(Alexandria, Virginia); Jane Walker
(Madrid); Felix Rosenthal (Moscow);
Robert Nickelsberg, Anita Pratap (New
Delhi); Elizabeth Brown (New York);
Michael Donath (Prague); Ann Wise
(Rome); Dick Berry (Tokyo); Traudl
Lessing (Vienna).

PUBLISHER: Joseph J. Ward

TIME FRAME
(published in Britain as
TIME-LIFE HISTORY OF THE WORLD)

SERIES EDITOR: Tony Allan

Editorial Staff for *Shadow of the
Dictators:*
Editor: Windsor Chorlton
Designer: Lynne Brown
Writers: Douglas Amrine, Chris
Middleton
Researchers: Paul Dowswell, Caroline
Lucas, Caroline Smith
Sub-Editor: Christine Noble
Design Assistant: Rachel Gibson
Editorial Assistant: Molly Sutherland
Picture Department: Patricia Murray
(administrator), Zoe Spencer (picture
coordinator)

Editorial Production
Chief: Maureen Kelly
Production Assistant: Samantha Hill
Editorial Department: Theresa John,
Debra Lelliott

U.S. EDITION

Assistant Editor: Barbara Fairchild
Quarmby
Copy Coordinator: Colette Stockum
Picture Coordinator: Robert H.
Wooldridge, Jr.

Editorial Operations
Copy Chief: Diane Ullius
Production: Celia Beattie
Library: Louise D. Forstall

Special Contributors: James Chambers,
Ron Coates, Alan Lothian, John Man
(text); Stephen Rogers (research); Roy
Nanovic (index).

CONSULTANTS

General:
GEOFFREY PARKER, Professor of Histo-
ry, University of Illinois, Urbana-
Champaign, Illinois

Europe:
DENIS MACK SMITH, former Senior
Researcher Fellow of All Souls College,
Oxford University, Oxford, England

The World at War:
H. P. WILLMOTT, Senior Lecturer,
Department of War Studies, Royal Mili-
tary Academy, Sandhurst, England

General and India:
CHRISTOPHER BAYLY, Reader in Modern Indian History, St. Catharine's
College, Cambridge University, Cambridge, England

China:
DENIS TWITCHETT, Gordon Wu Profes-
sor of Chinese Studies, Princeton
University, Princeton, New Jersey

**Library of Congress Cataloging in
Publication Data**

Shadow of the dictators: time frame AD 1925-
1950 / by the editors of Time-Life Books.
   p.   cm.—(Time frame)
  Bibliography: p.
  Includes index.
  ISBN 0-8094-6483-7.—ISBN 0-8094-6484-5
(lib. bdg.)
  1. History, Modern—20th century.
I. Time-Life Books. II. Series.
D443.S4678 1989
909.82—dc20   89-4992
                       CIP

Time-Life Books Inc. offers a wide range of fine
recordings, including a *Rock 'n' Roll Era* series.
For subscription information, call 1-800-621-
7026 or write Time-Life Music, P.O. Box C-
32068, Richmond, Virginia 23261-2068.

CONTENTS

THE GREAT DEPRESSION

"The fundamental business of the country is on a sound and prosperous basis," insisted U.S. President Herbert Hoover, speaking in the wake of Black Thursday, October 24, 1929, when panic gripped New York's Wall Street. The stock market had crashed, as 13 million shares were sold in one day's trading, and millions of investors suddenly found themselves destitute.

On the face of it, there was reason for Hoover's optimism. The United States had enjoyed a decade of unparalleled prosperity, with four years of surging "bull" markets pushing the New York Times stock index from 110 points at the beginning of 1924 to 331 in January 1929. Thousands of ordinary Americans had grown rich by investing in the country's thriving new industries. Although the events of Black Thursday were worrying, there seemed no good reason why the future should not be every bit as prosperous. Wall Street had shaken off the effects of serious crashes in 1893 and 1907, and it had overcome a severe setback in the early 1920s.

This time, however, there would be no quick recovery, for despite Hoover's reassurances, economic problems had been growing over the years. Prices for grain exports, a major source of U.S. wealth, had been falling for more than a year, driven down by competition from Europe. At home, there were signs that American workers, flush from years of wage increases, had bought just about all the consumer goods they wanted. Yet despite low demand, industry was still expanding.

The stock market, too, had been spoiled by success. Thousands were buying "on margin"—borrowing heavily to acquire stock, certain they could repay their loans from the handsome profits they expected to make on resale. With money pouring in, the market grew from strength to strength, buoyed up by its own self-confidence. But a moment had to come when the market could no longer float on euphoria alone.

The first signs of impending trouble became apparent more than a month before Black Thursday. The market began to falter in the first week of September, rising and falling unpredictably, unnerving a public familiar only with unbroken boom. By the middle of the next month, it was obvious that the market, while still uncertain, was on a gradual downward trajectory, and on October 21, the fall steepened. By Black Thurday, anxiety had turned to blind panic and investors sold as fast as they could.

Over that weekend, a chorus of eminent bankers, economists, and industrialists echoed Hoover's statement of confidence, but their soothing words, and intervention by the big banks to support prices, checked the momentum of the crash only momentarily. Within days, the banks themselves were joining in the selling. Many slid into bankruptcy, dragging with them some of America's greatest corporations.

The collapse of financial confidence was to affect all America. Millions of workers lost their jobs during the following months. Hoover had no answers to the problem. Although his administration eventually intervened to help tottering businesses, which usually only prolonged their agony, he was opposed to state welfare payments, believing that they would destroy self-reliance. As a result, the urban unemployed went hungry, unable to pay for food, while farmers across the country were left with livestock and crops they could neither sell nor afford to maintain.

And so the slump continued, until by 1933, more than 13 million Americans were unemployed, the ranks of the urban poor swollen by a massive influx of jobless agricultural workers. In the cities, armies of homeless people were reduced to living on the streets, begging, and sleeping under old newspapers—"Hoover blankets."

The effects of the crash were soon felt beyond the borders of the United States. The outside world had benefited from the years of American prosperity; Europe's industrial nations, especially Britain and Germany, had found a ready market in the booming United States—as had Japan. But the reduction in U.S. demand soon took its toll on exports, and Hoover's attempts to shield the domestic economy by setting up virtually impregnable tariff barriers worsened the situation, plunging the rest of the world into a nightmarish spiral of unemployment, poverty, and hunger. Protectionism backfired on the United States, however, because the impoverished foreign countries could no longer afford to buy American goods.

One of the few industrial nations to escape the Great Depression was Stalin's isolationist Soviet Union—although its citizens, caught up in the economic turmoil of the First Five-Year Plan, faced deprivations that were worse than any being experienced in the West. Elsewhere, political extremism—desperate remedies for desperate ills—flourished in all its forms. The United States was racked by industrial strife, and communism found increased support. Insensitive, dogmatic interference from distant Moscow, however, prevented any real consolidation.

Communism and the Left gained ground in Europe as well, but they were soon overshadowed in Germany by nazism, Adolf Hitler's ultraright nationalist movement. Reparations, imposed on Germany by the victors of the Great War, became an increasingly crushing burden as the world depression grew worse. Adolf Hitler, who for years had been a little-heeded prophet of doom, now gained credibility, his direst predictions all apparently coming true. On the other side of the world, Japan, too, was veering to the right, its military enraged at the straits to which liberalism and foreign trade had brought them.

Toward the end of the 1930s, the massive public-spending program of President Franklin Roosevelt's New Deal began to take effect, bringing the promise of renewed growth in the United States and of recovery for the world economy. The measures came too late, however, to redeem the deteriorating political situation. By then the world was already sliding inexorably toward war.

Only a few newspapers made the Wall Street crash a front-page story. Newspapers in the leading financial centers, New York and London, were unruffled—or strove to give that impression. But London's *Daily Mail*, in its continental edition, made the crisis headline news, and in the United States, the *Philadelphia Inquirer* reported the panic while attempting to present an optimistic gloss. The hoped-for upswing failed to materialize, however, as a sobering follow-up story from the Worcester, Massachusetts, *Evening Gazette*—printed the following Monday—indicates.

Unable to afford proper lodgings, homeless men in Berlin slump in exhaustion over a rope provided by a flophouse landlord.

Cattle gather around a trough on a prairie-state farm devastated by drought.

A street scene in a Tokyo slum conveys the despair felt by Japan's rural immigrants.

As the Depression deepened in the 1930s, it brought hunger and misery to town and country alike across the globe. In the Midwest, the severe economic problems were compounded by natural disaster in mid-decade, when freak winds following a scorching drought carried off the over-cultivated topsoil, turning nine million acres of the Great Plains into a Dust Bowl and badly damaging another 80 million. All over the world, ever-growing numbers of people joined the drift away from rural areas, searching for employment in the big cities. Unlike the countryside, the cities offered at least the hope of opportunity, however illusory. But the mass migration, which continued throughout the Depression years, placed intolerable burdens on communities already teeming with the urban destitute.

A MOUNTING TIDE OF MISERY

THE VOICE
OF PROTEST

Inevitably, the hardships of the Depression produced unrest and led to social conflict. With traditional politics apparently discredited, radical ideologies appealed as never before to the many people with little to lose and everything to fight for. Parts of the United States became an industrial battleground as workers campaigned in support of labor unions, which were resisted fiercely and often violently by employers, sometimes with the support of authorities. In France, a union of all the leftist parties into one popular front produced the country's first-ever Socialist government. In Britain, where some towns in the industrialized north suffered more than 75 percent unemployment, the jobless staged hunger marches to bring their plight to national attention. But radicalism was not the monopoly of the Left. In many democratic countries, the rhetoric of right-wing extremism found widespread support.

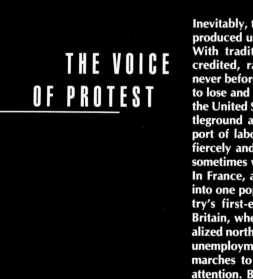

Unemployed shipyard workers from Jarrow, in northeast England, march on London in 1936 to present a petition on behalf of their town.

Police fight a running battle with pickets demonstrating for union representation at a Chicago steel company on May 30, 1937. Five workers were killed in the clash.

STORM CLOUDS OVER EUROPE

On June 14, 1934, Adolf Hitler flew to Venice on his first foreign visit as chancellor of Germany. He was worried about a proposed alliance between France and the Soviet Union, and he hoped to counter it by establishing a working partnership with his fellow dictator, Italy's Benito Mussolini, whose popularity was then at an all-time high.

On the face of it, the two leaders had much in common. From inauspicious beginnings, both men had risen to the supreme leadership of nations that were embittered by the terms of the Treaty of Versailles, which had been drawn up by the victors of World War I. Germany, branded the aggressor, had been saddled with the burden of paying reparations to its enemies, while Italy, though one of those enemies, had not received all the lands promised by its allies. Both leaders, addressing their compatriots in emotional terms that swayed millions, had won support by pledging to restore national pride, prosperity, and military power. For both Hitler and Mussolini, organized violence was an essential means to these ends. Virulently anti-Communist yet contemptuous of all forms of parliamentary democracy, they saw themselves as omniscient, the embodiment of the state, in which the rights of the individual were as nothing.

These very parallels made it unlikely that the two men could form any relationship based on trust. Hitler, who had been in power for little more than a year, had long admired Mussolini and the methods by which he had come to absolute rule twelve years before; but he still smarted under the rebuffs that Mussolini had administered during the Nazi leader's years in the political wilderness. Only five years earlier, when Hitler had requested an autographed picture of "this great man south of the Alps," the Italian dictator had snubbed him in typically bombastic fashion, instructing one of his aides to: "Please thank the above-mentioned gentleman for his sentiment and tell him in whatever form you consider best that the Duce does not think fit to accede to the request."

Now that they were meeting ostensibly on an equal footing, Mussolini still regarded his guest as nothing but an upstart—and a dangerous one at that, who was fomenting intrigue in Austria, a country that the Duce had promised to defend against "Prussian barbarism."

In any case, the visit was a disaster from the start. Hitler had requested a low-key meeting, but when he stepped out of his plane, dressed in a shabby overcoat and blue serge suit, he was confronted by the world's press and greeted by Mussolini attired in full Fascist uniform, complete with jackboots, black shirt, and a liberal garnish of gold braid. Mussolini's other attempts to upstage his visitor went embarrassingly awry; the military parades were sloppy, and the ceremonial concert degenerated into farce when the music became punctuated by organized shouts of "Duce, Duce."

Adolf Hitler, Germany's Führer, or "Leader," addresses his followers at a 1935 rally of his ruling Nazi party in Nuremberg. Like his fellow dictator, Italy's Benito Mussolini, Hitler used such massive rituals as a way of manipulating the emotions of his listeners to almost hypnotic effect. The awesome setting and the swelling roars of the half-million-strong crowd were calculated to reduce the participants to a single entity bewitched by the Führer's simplistic promises to resist communism, restore the nation's prosperity, and make Germany a great military power once again. At rallies such as these, Nazi propaganda chief Joseph Goebbels boasted, the individual was transformed from "a little worm into part of a large dragon."

15

By September 1, 1939, the day on which Germany's invasion of Poland triggered World War II, Hitler and Mussolini had created in central Europe an unstable "Axis" whose only rationale was further conquest. Germany's territory *(shaded red)* by now included the Rhineland, a demilitarized zone that Hitler had reoccupied in 1936; and Austria, which had been annexed in March 1938. Seven months later, Germany swallowed up the Sudetenland, Czechoslovakia's German-speaking border area; and in March 1939, German troops occupied the neighboring western provinces of Bohemia and Moravia and established a puppet regime in Slovakia. Italy's sole acquisition in Europe was Albania *(yellow)*, seized in 1937 as a springboard for an intended invasion of Greece.

Furthermore, Hitler was not impressed by the Italian navy when he saw sailors' laundry flying from the masts.

In their talks, it was Hitler who dominated the conversation, delivering lengthy harangues on subjects that ranged from his plans to start a European war by attacking France, to the "congenital weakness" of the British and the need to establish a pro-Nazi government in Austria. Visibly bored by Hitler's monologue during their last meeting, which had been held on a golf course, Mussolini later dismissed the German leader as a man who possessed neither intelligence nor dynamism, "a gramophone with just seven tunes."

Either Mussolini had seriously misjudged Hitler, or else his petulant denigration was the bluster of a man who felt himself to be in the presence of a demonic ruthlessness he could never emulate. For although the two would indeed prove to have a community of interests, Hitler would soon come to dominate the relationship. As his nightmarish plans unfolded through the 1930s, and then as Nazi armies stormed across western Europe during the first two years of World War II, Mussolini

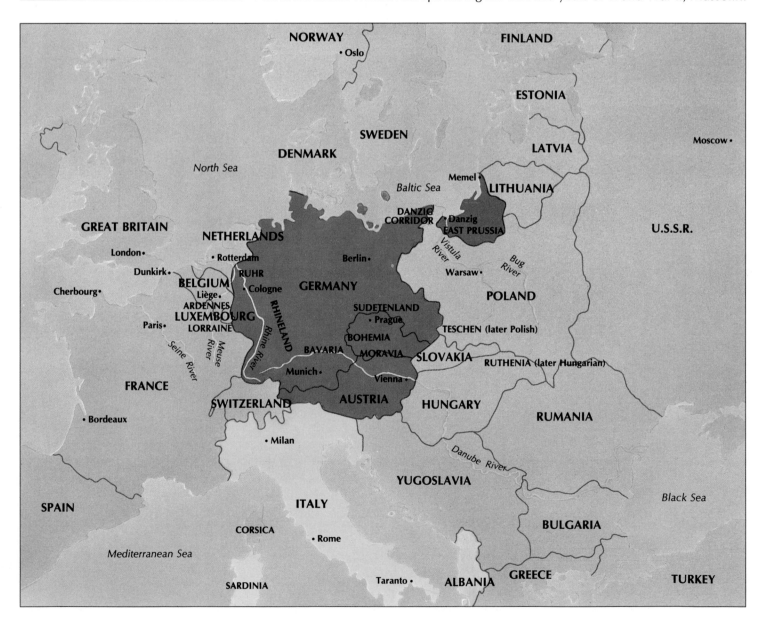

Unlike Hitler, Italy's Benito Mussolini sought to increase his nation's territory through colonial adventures outside Europe. When he came to power in 1922, Italy already possessed Eritrea, Italian Somaliland, and Libya. Mussolini, however, felt that compared with the larger holdings of Britain *(shaded green on the map)* and France *(pink),* the Italian possessions were no more than a "collection of deserts." Determined to enlarge them, in 1935, he invaded Ethiopia, a country he had previously championed when it applied to join the League of Nations in 1928.

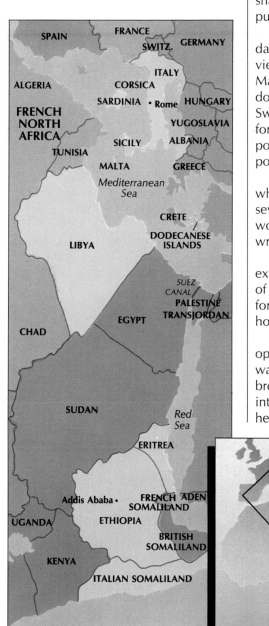

would find himself reduced to a mere vassal, his own attempts at creating an Italian empire leading to crushing failure and a humiliating reliance on the man he had once called a "mad little clown."

Being second best was something Mussolini had always sought to escape. He was born in 1883 to a devout Catholic schoolmistress and a hard-drinking blacksmith, an uneducated socialist who dabbled in anarchism and who kept discipline with a thick leather strap. Benito—he was named after the Mexican revolutionary Benito Juárez—shared his father's brutality; he was once suspended from school for stabbing a fellow pupil, and on another occasion he knifed one of his many girlfriends.

Before the First World War, Mussolini lived a bohemian existence, writing poetry, dallying with left-wing politics, and preaching violent revolution. He had no fixed views but adopted poses that suited the occasion, at one time claiming to be a Marxist, at another to have written a treatise on the history of Christianity. Abandoning a job as a temporary teacher in German-speaking northern Italy, he went to Switzerland, where he drifted between jobs and was sometimes reduced to begging for and stealing food. On several occasions he was arrested for vagrancy and for political agitation. The Swiss eventually expelled him, handing him over to the Italian police, who marked him as an "impulsive and violent" young man.

In 1909, he began a career as a journalist, editing small Socialist papers in Austria, where he was convicted five times for his ferocious libels. Back in Italy after only seven months, he continued his newspaper career, arguing strongly for international working-class solidarity and against Italian nationalism. "The national flag," he wrote, "is for us a rag to plant on a dunghill."

Driven by a desire for recognition and by an unfocused rage, he was forever experimenting with different roles, now unkempt and vulgar to appear as a champion of the proletariat, now dressed in modish patent-leather shoes and a silk-lapelled coat for some social occasion. In his commitment to violence as a political weapon, however, he was unwavering.

Sentenced to five months' imprisonment for antipatriotic agitation in 1911—he opposed Italy's imperial expansion into Libya—he emerged as a minor celebrity and was invited to edit the Socialist party's daily newspaper, *Avanti!* When the Great War broke out, he at first condemned it as a capitalist plot but then came to support Italy's intervention, hoping that the conflict would provoke the revolutionary "bloodbath" he craved. Turning against the Socialists, he resigned and started his own newspaper, *Il Popolo d'Italia (The Italian People),* subsidized by industrialists who stood to gain from war—the very people whom he had previously castigated. At the end of 1914, he took over a prointervention pressure group that called itself a *fascio,* a name inspired by the bundle of rods with an ax borne before ancient Roman magistrates as a badge of authority. When Italy entered the war in 1915, Mussolini was conscripted, serving for seventeen months and reaching the rank of sergeant before he was injured when a grenade thrower he was using exploded.

After the war, he found a political base among the many ex-servicemen who were disgruntled both by the failure of the Allies to grant Italy all it demanded at Versailles, and by the inflation, unemployment, and political paralysis that gripped the country. Sure that the parliamentary regime was doomed, Mussolini called a meeting in a Milan hall to formalize the fight against the nation's woes and launch the movement that would become the Fascist party. The assembly, held on March 23, 1919, was attended by a mixed bag of anarchists, Communists, unionists, Republicans, Catholics, and anticlerics. Not wishing to exclude any potential followers, he did his best to appeal to them all. He was, he said, "an adventurer for all roads." Over the next few months, he managed to recruit a private army of former servicemen and students whose methods would soon become familiar: destroying the printing presses of rival movements; beating up opponents and humiliating them by forcing castor oil—"Fascist medicine"—down their throats.

Acknowledging the adulation of a crowd in Venice's Piazza San Marco in 1934, Fascist leader Benito Mussolini adopts a typically aggressive and histrionic pose. A journalist before he came to power in October of 1922, Mussolini pioneered oratorical techniques and a use of propaganda and state pageantry that were to be assiduously copied by Hitler.

In the 1919 elections, the Fascists won not a single parliamentary seat, but from then on, their rise was rapid. To give the party a strong identity, Mussolini opted for a more right-wing image, using his paper to emphasize his "electric," "explosive" dynamism. Within a year, he had 320,000 members from all sections of society, and he enjoyed increased backing from employers who saw in him a possible national leader who would restore stability and growth. In the next elections, in May 1921, the Fascists received a helping hand from the dominant Liberal party, whose leader, the grand old man of Italian politics, Giovanni Giolitti, offered to include the Fascists in a coalition. With Giolitti's backing—and the help of strong-arm squads—thirty-five Fascists, including Mussolini, found themselves in Parliament, along with a dozen other diverse political parties, none of whom commanded a majority.

Mussolini, however, was not willing to share power. By promptly declaring himself to be against democracy, he made it impossible for the coalition to hold together. Giolitti resigned. For a while, local Fascist groups, sharing little but a love of violence and their blackshirt ex-servicemen's uniforms, became laws unto themselves. Many stockpiled bombs and firearms. In order to retain control of the movement, Mussolini tightened organization, grouping the squads into cohorts and legions under a hierarchy of commanders, with himself as the Duce. His aim was simple: to prove that democratic government could not defend law and order. In many areas, Fascist *squadristi* unleashed such violence that civil war seemed imminent. Anti-Fascists claimed that between 1920 and 1922, as many as 3,000 opponents of fascism were killed. The army, the police, and the magistrates, all seeing in the Fascists a force that could attain strong rule and an end to uncertainty, turned a blind eye. In February 1922, a new government under a feeble liberal, Luigi Facta, was formed, but it lacked the courage and foresight to challenge Mussolini's brutal tactics.

Events now played right into the Duce's hands. The labor unions declared a general strike, ostensibly to force the government to restore peace, but they accomplished precisely the opposite. Mussolini commanded his Fascists to break the strike, thus enabling himself to pose as the defender of law and order. Insurrection spread rapidly. Fascists seized control of half a dozen town councils, but still the government took no action. Mussolini, while maintaining contact with most factions in Parliament, suggesting to all that he might collaborate with them, held back until, on October 24, in Naples, he judged that the time had come to make his bid for power. "Either we are allowed to govern," he shouted at a cheering crowd of supporters, "or we will seize power by marching on Rome." He was greeted by ecstatic shouts of "To Rome! To Rome!"

Mussolini waited in Milan to see how events turned out, while some 30,000 Fascists assembled outside the capital and others occupied telephone exchanges and government offices in various parts of the country. This was a challenge that even Facta could not overlook: On October 28, he declared a state of emergency. Overnight, the army retook the occupied buildings, meeting little resistance. The Fascists who were camped around Rome were cold, wet, and hungry, and they were ready to head for home.

Then came an astonishing reversal. The king, Victor Emmanuel, a small, timid man, refused to ratify Facta's decree. Perhaps he lacked faith in Facta's ability to resolve the crisis, or perhaps he felt that the Fascists would provide a popular, effective government. In any event, the refusal was an extraordinary breach of convention by the constitutional monarch. Facta, his authority fatally undermined, had no choice but to resign.

The king's decision was a turning point, because it conferred respectability on the Fascists and made Mussolini's cooperation crucial to the formation of the next government. Facta's would-be successor, Antonio Salandra, in an attempt to form an administration, pleaded with Mussolini to come to Rome. The Fascist leader refused, however, gambling for higher stakes. The Duce would stay where he was, he said, unless he was allowed to form his own government. Salandra gave in. A day later, on October 29, Mussolini received a telegram from King Victor Emmanuel inviting him to be the next prime minister of Italy.

That evening, Mussolini caught the night train to Rome. Only later did his Black Shirts arrive, also by train, to find the Italian capital celebrating the end of the anarchy that they themselves had instigated. In Fascist mythology, the events of those five days, which became known as the March on Rome, quickly assumed heroic status. Soon government-sponsored history books provided Italian schoolchildren with stirring but utterly fanciful accounts of Mussolini arriving in Rome on horseback, of an

With a cameraman on hand to record his efforts, Mussolini makes a show of gathering in the harvest on a farm in the Pontine Marshes, near Rome, in 1936. This display of manly vigor was part of a drive to publicize Mussolini's campaigns to create more agricultural land by draining the malarial wetlands, thereby increasing wheat production. Both goals were achieved, helping to make Italy almost self-sufficient in grain. But the years of plenty were few, for good harvests depended on imported fertilizer, and yields slumped when war cut off the supply.

armed insurrection involving 300,000 Fascists, of 3,000 Fascists martyred by the army, and of Mussolini seizing power from an unwilling king.

With only thirty-two Fascist deputies in his administration, Mussolini was still far from wielding the absolute authority he sought. He at once demanded emergency powers to rule by decree for a year, and Parliament meekly acquiesced. A year after taking office, the law was changed yet again. By a huge majority—the opposition was now too cowed to resist him—Parliament agreed that any party obtaining at least 25 percent of the parliamentary vote would have an absolute majority. The only party that could win such a share was the Fascists. Thus a largely non-Fascist Parliament effectively voted to end parliamentary government.

Freed of the threat of civil war, the country responded as if by magic to Mussolini's show of strength and energy. Strikes ended. Production picked up. By 1924, confident that he enjoyed the massive support of the Italian people, Mussolini ordered new elections. In a campaign designed to increase the Fascists' electoral attractiveness, he opposed freemasonry to appeal to Catholics, halved estate taxes to win over the

middle classes, promised imperial expansion to please the nationalists, and privatized national industries to gain support from capitalists. To retain the loyalty of his squadristi, he gave them official status and wages, and students wounded in the Fascist cause were rewarded with university degrees without the necessity of passing an examination. That spring, Fascist candidates polled an astonishing 65 percent of the vote, winning more than two-thirds of the parliamentary seats—the greatest electoral victory in Italian history.

Undoubtedly, the result genuinely reflected public opinion, but the size of the majority struck at least one deputy, a moderate Socialist named Giacomo Matteotti, as fraudulent. When Parliament reassembled, he accused the Fascists of electoral fraud, presenting convincing evidence to support his claims. A few days later, Matteotti's mutilated body was found outside Rome. No one doubted that Mussolini had connived at, if not actually ordered, the murder. In the outcry that followed, most of the non-Fascist opposition withdrew from Parliament.

Once again, however, Mussolini's enemies only provided him with another chance to extend his power. On January 3, 1925, he boldly claimed responsibility for the assassination of Matteotti and challenged anyone to impeach him. No one took up the challenge.

Mussolini's undeviating aim had been to seize absolute power, but he had given little thought to how he would wield it, and from the start, his rule was as much show as substance. He claimed that government was "ninety-seven cents' worth of mere public clamor and three cents' worth of solid achievement," and he once remarked that to govern Italy, "you needed only two things: policemen and bands playing in the streets." A few weeks after assuming office in 1922, he had insisted on taking part in a congress in Switzerland so that he could display himself in public surrounded by a phalanx of Black Shirts. Although he had nothing to contribute to the congress—which was held to ratify a treaty between Greece and Turkey—he held eleven press conferences. At one of them, the author Ernest Hemingway, who was then a foreign correspondent, found Mussolini frowning ostentatiously at a weighty tome as the journalists were admitted. It was, Hemingway noticed, a French-English dictionary held upside down.

But once he was installed as dictator, Mussolini realized that his regime needed at least the semblance of a positive program if it was to maintain its impetus. His plan was to extend fascism into as many facets of Italian society as possible. Predominantly, this was to be achieved by establishing a score of huge corporations that combined the roles of labor unions and employers' federations. In addition, each major institution had a parallel Fascist organization: Fascist militia were attached to the army; Fascist tribunals worked alongside the courts; Fascist secretaries oversaw provincial administrators. Allegedly, the purpose of this massive upheaval was to create prosperity and self-sufficiency. In fact, the moves had a twofold political purpose: to exercise control over the entire work force and to provide jobs for the immense Fascist hierarchy.

For a while there were some notable successes. Vast sums of money were poured into a succession of economic "battles"—for food, for agricultural land, for higher population. Several hundred thousand acres of marshland were reclaimed, wheat production raised by 30 percent, roads built, and—in a catch phrase used by English-speaking people to summarize the positive results of fascism—the trains were made to run on time.

Sentenced to Landsberg Prison after his failure in 1923 to seize power in Bavaria, Adolf Hitler *(far left)* faces the camera with fellow-Nazi conspirators, including Rudolf Hess *(second from right)*, his secretary and future deputy. Reflecting official sympathy with Nazi aims, the prison authorities granted the inmates remarkable liberties. In this picture—taken by one of their many visitors, Hess's future wife—they appear confident, well fed, and smartly dressed in the Bavarian style. Their confidence was well placed: Within a year, they had all been released, and Hitler was rebuilding his political career.

Such feats were little more than window dressing, however. The increase in home-grown wheat, for example, allowed grain imports to be cut, but Italians paid 50 percent more for their wheat than Americans paid for theirs. The corporations were overstaffed by armies of Fascist bureaucrats who supplemented their low salaries by creaming off a percentage of the businesses they controlled and by selling their influence to the highest bidder. Corruption was endemic.

Steadily, fascism intruded into the daily lives of ordinary Italians. People were urged to date events from the *anno primo* of 1922 and were encouraged to use the "hygienic" Fascist salute instead of shaking hands. Children from the age of four were expected to join Fascist youth clubs. Roadside billboards displayed Mussolini aphorisms such as Mussolini Is Always Right and Better to Be a Lion for a Day Than a Sheep for 100 Years.

That such a system not only survived but also was generally popular was due in large part to the personality of the Duce as he presented himself to the public. He used his histrionic talents—he had a fine baritone voice and an actor's way with expression and gesture—to project an image of wisdom, industry, and urgent activity. His sixty-five-by-forty-foot marble office in the Palazzo Venezia was designed to awe visitors, and he habitually left the light burning late, suggesting to admirers outside that he was working into the night, when in fact he was asleep. Carefully edited photographs and press releases gave the impression that he was a gifted violinist, expert pilot, daring horseman, penetrating intellectual—"pardon my learned references" was one of his favored asides—and a devil-may-care free spirit. Foreign journalists could be expelled for mentioning that he wore glasses or had an ulcer. Mussolini claimed that he was greater than Napoleon and that, like Napoleon, he was more than capable of leading in both peace and war.

This playacting, much of it absurd, could not disguise his inadequacies as an administrator. He surrounded himself with yes-men who would never disagree with him or point out his errors: To do so, he said, would only divert "me from what I know to be the right path, whereas my animal instincts are always right." Disdainful of anyone else's political abilities, he found it impossible to delegate, personally holding eight government offices in 1926; among other positions he held, the Duce was prime minister, foreign minister, interior minister, and minister for all three armed services. Consequently, he was unable to concentrate on any one area of policy for long. He would contradict himself to avoid acknowledging failure. "The ideals of democracy are exploded," he wrote on one occasion, and on another, "Fascism is the purest kind of democracy."

As the economy failed to measure up to his initial promises, he adjusted his message. Instead of boasting about his commitment to prosperity, he began to preach on the restorative virtues of adversity. "Fortunately," he said dismissively, when informed that food production had fallen, "the Italian people are not accustomed to eat much." As the benefits of corporatism continued to elude the country, Mussolini found another catchword, "autarchy," self-sufficiency, which he repeated like an incantation: Henceforth, he declared, Italy was to be self-sufficient not only in food but also in industrial products. At the same time, however, he initiated a major rearmament program that would inevitably make Italy, which was deficient in the raw materials required for the waging of war, more dependent on imports. He needed weapons for a campaign of imperial expansion in Africa: 1935, he stressed, was to be the year when he would be ready to go to war.

Although Hitler was the newcomer when he met Mussolini in 1934, he was already regarded by millions of Germans as the embodiment of Germanic culture. But Hitler was not German by birth. He was born in 1889 and raised near Linz in Austria. His father, a customs official for the Hapsburg empire that linked Austria and Hungary, died when Adolf was only thirteen. Left in the care of his fond, simpleminded mother, he became solitary and rebellious, showing interest in little but drawing. When he was eighteen he went to Vienna, where he failed to win admission to the Academy of Fine Arts. His mother died of breast cancer, and he was reduced to living in

Dictated by Hitler during his time in prison, *Mein Kampf—My Struggle*—is a manifesto in which he set out his racist theories and dreams of empire. After he came to power, six million copies were sold or distributed free; all newlyweds, for example, received one from their local government. Copies were often kept in presentation boxes, such as the one shown here, which is carved with the lightning flashes of the SS, the Schutzstaffel, Hitler's elite personal bodyguard.

flophouses, eking out a meager allowance by painting advertisements and postcards.

These were unhappy years, and formative ones. Lazy, moody, at odds with society, he had one consuming passion: talking politics. He was an intense admirer of German culture, for Germany, a young and strong nation, offered a brighter future than the Austro-Hungarian empire, undermined as it was by the nationalist demands of its subject peoples. He was particularly resentful of Vienna's Jews, believing that they threatened the fabric of German culture. His narrow, powerful mind, stimulated by an anti-Semitism that was endemic in Vienna's gutter press, conceived a catchall explanation of the sickness—as he saw it—of the modern world: All true ideals, all good government had been weakened by a worldwide Jewish conspiracy, operating through Social Democracy, Marxism, and Christianity. Avidly skimming books by the hundreds, he absorbed those ideas that confirmed his prejudices. Acquaintances later

In a sequence of studio photographs taken in 1925, Hitler strikes dramatic attitudes intended to increase the impact of his oratory. It was practice well spent. His speeches, delivered with theatrical gestures and rising intensity, induced in audiences a sort of hysteria that overwhelmed the critical faculties of most listeners.

recalled him as a brooding, wild-eyed figure, bursting out of dark moods into violent, bitter diatribes.

In 1913, Hitler moved to Munich, a city he loved, and when war broke out, he enlisted in the German infantry, serving as a dispatch runner in Flanders throughout most of the conflict. Never rising above the rank of corporal, he did, however, prove himself a brave soldier, winning the Iron Cross, First Class—a rare distinction for a combatant of his rank. Transferred to Germany after falling victim to a gas attack in October 1918, he was shocked to the core of his being by Germany's sudden capitulation the following month.

He returned to Munich through a country in ruins. Germany's postwar Republican government, named after Weimar, the town in which the national assembly first met, was in disarray. While left-wingers hoped for revolution, millions of others—especially disaffected veterans like Hitler—could not accept the armistice, claiming that Germany had been "stabbed in the back" by its own Republican politicians,

abetted by Socialist agitators, by Jews, and by war profiteers. The peace treaty signed at Versailles in 1919 was seen as another betrayal. Only some new movement, backed by the army, could hope to restore German national pride.

Bavaria in particular, which was the largest of Germany's constituent states, was on the brink of revolt. Independent until 1866, with their own monarch until the previous year, Bavaria's Catholic people disliked Protestant Berlin. There were many who would have preferred a South German Union with Catholic Austria, which had emerged as an independent country after the dismantling of the Austro-Hungarian empire in 1918.

Hitler was given work in the army's political department and assigned to investigate a small right-wing group, the German Workers' party. It interested him, because its few dozen members turned out to be fervently patriotic, reflecting opinions that

were popular among the Bavarian police and army, as well as eager for working-class support. Hitler accepted an invitation to join the party's committee and was placed in charge of propaganda.

In his new role, the Führer revealed two exceptional gifts: He could organize others, and as a speaker, he could sense and express the mood of an audience, articulating their own hopes and fears and thus personifying their raw emotions. "He could play like a virtuoso on the well-tempered piano of lower-middle-class hearts," said one of his later associates. When he was in public, his customary moroseness suddenly dropped away, his pale blue eyes took fire, and he acquired a compelling, utterly self-assured passion.

He quickly dominated the party and began to rebuild it, changing its name to one taken over from a minor Austrian group, the National German Workers' party—Nazi for short. From the same source, he adopted as the party symbol an ancient cross motif known as the swastika. He insisted on a ritual greeting, "Heil!," which means

"Hail!," but which also evokes concepts of wholeness, salvation, and health. Most important of all, he formed a private army of thugs, known as the Storm Section—the Sturmabteilung, or SA—to intimidate political opponents. It was led by a local army officer, Captain Ernst Röhm, a scar-faced tough who persuaded his ex-commander to divert secret army funds for the purchase of a virulently racist local newspaper, the *Völkischer Beobachter,* or *National Observer.* Under the editorship of Alfred Rosenberg, it became a vehicle for Hitler's ultranationalist views.

Conditions soon favored the burgeoning party. Reparations payments were proving such a burden that the German economy collapsed. To enforce payments, in January 1923, France occupied Germany's industrial heartland, the Ruhr. The government responded by backing a general strike, financing it by printing more money. Confidence in the currency began to slip, and within months, rampant inflation, the worst in German history, set in. In November, the exchange rate peaked at four trillion marks to the dollar. Savings were worthless, property was unsalable, labor had no rewards. The very foundations of the state seemed about to vanish.

In February 1934, Hitler defers to President Paul von Hindenburg at a memorial service for the dead of World War I. Hitler had been appointed chancellor the previous year, after unsuccessfully challenging the popular Hindenburg for the presidency. The eighty-seven-year-old former field marshal possessed a constitutional right to veto Nazi legislation, but Hitler used the threat of Communist subversion to push through his party's program by decree. When Hindenburg died in August 1934, the Führer simply assumed his office and thereafter ruled supreme.

In these chaotic circumstances, many in Bavaria were ready to back an army revolt against the republic. Hitler had already discussed the possibility with several people, including the eminent World War I commander General Erich Ludendorff, who was living in retirement in Munich. For the moment, however, sympathetic military leaders urged restraint on the plotters. The time was not ripe: There were signs that the Republican government could, after all, surmount the crisis. But Hitler was not to be deterred. He determined to seize the initiative, take over the army, police, and government, and use Bavaria as a springboard to national power.

On November 8, 1923, a group of government officials, military leaders, and civil servants gathered in a large Munich beer hall, the Bürgerbräukeller, to hear the Bavarian state commissioner deliver a lecture on the moral justification of dictatorship. Only twenty minutes into the meeting, twenty-five armed SA men burst in—the signal for Hitler, who had been waiting inconspicuously by a pillar, to fire a shot into the ceiling and yell that the national revolution had begun. After bundling the senior officials into a back room, he returned to the main hall and announced to the startled audience that he was setting up a national government with the help of Ludendorff. The general knew nothing of the plan, but when hastily informed of events, he agreed to back the Nazis. He went to the hall, where Hitler, after delivering a brief, impassioned speech that roused his hostages to cheers, let the officials go.

Hitler had totally miscalculated. The next morning, when he and Ludendorff led a march of more than 2,000 men through the streets toward the Bavarian War Ministry, believing that the city would fall to him, the police barred their way. Shots rang out. Sixteen Nazis fell dead, and the rest fled, only to be arrested at a later date. Ludendorff was released, but Hitler and several others were imprisoned.

He put his year in prison to good use, reading voraciously and dictating his thoughts to his closest associate, Rudolf Hess. The result was the book that would eventually become the Nazi bible, *Mein Kampf (My Struggle).* In this turgid work, he expressed the thoughts, aims, and methods that became the heart of nazism.

In the past, he argued, successful cultures—such as the classical world and medieval Europe—had been weakened by an "effeminate" Jewish-Christian ethic. The same destructive ethic, compounded by insipid leadership, had enfeebled postwar Europe. The culture that would revitalize it was Germanic, or "Aryan," as he termed it. The Germans had acted as "culture-bearers" after the fall of Rome, and they would do so again, not under any milksop democracy, but under a single messianic figure of iron will. Such a person could change the course of history; indeed, Mussolini, "that unparalleled statesman," had shown how with the March on Rome.

Hitler himself, of course, was the new messiah—a unique combination of politician, philosopher, and military strategist. Working through the Nazi party, he would unite all German-speaking people into a new empire that would dominate "lesser" races, in particular the Slavs, and seize new lands to the east—as German Crusaders had in the thirteenth century. Germany "must again set itself on the march along the road of the Teutonic Knights of old, to obtain by the German sword sod for the German plow and daily bread for the nation." In the Soviet Union, Germany would find the lebensraum, the living space, its people needed. The Soviet Union was Germany's natural enemy, more so now than ever, for it was in the hands of a rival ideology, Marxism, behind which—according to Hitler—stood the Jew, the incarnation of all evil. The real battle would be with the Soviet Union and the "half beast, half giant" Stalin; it would be an apocalyptic struggle that would decide the fate of Europe for centuries to come. The Soviet Union was to be utterly crushed, its cities leveled, its people enslaved. In this new empire, the Jewish "problem" would find its "final solution" in the total eradication of Jewish culture.

Compared with the grand scheme of expansion to the east, war with the nations to the west, though possibly unavoidable, was a small matter. Liberal democracy was so debilitated it would collapse of its own accord. France would be defeated—and in this, Italy would prove an ally. Britain, which was itself a Germanic nation, would offer no opposition and would come to an understanding.

To achieve these ambitions, Hitler would direct the German people through propaganda. "To be a leader," he said, "means to move masses." This could never be done by rational means, but only by using the spoken word to create emotions of hysterical intensity. The leader must recycle a crowd's emotions, feeding the people with their own feelings, reinforced by utter self-confidence. There must be no hesitation, weakness, or concession. He must lie, if that serves his purpose, and make the lies big, "because in the big lie there is always a certain force of credibility."

This oratorical technique would be backed by two other elements: paraphernalia and ritual that would create a sense of power greater than the individual; brute force to ensure that no opposing voices would be heard.

It was a vision devoid of humanity, spirituality, or creativity; it was a barbaric

This badge identified its owner as a member of the National Socialist German Workers'—or Nazi—party. The party symbol, later adopted as the national emblem of the Third Reich, was the swastika, or *Hakenkreuz* (crooked cross). A good-luck charm in ancient Asian cultures, the swastika was used by early Christians as a distorted form of cross to disguise their religious affiliations. Hitler borrowed it, along with the party name, from a tiny Austrian Nationalist party that he joined after World War I.

Joseph Goebbels, who orchestrated Hitler's campaign for office in the 1920s, gives the camera a baleful glance during a 1933 visit to the League of Nations' Geneva headquarters. An academic turned journalist, Goebbels built up support for the Nazis in Berlin by means that included—by his own admission—"slanderous agitation and all the vile cunning of the gutter press." He was largely responsible for creating the myth of Hitler's infallibility and was rewarded in 1935 with control of the Ministry of Information and Propaganda. In that capacity, he also exercised strict supervision of the press, radio, cinema, theater, and literature.

vision, deliberately so, for it was through barbarism, Hitler believed, that the dynamic, healthy new culture would replace the degenerate old one. "We are barbarians!" he proclaimed. "We want to be barbarians! It is an honorable title. We shall rejuvenate the world!"

It was a vision conceived against all the odds. When Hitler was released in December 1924, he appeared to be finished as a political force. Within nine years, however, he was ready to re-create his nation, along with the rest of Europe, in his own terrible image.

His methods would not be those that had failed him in Munich. He would not again challenge authority directly. He would establish his own political organization and work his way to power legally. "Democracy," he declared, "must be destroyed by the weapons of democracy."

For a while, conditions did not favor him. For one thing, he was still on parole and banned from making public speeches. For another, the economy revived. After the horrors of the 1923 inflation, a new currency restored stability. Reparations payments were reduced, and France evacuated the Ruhr. International confidence was further restored by the election of Field Marshal Paul von Hindenburg as president; he was the last chief of the general staff, who had with Ludendorff effectively controlled military and civilian policy during the last two years of the war. Generous dollar loans poured in from America.

All Hitler could achieve in these years was a slow growth in party membership—up to 178,000 in 1929—and the establishment of a national organization. The Nazis won their first seats in the Reichstag (Berlin's Parliament building) in 1928; among the twelve successful candidates were the swaggering former Luftwaffe pilot Hermann Göring, whose contacts with industrialists would prove important to Nazi finances, and the brilliant propagandist Joseph Goebbels.

Not until 1929 did the tide turn in Hitler's favor. When the American stock market crashed, U.S. banks called in their loans. Dole lines lengthened, businesses closed, properties were repossessed, public works ended. In 1930, unemployment rose to four million. A second plan for reparations rescheduled payments at a lower level, but for a forbidding sixty years.

In the 1930 elections, the Nazis broke through, winning 107 seats and six million votes, second only to the Social Democrats. With the party's leader now a figure of national importance, Nazi membership rose to 800,000. The next elections, in 1932, were for the presidency, when Hitler challenged the venerable Hindenburg, now eighty-four. Hitler lost, but as luck would have it, Hindenburg failed by 0.4 percent to achieve the overall majority required by law. A second campaign followed, which allowed Goebbels to mastermind an unprecedented publicity campaign: Hitler covered the country by plane, speaking in twenty towns in a week. Hindenburg won again, but Hitler increased his vote and was in a strong position for the forthcoming parliamentary elections.

With unemployment now around the six million mark, Hitler's extremist views and simplistic solutions had wide appeal to almost all sections of German society. Again he toured the country by air, covering fifty cities in the second half of July. In each, SA troops paraded though the streets, breaking up rival meetings and beating up opponents. This time the Nazis won the most seats, 230 out of 608—still not an absolute majority, but large enough to make Hitler the most powerful figure in

German politics. The chancellor, the aristocratic Franz von Papen, offered him the post of vice-chancellor.

But Hitler, like Mussolini in 1922, was determined to play for higher stakes. Spurning Papen's offer, he demanded the chancellorship itself. Papen and Hindenburg turned him down unconditionally. Fortunately for Hitler, there then followed months of political deadlock, until finally Hindenburg, fearing civil war, backed down and offered Hitler the position he wanted. Nevertheless, there were conditions attached: Hitler would have to accept Papen as his vice-chancellor and appoint no more than three Nazis to the cabinet.

One of these Nazis was Göring, who as Prussian minister of the interior immediatley began a drastic purge of the Prussian administration, replacing hundreds of officials with party members and establishing an auxiliary Nazi police force of 50,000—the Gestapo.

Still not satisfied, Hitler demanded yet another election. Events now played dra-

Members of the Nazi Labor Corps drill with shovels soon after Hitler came to power. The corps had a dual purpose. It trained potential soldiers at a time when the official German army was limited to a strength of 100,000 by the terms of the Treaty of Versailles, drawn up by the victors of World War I. It also provided a cheap labor force for industry and public works programs and was instrumental in lowering unemployment, which dropped from some six million in 1933 to less than three million the following year.

matically into his hands. On February 27, 1933, Hitler was dining with Goebbels when news came that the Reichstag was on fire. A young Dutch Communist, Marinus van der Lubbe, was arrested shortly before Göring—by apparent coincidence—arrived at the scene of the crime. Hitler seized his opportunity. Claiming that the fire was a signal for a leftist uprising, he insisted on an emergency decree suspending civil rights. Göring's Gestapo arrested 4,000 Communists. Van der Lubbe was tried, found guilty, and executed.

At the next elections, in early March, the Nazis increased their seats to 288, polling 43.9 percent of the votes. Despite the near monopoly of propaganda they now enjoyed and the intimidating tactics of the SA, this was still not a majority. But it hardly mattered. Hitler demanded the right to rule by decree for four years under a so-called Enabling Act. In a parliamentary chamber dominated by a huge swastika and ranks of SA troops, the frightened deputies granted him dictatorial powers by a large majority. (They had good reason to be frightened: Of the ninety-four dissenters, twenty-four were subsequently murdered.)

As the Nazi revolution got under way, there remained one additional possible source of opposition: the street-brawling Storm Troopers who had bludgeoned Hitler's opponents into silence. The two million SA outnumbered the army many times over, and their coarse, outspoken boss, Ernst Röhm, was eager to take over the army completely. But Hitler was already thinking of conquests outside Germany, and for that he would need the regular army, not a mob of sadistic hooligans. To deal with Röhm, he called upon his own newly formed bodyguard, the Schutzstaffel (Protection Squad), or SS, a small, elite corps that was later to become an army in its own right.

On the night of June 29 to 30, 1934—the Night of the Long Knives—the SS arrested Röhm and many other Hitler rivals and opponents, inside and outside the Nazi party. No one knows how many were killed: 82, according to Nazi sources; more than 400, according to more objective estimates. "So! Now I have taken a bath and feel clean as a newborn babe again," Hitler told his private secretary.

Five weeks later, the ailing Hindenburg died, and in a move prearranged with the grateful leaders of the army, Hitler had the chancellorship merged with the presidency, which carried with it supreme command of the armed forces. Designating himself Führer (Leader) of the German people, Hitler demanded that officers and men swear an oath of "unconditional obedience," not to the state or any of its offices, but to him personally. Finally, to rubber-stamp his actions, he held a plebiscite: 90 percent of the population approved. "Thus I have conquered the German people," he boasted.

There was now nothing to prevent Hitler from starting on the course he had mapped out for the creation of a greater Germany under his sole authority. A process of "coordination" legalized

These toy soldiers, about two and one-half inches high, were produced by the millions in the 1930s and helped spread the cult of Nazi militarism among children of the Third Reich. The models represent Hitler himself, with an arm that rotates to give the Nazi salute, and four standard-bearers. From left to right, they portray members of the Labor Front, the only legal union; the Air Sports Club, which trained military pilots in contravention of the ban on a German air force imposed after World War I; the League of German Girls, a Nazi youth organization; and its male equivalent, the Hitler Youth.

his efforts, bringing all organized life under the control of the Nazi party. Local parliaments, administrations, and police forces were all given Nazi leaders. All political parties save the Nazis were outlawed. A new people's court held trials for treason—a crime defined by the court itself. SA gangs were immune from prosecution. A new Labor Front replaced unions. The first concentration camps were set up. In 1935, by the infamous Nuremberg Laws, Jews were barred from businesses and professions and forbidden to marry German "nationals." Teachers were required to join the Nazi Teachers League, and all children from the age of six were coopted into the Hitler youth organizations. The Protestant church came under state control, and an agreement with the Vatican forbade Catholic clergy from engaging in politics.

For a while the Nazi revolution seemed to provide precisely what had been promised. Although Hitler knew nothing of economics, he did know what the people wanted: work and pride in their country. In some areas, Nazi measures did strengthen the economy. Strikes were forbidden, and labor schemes—principally in the armaments, agricultural, and building industries—helped reduce unemployment from six million to 1.7 million by 1935. In general, however, Germany's economic revival

owed more to the country's clever financial administrators and industrial managers than to Nazi initiatives. Under the guidance of Hjalmar Schacht, who was president of the Reichsbank as well as economics minister, foreign debts were again rescheduled, export subsidies granted to boost foreign trade, and barter agreements reached to give access to vital raw materials. As a result, production per head rose 64 percent in the first six years of Hitler's rule. Domestic production of oil, plastics, fibers, and synthetic rubber rose as much as tenfold in the late 1930s.

Most of Germany's newfound prosperity was diverted into rebuilding the nation's military strength. Hitler had made his priorities clear within a few weeks of becoming chancellor: "Every publicly supported project for creating employment must be judged by one criterion alone: Is it or is it not requisite for the restoration of the German nation's fighting capability?" By the Treaty of Versailles, Germany was allowed an army of no more than 100,000, a token navy, and no air force at all. Hitler had always declared these sanctions to be iniquitous. Now he demanded equality of status. Perhaps, he suggested, other countries should disarm down to Germany's level. When that suggestion was rejected, he withdrew from the League of Nations, the international organization set up by the Treaty of Versailles to preserve world peace. At first secretly, and then openly, he oversaw a massive program of rearmament designed to make Germany capable of waging an aggressive war by 1940. In 1936, he announced his intention to multiply arms expenditure almost sixfold, from almost six billion marks to more than 32 billion in 1939.

On November 5, 1937, Hitler revealed his long-term ambitions in Europe during a secret conference with his military chiefs. The need for lebensraum was paramount, and so it was vital that in the period between 1938 and 1943, Austria and Czechoslovakia be taken over by Germany, Poland be overrun, and finally that the Soviet Union be invaded and conquered.

When Hitler met Mussolini in 1934, he was already thinking about his first foreign adventure, the annexation of Austria. Since his rise to power, Vienna's Nazi party had been preparing for Germany to forge an indissoluble union—Anschluss—with the country of Hitler's birth. In July 1934, a group of party members dressed as Austrian soldiers shot dead the Austrian chancellor, Engelbert Dollfuss, a dictatorial character who hated Nazis and Communists alike. But the Austrian army and government failed to back the plotters. They were arrested, and Mussolini, guarantor of Austria's independence, sent 50,000 troops to guard the country's borders. Hitler was shocked: He thought that he had won the Duce's compliance in Venice the previous month. For the moment, he pulled back from further action, disclaiming any connection with the murder, and set about weaning Mussolini from his commitment to Austria.

The next two years were frustrating ones for Hitler. It was not until 1936, by which time his army had grown to more than half a million men, that he achieved his first coup in foreign policy. On March 7, columns of goose-stepping infantrymen marched into Cologne and other major cities between the Rhine and the French border. Under the Treaty of Versailles, the whole Rhineland was declared a buffer zone, off-limits to German soldiers. Hitler had in effect torn up the treaty. German crowds roared their delight, and in a subsequent plebiscite—which was now an established tactic to display his popularity—the people of the Rhineland approved his action by an overwhelming 98.8 percent.

France and Britain protested but did nothing: No one was willing to believe that

Hitler was actively preparing for war. Most government leaders preferred to think that he was merely undoing the worst humiliations of Versailles—humiliations that many had regarded as unfair in the first place. If France had sent in its own troops, Hitler's token force would have had to withdraw, but no one had the stomach to wage war against Hitler for marching into German territory. As the London *Times* remarked, Hitler had done nothing more than go "into his own back garden."

Mussolini, meanwhile, had turned his gaze farther afield. As Italy's economy faltered in the 1930s, he sought to extend the country's possessions in Africa, where Italy's colonial holdings—Eritrea, Italian Somaliland, and Libya—were, in the Duce's words, mere "crumbs from the sumptuous booty of others." On Somaliland's border lay a likely victim, Ethiopia, which was, he declared, a treasure house of gold, platinum, oil, coal, and agricultural wealth. In October 1935, some 300,000 Italian troops equipped with artillery, bombers, and mustard gas invaded Ethiopia. Their ragged, poorly armed opponents proved easy victims. Among the combatants was Mussolini's son, Vittorio, a pilot, who wrote that every Italian boy should try his hand at warfare some day because it was the most thrilling of sports. He found it particularly "diverting" to bomb Galla tribesmen and see the group "bursting out like a rose after I had landed a bomb in the middle of them." On May 5, 1936, Italian tanks rolled unopposed into Addis Ababa: The emperor, Haile Selassie, along with his family and hundreds of retainers, had fled to exile in Britain.

Other countries expressed shock but did not intervene. The League of Nations proved woefully inadequate at inflicting international constraints. It branded Mussolini an aggressor and imposed economic sanctions. From the start, however, these trade restrictions were a dead letter, for no one wanted to drive Mussolini into starting a European war either on his own or—far worse—in alliance with Germany, the other threat to international peace. As a result, the sanctions were never meant to be punitive. They did not include such essential commodities as coal, steel, and oil; they did not even involve forbidding Italy to use the Suez Canal, which was the main conduit of Italian overseas imports.

In any case, the result of the sanctions was precisely the opposite of what had been intended. Angered by criticism from France and Britain, which hitherto had enjoyed reasonably amicable relations with Italy, Mussolini spoke bitterly of European governments preferring "a horde of barbarian Negroes" over the "mother of civilization." Moreover, he began to see in Hitler a possible ally. In late 1936, after both countries had sent military support for the Nationalists in the Spanish Civil War, a bitter conflict between Communist-backed Republicans and the right-wing forces of General Francisco Franco, Mussolini spoke for the first time of a Rome-Berlin "Axis." The following year, he made a state visit to Germany, where Hitler laid on an SS parade, military maneuvers, and a Berlin rally of one million people, all roaring support for the two leaders. After that, Mussolini's doubts about Hitler vanished, as did his commitment to Austria's independence. "Austria," he said not long afterward, "is German State number two."

At last Hitler was free to settle the unfinished business with his country of birth. On February 12, 1938, he invited the Austrian chancellor, Kurt von Schuschnigg, to his mountain retreat at Berchtesgaden, southeast of Munich. There he subjected him to a two-hour tirade, demanding that a team of named Nazis be included in the Austrian government and that all arrested Nazis be released. He then produced an ultimatum:

Boys of the Hitler Youth *(below)* adopt the steely gaze and rigid posture expected of them as future soldiers. Hitler was determined to create a male generation that was imbued with physical fitness, martial courage, and dedication to their leader as the hero and savior of his people. Their female counterparts were expected to be paragons of "femininity," an ideal implicit in the dress and deportment of members of the League of German Girls *(opposite)*. Legally excluded from holding high party office, university professorships, or judicial posts, women were encouraged to seek no role other than that of devoted mothers. "With each child that she brings into the nation," Hitler declared, "she is fighting her fight on behalf of the nation."

Schuschnigg must sign a prepared agreement conceding Hitler's demands, or the issue would be settled by force. "Think it over, Herr Schuschnigg, think it over well. I can only wait until this afternoon. If I tell you that, you will do well to take my words literally. I don't believe in bluffing. All my past is proof of that." After thinking it over, the browbeaten Schuschnigg signed.

Back in Vienna, however, his courage revived, and he announced that there would be a plebiscite for the people to decide whether or not Austria should remain independent. The enraged Hitler demanded that he cancel the plebiscite or face invasion. Schuschnigg capitulated, then resigned. His provisional successor, Interior Minister Arthur Seyss-Inquart, a Nazi stooge acting on orders from Berlin, promptly requested a German invasion to "restore order."

Before he acted, Hitler took pains to clear his decision with Mussolini, who offered

no objections. Hitler was delighted. "I shall stick with him whatever may happen," he said—one of the few promises he would keep.

German troops crossed the border on March 12 and enjoyed a tumultuous reception. Hitler followed two days later, making a triumphant return to the city where he had once starved in obscurity. A month later, in a plebiscite, 99.75 percent of Austrians approved the Anschluss. Socialists, Communists, and Jews were publicly humiliated. Schuschnigg was sent to a concentration camp.

Again, no country took action. Just as with the Rhineland, Hitler had publicly declared his commitment to peace, gambled that other countries would not want violence, and then taken what he wanted. The first of the targets he had listed to his generals had been acquired without a shot being fired; now he was thinking about the next. On the flight back to Germany from Vienna, Hitler showed a crumpled news cutting to his chief of staff, Wilhelm Keitel. It was a sketched map of the Reich's new frontiers, which now hemmed in Czechoslovakia on three sides. Placing his left hand on the map so that his forefinger and thumb were on Czechoslovakia's frontiers, he winked at Keitel, slowly pinching finger and thumb together.

The nations most concerned about Germany's expansion were the old wartime allies, France and Great Britain. Yet apart from increasing their own military strength, they took no positive steps to thwart Hitler. True, the French and the British were not in a position to impose their will on Germany by force. French generals had opted for a defensive military strategy, believing themselves to be safe behind the concrete blockhouses of the Maginot line that guarded their eastern border, while British leaders put their faith in a deliberate policy of "appeasement," by which was meant an understanding response to legitimate grievances and a way to reconcile former enemies. At the time, the policy was seen as a noble ideal: magnanimous, sound security, good business.

Appeasement had a tireless champion in Neville Chamberlain, a former businessman and lord mayor of Birmingham who became British prime minister in May 1937. Courageous and self-confident, he was determined to go down in history as a great peacemaker, and for this, according to Winston Churchill, Chamberlain's successor and Hitler's implacable foe (but only an ordinary member of Parliament in 1937), "he was prepared to strive continually in the teeth of facts." It never occurred to Chamberlain that Hitler did not want peace, that his whole personality, the personality of the Nazi regime, demanded the waging of war.

In the event of war with Czechoslovakia, Hitler's generals cautioned, conquest was not a foregone conclusion. Though a young country, carved from the ruins of the

LEGITIMIZING RACIAL HATRED

Anti-Semitism was Hitler's emotional bedrock. As a youth in Vienna, he had convinced himself that Jews were responsible for all the political and economic woes that beset European society, and when he came to power, he introduced drastic measures to eliminate them from public life. Jewish shops, lawyers, and doctors were officially boycotted. Jewish children were banned from state schools, where Nazi ideas about race were introduced into the curriculum. Some of the most odious anti-Semitic children's literature was published by Julius Streicher, a sadistic pornographer whose tabloid newspaper, *Der Stürmer (The Storm Trooper),* had been a mouthpiece for Hitler's racist views since the 1920s.

In 1935, Hitler formalized his prejudices in the notorious Nuremberg Laws, which deprived Jews of their citizenship and forbade intermarriage between Jew and "Aryan"—the Nazis' term for the hypothetical German ethnic type.

But how did one tell Jew from Aryan? Pseudoscientists were soon found to define Aryan and Jewish physical characteristics. By such means, Hitler isolated the Jews from the rest of society, leaving them defenseless against the Nazi violence that would culminate in their genocide.

Schreibers rassenkundliche Anschauungstafel: Deutsche Rassenköpfe
Bearbeitet von Dr Alfred Eydt

Nordisch

Westisch

Fälisch

Dinarisch

Ostbaltisch

Ostisch

In an attempt to confer respectability on a pseudo-science, a Nazi "race-identification table" used for classroom display *(left)* purports to portray typical heads of the German "races." The classification is quite without basis in anthropology.

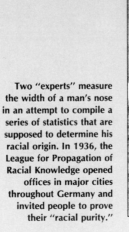

An illustration from one of Julius Streicher's anti-Semitic children's books shows blond Germanic pupils rejoicing as grossly caricatured Jewish children and their teacher are expelled from school so that "order and discipline" can be restored.

Two "experts" measure the width of a man's nose in an attempt to compile a series of statistics that are supposed to determine his racial origin. In 1936, the League for Propagation of Racial Knowledge opened offices in major cities throughout Germany and invited people to prove their "racial purity."

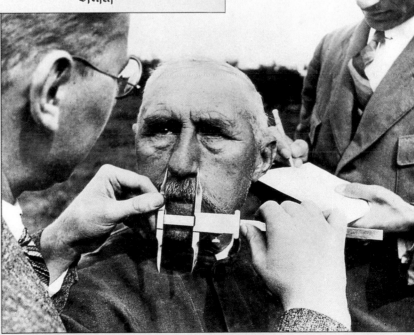

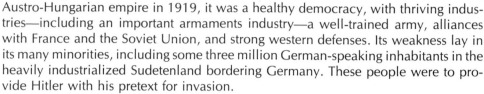

Austro-Hungarian empire in 1919, it was a healthy democracy, with thriving industries—including an important armaments industry—a well-trained army, alliances with France and the Soviet Union, and strong western defenses. Its weakness lay in its many minorities, including some three million German-speaking inhabitants in the heavily industrialized Sudetenland bordering Germany. These people were to provide Hitler with his pretext for invasion.

Only two weeks after the seizure of Austria, Hitler briefed the Sudetenland leader, Konrad Henlein, on how to proceed. "Always demand so much that we can never be satisfied," he said. Refusal could then be met by outrage and civil unrest—subversive action that would be supported by Germany. Henlein therefore demanded of Czechoslovakia's president, Edvard Beneš, nothing less than independence for the Sudetenland. Beneš made counteroffers guaranteeing greater freedom for the Sudeten Germans, but since Henlein always found something to object to, the president turned for support to his principal ally, France. The premier, Édouard Daladier, appealed to Chamberlain to find a solution.

To Hitler's delight and astonishment, the British prime minister at once sent a message proposing that he should fly to Germany for talks to settle the dispute. On September 15, 1938, after a seven-hour flight—his first—he was greeted by the Führer at Berchtesgaden. Hitler reiterated his intention to see justice done for the Sudeten Germans, even if it meant backing Henlein with an invasion. Chamberlain became impatient. Why had Hitler let him come, if he was determined to settle the matter by force? Hitler's mood softened. He suggested that the cession of the Sudetenland to Germany might offer a way out of the impasse. Chamberlain agreed in principle and departed, leaving Hitler confident that Czechoslovakia would never agree to such a proposal. Preparations for invasion, set for October 1, continued.

But Beneš, under pressure from the British as well as the French, did agree. Delighted, Chamberlain again flew to Germany on September 22 and told the Nazi leader that the Czech president had accepted his terms. It was precisely the opposite of what Hitler wanted; his plan had been to take all of Czechoslovakia. "I am exceedingly sorry," he told the bemused prime minister, "but after the events of the last few days, this solution is no longer any use." Now he demanded immediate German occupation of the Sudetenland, moving the date up to September 28. Chamberlain protested, at which Hitler agreed to a delay of three days—until October 1.

Beneš rejected this new set of demands. France at last stated that it would stand by its obligations and defend Czechoslovakia. Britain, too, prepared for war. "How horrible, fantastic, incredible it is," Chamberlain said in a broadcast to the nation "that we should be digging trenches and laying gas masks here because of a quarrel in a faraway country between peoples of whom we know nothing."

On September 26, Hitler addressed a huge crowd in Berlin's Palace of Sport. In a speech full of extreme distortion and invective, he painted a lurid picture of Sudeten Germans being forced to flee a ravaged countryside, portraying himself as a simple,

Barefoot Ethiopian troops parade before marching off to fight the Italian armies that invaded their country in 1935. The poor state of the nation's forces convinced Mussolini that what he called the "greatest colonial war in all history" would be a "war without tears." Although the Ethiopian defenders never had a chance against the Duce's motorized columns, bombers, and poison gas, it took the Italians eight months to take the capital, Addis Ababa. During the campaign, the Italian side lost about 5,000 soldiers. They were mostly troops from Italy's African colonies—a fact that prompted Mussolini to comment that he wished more Italians had been killed so as to make the war seem more serious.

JAPAN TAKES THE PATH TO WAR

Japan seemed to be set on a course toward parliamentary democracy until, in the early 1930s, the Great Depression brought it to economic ruin. Rejecting the liberal policies that were favored by the government in power at that time, ultranationalist groups led by the armed forces embarked on a campaign to establish a military dictatorship whose ultimate aim was Japanese hegemony in the Far East.

Their first target was Chinese Manchuria and its plentiful supply of natural resources, which the Japanese war minister—a serving officer who was outside government control—believed to be a prerequisite for the successful waging of war. In 1931, army officers acting without the approval of the Japanese cabinet provoked an incident that they used as an excuse to seize Manchurian towns.

Japanese politicians who were opposed to the Manchurian venture were assassinated by young officers dedicated to the code of *bushido,* the way of the warrior. When the League of Nations condemned Japanese aggression in 1932, Japan simply resigned from the league. Supported by a surge of nationalist sentiment back home, the Japanese army took over the whole region of Manchuria by 1933.

Four years later, the military fabricated an excuse to launch a full-scale attack on China, beginning an undeclared war that would last eight years. As pressure to resist Japanese expansion mounted in the United States, the Asian warlords looked for allies overseas. On December 27, 1940, Japan joined with Germany and Italy in a tripartite pact, by which each recognized the other's imperial ambitions.

General Hideki Tojo, the Japanese war minister, bows to Emperor Hirohito at a military review in October 1940. The real balance of power, however, was the other way around. Hirohito, though idolized by the Japanese, had little part in shaping their foreign policy, whereas Tojo, former chief of staff of Japanese forces in Manchuria, was a major force behind the growth of Japanese militarism. A year later, he would become prime minister and lead his country into war with the Western Allies.

pacific German and Beneš as a lying, cheating warmonger. Beneš, he yelled, pounding the lectern, must agree now to hand over the Sudetenland. This "is the last territorial claim that I have to make in Europe. . . . The decision now lies in his hands: peace or war." The deadline was 2:00 p.m. on September 28.

Hours before the deadline expired, feverish representations from the British government persuaded Mussolini to intervene with a last-minute appeal to Hitler for a twenty-four-hour delay in his war plans. Chamberlain, Mussolini explained, wanted a conference to discuss a negotiated settlement. Hitler agreed, provided that the meeting was held within the twenty-four-hour period. Invitations were sent to Chamberlain and Daladier. The president of Czechoslovakia was not invited.

On September 29, the leaders of the four powers gathered in Munich to consider a draft treaty that had been presented by Mussolini (but prepared by the German foreign ministry and by Göring). In substance, the treaty merely repeated the demands made by Hitler at his last meeting with Chamberlain: The Czechs were to complete their evacuation of the Sudetenland by October 10. Just after midnight on September 30, the leaders of Great Britain and France agreed to the proposals. Czechoslovakia was to be partitioned.

Chamberlain returned to Britain convinced that he had averted war—the more so because he had persuaded Hitler to sign another sheet of paper, hastily typed, recording "the desire of our two peoples never to go to war with one another again." Arriving at London's Heston airport, Chamberlain uttered words that were soon to be given a tragic irony by events: "I believe it is peace for our time," he said, waving his piece of paper. "Peace with honor."

Once again, Hitler was assured of a major prize without firing a single shot, but it was not the way he wanted it. "That fellow Chamberlain has spoiled my entry into Prague," he complained to his SS entourage back in Berlin. Nevertheless, Czechoslovakia was a corpse, ready for dismemberment. Beneš resigned and went into exile in Britain. In March 1939, Hitler and his aides lambasted the new president, the ailing Emil Hácha (at one point the old man actually fainted when Göring threatened to destroy Prague with bombs), until he agreed to surrender the other western provinces of Bohemia and Moravia. Hours later, after encountering no resistance, German troops rolled eastward.

There were other nations, too, that were eager to tear at the dying country. Poland seized a northern pocket known as Teschen; Hungary grabbed a strip along the border, and then the eastern province of Ruthenia. All that was left was a rump, Slovakia, with nominal independence as a German protectorate. Czechoslovakia had simply ceased to exist.

Hard upon Munich, more German demands followed. First Hitler forced Lithuania to cede the German-speaking city of Memel. Next he turned to Poland. The root of dissension here was the Baltic port of Danzig, a city of Germans isolated within Poland. Hitler demanded that a corridor be established between Danzig and the Reich. Confident that the Poles would not refuse, at first he did not even contemplate using military action.

But at this moment—March 31, 1939—Chamberlain, seeking ways to counter criticism of his betrayal of Czechoslovakia, offered to guarantee Poland's security. He still did not believe that Hitler would actually go to war, but he had become convinced that Britain needed an ally in eastern Europe. That ally could have been the

THE SPANISH CRUCIBLE

In 1936, when civil war erupted in Spain, it seemed that the ideologies dividing Europe—fascism and communism—were formally opposed for the first time.

But the conflict, which began when army commanders in Spanish Morocco revolted against Madrid's Republican government, was a far more complex affair—of employers against workers, landless peasants against property owners, church against state, armed forces against civilians.

The government was a diverse coalition of left-wing groups. The rebels, alarmed that the country was about to surrender to communism, were supported by the Catholic church, the middle class, and a small Fascist party, the Falangists. They were eventually welded together by the austere General Francisco Franco—portrayed in the postwar mural above as a crusader who united army and church.

With aid from Hitler and Mussolini, Franco rapidly gained control of the west and south of Spain. Hitler had a particular interest in the war: Here he could test his new air force. German planes ferried Franco's troops from Africa, and the 100 aircraft of the Condor Legion gave the Nationalists command of the air. Mussolini, eager not to be outdone, sent almost 50,000 troops to fight for the Nationalists.

None of Europe's democratic governments responded to Republican pleas for assistance, but individuals did: Some 40,000 of them enlisted in the International Brigades that were organized by the Communist International. The Soviet Union also sent military aid; in October 1936, Soviet aircraft and tanks temporarily saved Madrid for the Republicans.

Both sides fought with equal brutality and with scant regard for the lives of noncombatants. In one notorious atrocity that foreshadowed the terrors of World War II, Guernica, the Basque capital, was destroyed by German bombers, with heavy loss of civilian life.

The war dragged on for more than two years, until Franco's better-disciplined, better-equipped forces cut through depleted Republican lines. By April 1939, it was over, leaving almost one million Spaniards dead, with Franco the dictator of a new military regime. Shattered by the conflict, Spain remained neutral throughout World War II, recovering slowly thereafter under Franco's stern control.

Soviet Union, which had made overtures to Britain, but West and East were divided by a gulf of mistrust. The West had sought the destruction of Bolshevik Russia in 1918; and the Bolsheviks were in theory committed to undermining capitalist countries. Besides, Western politicians were certain that Stalin was a savage, his armies in tatters, his political system on the verge of collapse. In brief, the Soviet Union was both too dangerous and too weak to be considered as an ally.

Poland's foreign minister, Józef Beck, accepted Chamberlain's offer instantly and firmly rejected Hitler's demands. The Führer was astonished by the appeaser's newfound resilience. "They are little worms," he said. "I saw them in Munich." And again, in fury: "I'll cook them a stew they'll choke on!" The stew was nothing less than war on Poland. The date was set for September 1.

That summer, Hitler received a much-needed reassurance. A perpetual worry for Germany was the possibility of war on two fronts—in the west against France and Britain, and in the east against the Soviet Union. The problem had dominated German planning before World War I, and it remained a nightmare for German generals—or would have, had not the Soviet Union itself signaled a desire to improve relations. It did so because Stalin had finally given up the idea of an alliance with Britain.

Exuberant Londoners cheer Prime Minister Neville Chamberlain on the night of September 30, 1938. Two days earlier, the British premier had signed the Munich Agreement, conceding Hitler's demand that German troops be permitted to occupy the Sudetenland, Czechoslovakia's German-speaking border area. Although one of Chamberlain's cabinet colleagues resigned in protest at this betrayal of a friendly democracy, the prime minister's belief that by sacrificing Czech territory he had won "peace for our time" was widely shared—and not only in England. In Germany, where the military had been openly dubious about the prospects of conquering Czechoslovakia, a wave of relief swept the country. Hitler, however, saw Britain's policy of appeasement as a sign of weakness that encouraged him to make additional territorial demands.

Though long-term enemies, Hitler and Stalin both had a cynical interest in a short-term alliance. It would ensure that Hitler would not be faced with a conflict on two fronts should Britain and France actually fight on behalf of Poland; and it would give Stalin the time to rebuild his army, seriously weakened by ideologic purges. Neither had any illusions about the other's long-term aims. "Everything that I undertake is directed against Russia," Hitler said. "If the West is too stupid and too blind to understand this, then I will be forced to reach an understanding with the Russians, smash the West, and then turn all my concentrated strength on the Soviet Union." "I know what Hitler's up to," Stalin confided to a colleague. "He thinks he's outsmarted me, but actually it is I who have outsmarted him."

On August 23, Nazi Germany and the Soviet Union signed what was ostensibly a nonaggression pact. But under a secret protocol, the two simply divided up Poland and other territories. Hitler would take western Poland, and Stalin would seize eastern Poland, part of Finland, the Baltic states of Lithuania, Latvia, and Estonia, and part of Rumania. It was perhaps the most astonishing event of an astonishing decade. Both leaders had simply tossed all their well-rehearsed convictions aside, and the political world was turned upside down.

Only Chamberlain's guarantee to Poland could deter Hitler now, but convinced

Registering dull shock and helpless anger, a crowd of Czechs watch German troops entering Prague on March 15, 1939. After their country's frontier defenses had been signed away at Munich, the Czechoslovak government tried rigorously to comply with the terms of the agreement so as to save the rest of the country from annexation. But Hitler, whose intention had always been to seize the entire Czechoslovak state, used the excuse of a Slovak separatist uprising to occupy Prague less than six months after the occupation of the Sudetenland. In violation of the Munich Agreement, most of the country was declared a German protectorate, but Britain and France again did nothing, arguing that the voluntary severance of Slovakia from the country nullified their guarantee to protect the integrity of the Czechoslovak state.

that Britain would do no more than "just put on an act of waging war," he set zero hour for 4:45 a.m. on September 1. "I've given the order," he told his foreign minister. "I've set the ball rolling."

This time, though, the Führer lost his gamble. Chamberlain was still talking about a negotiated settlement when German bombs fell on Warsaw, but the House of Commons had had enough. Under pressure, Chamberlain sent an ultimatum to Hitler telling him to desist by 11:00 a.m. on September 3. When the ultimatum expired, Britain announced that it was at war with Germany, and France unwillingly followed suit that afternoon.

Hitler's weapon against Poland was blitzkrieg (lightning war)—a concept that emerged in the 1920s and 1930s among strategists who sought to avoid the dogged stalemates that had characterized the battles of World War I. In Germany, a number of generals—notably Heinz Guderian—devised strategies based on fast-moving armored units of tanks, trucks, and self-propelled artillery. The ground forces would be

Armed with lances and sabers, a Polish cavalry unit practices maneuvers in April 1939, four months before the German invasion of their country that was to pit them against fast-moving tanks and screaming dive bombers. During the early days of the attack, some Polish cavalry charged the tanks in the belief that they were nothing but cars covered by painted plywood—a training device used by the German army before it had proper armored vehicles. Hitler's invasion of Poland finally led Britain and France to declare war on Germany. But the two powers could do little to aid their far-off ally, and within a month, Poland was vanquished, its lands divided between Nazi Germany and Germany's new, short-term ally, the Soviet Union.

supported by aircraft, including reconnaissance planes, fighters, and dive bombers, which would act as airborne artillery. A few radical military thinkers in England, Italy, and France (among them an abrasive young Staff College lecturer named Charles de Gaulle, the future president of France) shared this vision, but they were outnumbered by traditionalists who insisted that battlegrounds were still the domain of infantry and static defenses. Hitler, on the other hand, had quickly seen the advantage of fast, decisive campaigns.

Put to the test against Poland, blitzkrieg proved an overwhelming success. First, bombers droned deep behind enemy lines to destroy airfields, railway stations, bridges, and fuel dumps. All along the front, Polish troops were assaulted by the terrifying Junkers-87 *Sturzkämpfer* (dive bomber), better known as the Stuka, which plunged almost vertically, siren wailing, to release bombs with devastating accuracy. Then came the tanks, bursting through weak points, fanning out to split enemy forces, wheeling to destroy and capture. If the enemy stayed to fight, they were surrounded; if they retreated, they ran into the chaos caused by the bombers.

Even the weather was on the side of the Germans. Clear, sunny skies baked the ground hard for the tanks and kept the rivers—Poland's only natural lines of defense—low. Within days, western Poland was in German hands. Any hopes that the Poles could regroup in the east were dashed on September 17, when Stalin, fulfilling his agreement with Hitler, invaded across the eastern frontier. The armies of the two aggressors met at the Bug River, the new demarcation between the Third Reich and the Soviet Union.

In the west there was a brief flurry of activity. The French mobilized five million troops. The British started a blockade of German ports and dispatched two divisions, the British Expeditionary Force (BEF), to help the French. Then all fell quiet. Tradition dictated that no attack could be mounted without massive artillery bombardments, and the guns were not yet ready. The Polish campaign was over, and the German army was prepared to take on any threat in order to prevent the Western Allies from doing anything effective.

Hitler was all for making a preemptive strike, aiming to occupy the Low Countries and the Channel coastline down to Calais; but his generals, who had counted on several weeks' lull to build up strength, were so appalled that some of them considered deposing him. In the end they simply stalled for time, then produced an unoriginal plan involving a massive thrust through Belgium, similar to the German opening advance of 1914. Hitler did not like it; he favored a push through the hilly, forested Ardennes region of southern Belgium, an area that his experts assured him was impenetrable by heavy armor. The onset of winter forced a postponement, but essentially the conservative plan was accepted—until, in January, it fell into Allied hands when a Luftwaffe plane crashed in Belgium. In something of a panic, the Germans went back to the drawing board.

So for nine months, neither side did anything of strategic importance. A U-boat sank the battleship *Royal Oak* at anchor in the Orkneys. The British distributed gas masks, sent children out of London to live in foster homes where they would be safe from the threat of bombs, and banned the use of car headlights at night (thereby

In a work entitled *Rendezvous,* the British cartoonist David Low portrays Adolf Hitler and Joseph Stalin greeting each other over the prostrate body of a defeated Poland. On August 23, 1939, the two dictators—for long the bitterest of ideological enemies—had made a secret agreement to partition Poland as part of a hastily negotiated nonaggression pact. Thereby, Stalin bought time to build up his armed forces, and Hitler secured his eastern frontiers, enabling him to plan his 1940 invasion of Belgium and France. The Führer's hatred of Soviet communism remained undimmed, however, and within two years of signing the pact, he was to launch a full-scale invasion of his supposed ally.

Soldiers of the British Expeditionary Force wade away from the beaches at Dunkirk, in northern France, to a waiting ship—one of the 900 small vessels that helped rescue more than 300,000 Allied troops between May 27 and June 4, 1940. Trapped in a German pincers, these men would have had no alternative but surrender had Hitler not stopped his commanders' advance. He wanted to save his armor for a final offensive against the French, whose defeat he felt sure would bring Britain to the negotiating table. In addition, he was under pressure from Hermann Göring to leave the rest of the battle to the German air force. Two days later, Hitler reversed his decision, but the British had used the respite to strengthen their defenses, enabling them to hold off the Germans long enough to complete one of the most dramatic evacuations in military history.

doubling the number of traffic accidents). But that was about all. If this was war, it was a very odd one. The Germans called it sitzkrieg, the sitting war. In Britain, it was dubbed the Phony War.

Prewar apathy regained its hold. The Belgians refused to allow Allied troops on their soil; it would, they said, compromise their neutrality. The French commander in chief, General Maurice Gamelin, buried himself in the ancient fortress of Vincennes on the outskirts of Paris, making little contact with his officers. Mussolini, though Hitler's ally, had declared Italy nonbelligerent. When Churchill, who was appointed first lord of the admiralty on the outbreak of hostilities, said the war was not really about Poland—"We are fighting to save the whole world from the pestilence of Nazi tyranny"—few took him seriously. It was widely assumed that Hitler had made a fatal error in not attacking westward immediately after Poland fell. He "had missed the bus," said Chamberlain, in another famous phrase.

But it was Hitler, again, who seized the initiative. His more radical generals shared his belief that it would be possible to make an armored thrust through the Ardennes, and that tanks could cross the Meuse River and penetrate the light French defenses there. Hitler was delighted to have his earlier suggestion fed back as a full-fledged plan. The attack was set for May 1940.

Before then, however, he conceived another action that would give Germany a strategic edge. The Führer planned to invade neutral Norway in order to safeguard imports of Swedish iron ore shipped either from the Baltic or from the ice-free Norwegian port of Narvik. Britain, too, planned an invasion of Scandinavia, but Hitler was one step ahead of the Allies. Even as British troops were embarking in the Firth of Forth on April 9, 1940, German invaders were slipping ashore at various points along the Norwegian coast. Early the next morning, German forces also entered neutral Denmark. Surprise was total. In Denmark, there was virtually no resistance. The Norwegians resisted bravely—most dramatically by sinking the heavy cruiser *Blücher* in the Oslo fjord, with the loss of 1,000 lives. Allied naval actions sank two German cruisers and ten destroyers, but on land the small British relief force was repelled. The Norwegian king, Haakon, escaped to Britain, and the German troops marched into Oslo unopposed.

In Britain, the fall of Norway had a dramatic effect. The public had become deeply dissatisfied with the bumbling complacency that had marked the Phony War. Now they were confronted with military failure. On May 7, an aging conservative, Leo Amery, put the powerful feelings of many into words. Turning to Chamberlain in the House of Commons, he quoted Oliver Cromwell's words when he dissolved Parliament in 1653: "Depart, I say, and let us have done. In the name of God, go!" Already ill with a cancer that would soon kill him, Chamberlain resigned, to be replaced three days later by Winston Churchill at the head of a wartime coalition government. On the same day, the German armed forces swept westward.

Gamelin had been expecting an attack, and expecting it through Belgium. Nor were his preconceptions disappointed at first, for Hitler had devised a brilliant feint to disguise his true intentions: The German army would lure the French north with an invasion of Belgium and Holland, then Guderian's panzers—armored divisions—would attack through the Ardennes, race for the sea, and slice the Allies in two.

Holland capitulated after four days. Spirited resistance was broken by German threats to bomb Rotterdam; two hours before the deadline expired, the Germans bombed the city anyway, killing almost 1,000 people. Queen Wilhelmina and her court fled to London. Belgium fell almost as quickly. Supposedly, the way into Belgium was barred by a great fortress, Eben Emael, north of Liège, which could pour devastating fire for miles in any direction—except upward. German parachutists, delivered silently by gliders, landed directly on the fortress, crammed explosives into its fire slits, and blasted and burned out its occupants.

Allied divisions sped north to reinforce the Belgians, while Hitler rejoiced. "I could have wept for joy," he said. "They have fallen into my trap." Even as the fighting in Belgium continued, the main German force advanced through the weakly defended Ardennes. On May 13, it crossed the Meuse into France, then swung north to slice into the flank of the Allied forces advancing into Belgium. Protected from above by Stukas, seventy-one German divisions whipped across France, cutting the Allied armies in half, scattering tens of thousands of refugees.

The Allies, their entire war plan shattered by the brilliance of the German advance, were left in total confusion. The only conceivable response—to cut the German arrowhead from its narrow shaft—was impossible, because most units were exhausted and short of supplies. The French reserves were already cut off in Lorraine, far to the southeast, and the French commanders were always a beat behind events. The ineffectual Gamelin was replaced by General Maxime Weygand, an elderly World War I hero. He was still issuing confident orders and encouraging messages when the Germans reached the Channel. It had taken them just a week.

Meanwhile, the Allied forces in Belgium and northern France were in rapid retreat. For the British there was only one thing to do: evacuate. Commanders back in London were still swayed by Weygand's optimism, but the BEF commander, General Lord Gort, a stolid realist, knew better. On May 27, he withdrew the British into the last coastal pocket around Dunkirk.

While Hitler inexplicably hesitated to attack the enclave, an extraordinary rescue operation went into action. It would take an armada to save the British troops,

One month after the German invasion of France on May 13, 1940, a field gun lays down covering shellfire to protect forces about to cross the Seine River at Rouen, on their way to Paris. The capital fell in just five weeks, largely because the French military planners had deployed their troops in expectation of an attack from the coastal plain of Belgium. The German high command took them by surprise by attacking from southern Belgium, sending their armored divisions through the hilly and forested Ardennes and prying open weak links in the Maginot line, the supposedly impregnable chain of defenses protecting France's eastern border.

and since only forty-one of the Royal Navy's destroyers were available, a call went out for all ships that could sail to lend assistance. The response was astonishing. Hundreds of civilian owners made ready trawlers, paddle wheelers, barges, ferries, launches, schooners, ketches, and private yachts. Braving mines, shellfire, and dive bombers, guided by the columns of smoke from Dunkirk, 900 vessels maneuvered inshore toward the lines of men waiting on Dunkirk's jetties and beaches. During the next eight days, more than 200,000 British and more than 100,000 French, Belgian, and Dutch troops were rescued in an operation that became a byword for heroism in the face of defeat.

But France now stood ready for conquest; already, 370,000 French were dead, wounded, or taken prisoner. In the first half of June, both German army groups wheeled south, broke the French lines, and scattered what remained of the French army. The roads leading south were choked with as many as 10 million refugees and thousands of cars, abandoned when they had run out of fuel. Officers' vehicles tried to force a way through the disordered procession, while German planes roared unopposed above, strafing the columns.

There were three possible courses that Premier Paul Reynaud could follow: He could capitulate, he could accept even more destruction in a futile defense of the nation, or he could set up government-in-exile in North Africa. Those who favored capitulation looked to the new vice-premier, Marshal Henri Philippe Pétain, an eighty-four-year-old hero of World War I, to negotiate a surrender. Others, notably the young under secretary of state for national defense, Charles de Gaulle, refused to admit defeat. He was all for continuing the war from North Africa or from anywhere French forces could be rallied.

Paris emptied. After a final few days of bittersweet normality—the cafés crowded, the theaters full—two million Parisians spilled southward, in an "interminable treacle" of lines, going they knew not where. The French government fled to Bordeaux, while the remaining British troops dashed for Cherbourg, where they steamed out of port just in front of General Erwin Rommel's 7th Panzer Division. On June 14, three days before Pétain capitulated, the Germans entered the capital, goose-stepping down the Champs Élysées.

"Our most dangerous enemy is Britain," Hitler had said after the defeat of Poland. Britain now had to be eliminated before he could turn to his main objective, the Soviet Union. He tried to secure a negotiated peace but was coldly rebuffed. In August, he reluctantly decided that there was no alternative to an invasion, which was set for September 15. That meant first securing control of the skies—a task that the vainglorious Reichsmarshal Hermann Göring, commander of the Luftwaffe, claimed would be fulfilled in four days.

The Battle of Britain, as it came to be called, started on August 12, with the first of many aerial attacks on coastal radar stations and air bases. The German planes were met by the Royal Air Force's single-engined Hurricanes and Spitfires, which were not as heavily armed as the Messerschmitt 109s that escorted the German bombers, but which were more maneuverable. Another advantage enjoyed by the RAF fighters was an excellent system of radar stations that could direct the aircraft to intercept enemy formations quickly and accurately, allowing the pilots to remain on the ground until the last minute, thus saving fuel for combat. The German pilots, lacking adequate radar guidance themselves and operating at the limits of their range, were at an

At once conqueror and tourist, Hitler strolls away from the Eiffel Tower on June 23, 1940, the day after he had accepted the surrender of France. The document was signed in the Forest of Compiègne, at the exact spot where, in a restaurant car on a railway track, the Allies had imposed armistice terms on the German army in 1918. To complete the revenge he had promised his followers, Hitler ordered the same railway car to be brought from a Paris museum for the occasion. He then spent a day sightseeing in Paris, which he called "one of the jewels of Europe," before leaving, never to return.

immediate disadvantage. By the end of August, the Luftwaffe had lost more than 600 fighters and bombers for the loss of fewer than 300 RAF fighters. Then, by concentrating his raids on airfields, Göring began to redress the balance.

But before it could tip firmly Germany's way, Hitler intervened. Incensed by a Bomber Command raid on Berlin, he diverted the Luftwaffe to attacks on London. On September 7, almost 400 German bombers, escorted by 600 fighters, attacked London's East End, killing 1,500 people. Hitler's purpose was to destroy the Britons' determination to resist, but the "blitz" had the opposite effect and, more important, gave the Royal Air Force time to rebuild its airfields and train new pilots. As a consequence, additional raids on civilian targets were broken up with heavy losses by Fighter Command.

Realizing that Göring could not win control of the skies, Hitler canceled the invasion of Britain—a project that had never excited his enthusiasm. On September 17, it was postponed "indefinitely," and two days later, Hitler ordered the invasion fleet to be dispersed. The night-bombing raids would continue, as would U-boat attacks on British shipping, but for the remainder of 1940, Hitler concentrated his attention on plans for the invasion of the Soviet Union.

Far to the south, offstage, Mussolini had watched Hitler's successes with growing envy. He wanted to share what he called the "booty" with "those who keep ferociously to themselves all the riches and all the gold of the earth." After the British defeat in Scandinavia, he announced that he could no longer delay his "appointment with history," but he waited until the French army had been broken before entering the war on Germany's side. Neither the Italian economy nor the army was in any shape to sustain a war, but Mussolini was convinced that Germany would emerge as the victor, giving Italy the opportunity to win its own "living space" in the Mediterranean. Indeed, he had already undertaken a quick little campaign against near-helpless Albania, seizing it in five days in April 1939. Now he declared war on France, hoping to annex a few border areas in the south; his troops, however, were stopped dead in the Alps by snow and by the few French troops that were still guarding the passes.

Mussolini blamed the failure on the "softness" of his troops—a defect that would be remedied in a "parallel war" against Britain in the Mediterranean and African theaters. He had sizable forces in Africa—215,000 troops in Libya and more than 250,000 in Italian East Africa—which he planned to throw against British-held Egypt. But they were woefully short of supplies, and when the Libyan troops did invade, they came to an ignominious halt in the desert when they ran out of fuel sixty miles across the border. And after the East African troops had taken British Somaliland in August—Italy's only single-handed success on land during the whole war—they, too, ran low on supplies and were rendered incapable of further attack.

In the light of Italy's military weakness, Mussolini's next actions were little short of mad. He planned simultaneous invasions of Switzerland, Yugoslavia, and Greece. Fortunately, he did not have troops for all three, and on advice from his commanders, he abandoned his plans against Switzerland and Yugoslavia. That left Greece. Angered by an understanding that Hitler had secretly reached with Rumania in September 1940, Mussolini blurted to Count Ciano, his son-in-law and foreign minister: "Hitler always faces me with a *fait accompli*. This time I am going to pay him back in his own coin. He will find out from the newspapers that I have occupied Greece.

Vapor trails mark the pattern of an aerial dogfight over London during the Battle of Britain in August 1940. The Luftwaffe never managed to dominate the skies, partly because its fighter planes, operating at the limits of their range, could not provide adequate protection for its bombers, and partly because of the quality of the Royal Air Force's pilots. This tight-knit team—some 1,500 in all, including many Polish, Czech, and Commonwealth fliers—succeeded in thwarting Hitler's plans to invade Britain at the cost of more than 400 lives. Churchill acknowledged his compatriots' debt in a succinct, much-quoted phrase: "Never in the field of human conflict was so much owed by so many to so few."

In this way the equilibrium will be reestablished. I shall send in my resignation as an Italian if anyone objects to our fighting the Greeks."

Italian troops invaded from Albania on October 28 and were expelled within a week. This humiliation, combined with a British raid on the port of Taranto that destroyed much of the Italian navy, plus a British counterattack on Libya in December, convinced Hitler that Mussolini must have German help. Over the next few weeks, German troops arrived to support Italy in Greece, Libya, and Sicily (to strengthen Italian attacks on British ships in the Mediterranean). Not only was Libya held and Greece taken, but Yugoslavia, too, was overwhelmed.

These conquests, so vital to Mussolini, were a strategically irrelevant distraction for Hitler, who by now had approved the plans for Operation Barbarossa, the invasion of the Soviet Union. In readiness for the attack, he withdrew Luftwaffe units from Sicily to the Eastern Front, with catastrophic results for Italy. Operating out of Malta, the British air force and navy destroyed many Italian convoys to North Africa. Once again, Hitler had to come to the rescue, giving Field Marshal Albert Kesselring the task of capturing Malta and winning all North Africa for the Axis.

In the end, there was no German invasion of Malta, and the British in Egypt held firm, retaining a foothold in Africa that would become the springboard for a subsequent Allied invasion of Europe through Italy. Mussolini's involvement in the war had been disastrous for Germany, as Hitler himself admitted. "My unshakable friendship for Italy and the Duce may well be held to be an error on my part," he wrote. "It is in fact quite obvious that our Italian alliance has been of more service to our enemies than to ourselves."

In particular, the Nazi leader claimed—aided by the wisdom of hindsight—the unplanned intervention of Germany in the Balkan States had "led to a catastrophic delay in the launching of our attack on Russia. Ah, if only the Italians had remained aloof from this war!"

Almost certainly, Hitler was exaggerating. In June 1941, there were only seven German divisions in the Balkans, compared with some 150 along the border with the Soviet Union. At that moment, before the release of the greatest invasion in history, Hitler was supremely confident of victory.

THE RED CZAR

When Vladimir Ilyich Ulyanov Lenin, first leader of the Soviet Union, died after a twenty-month illness on January 21, 1924, all the funeral arrangements were made by the one man he did not want to succeed him—former seminarian and Bolshevik revolutionary Joseph Stalin, photographed here at his leader's left side in 1922.

Lenin was so opposed to Stalin—whom he regarded as too crude for high office—that he had recommended in a letter to the Communist Party Central Committee that the shoemaker's son from Georgia should be stripped of his post as its secretary-general. But Stalin, a brilliant political tactician, had recruited so many of his own supporters for the committee that it voted to ignore even the deathbed wishes of the Soviet nation's founder.

This crucial hurdle overcome, Stalin spent the next four years consolidating his personal power. He eliminated rivals by first allying himself with them against political opponents and then abruptly shifting his allegiance, isolating his former supporters and exposing them to charges of political divisiveness that he himself would bring. In this way, he disposed of his most formidable rival, Leon Trotsky.

In 1928, Stalin abandoned Lenin's New Economic Policy, which permitted small-scale private enterprise, replacing it with forced "collectivization" of small peasant plots. Collectivization was accompanied by a program of industrialization forced through at breakneck speed. In a single decade, the Soviet Union aimed to reach levels of industrial productivity that it had taken the Western democracies more than a century to achieve.

But the upheavals that the economic revolution set in motion caused horrendous suffering and widespread discontent. Fearing conspiracies everywhere, Stalin launched a mass terror campaign in the 1930s to crush all opposition. In a climate of fear whipped up by government propaganda, two-thirds of the Communist Party Central Committee, half the army officers over the rank of major, and most managers holding key industrial posts were eliminated as "enemies of the people."

The Great Purge ended only when it became clear that the Soviet Union's internal convulsions had sharpened the predatory intentions of Stalin's fellow dictator, Adolf Hitler. In the absence of European allies, Stalin abandoned his anti-Nazi stance and signed a nonaggression pact with Hitler, hoping that a temporary peace would give him time to build up the Soviet Union's industrial and military muscle for the inevitable confrontation with Germany.

FORCING THE PACE OF PROGRESS

In terms of numbers of workers and raw materials, post-revolutionary Russia was a giant, but compared with the Western powers, it was woefully deficient in skilled labor, machinery, and efficient management. Very well aware of the Soviet Union's weakness, Stalin ordered an entire overhaul of the economy, launching a series of Five-Year Plans that were designed to turn the Soviet Union into a major industrial power. Failure to meet the targets was considered a crime against the state and punished accordingly.

As a first step toward industrialization, Stalin ordered the collectivization of agriculture. Small farms were combined into units large enough to make mechanization cost-effective; peasants who resisted were dispossessed of their holdings, deported to labor camps, or summarily executed. Some farmers slaughtered their livestock and fled the countryside for the towns, where they were hired at miserable wages in factories partly financed by the export of agricultural output extracted from the state farms at rock-bottom prices. Food production by the demoralized and alienated farmers actually fell, and poor distribution of the harvest meant that millions of people went hungry. Farm output did not rise to precollectivization levels until 1938, but by 1937, Soviet industrial output was second only to that of the United States.

A portrait of a steadfast Stalin dominates this poster celebrating the construction of a steel plant in the Ural Mountains, 900 miles east of Moscow. Exhorted by slogans such as The Victory of Socialism Is Achieved in Our Country, Soviet workers did fulfill some of the economic goals set by the first two Five-Year Plans, which concentrated on what Stalin referred to as "the means of production." Between 1929 and 1938, coal output rose by 230 percent, electric-power generation by 540 percent, and motor-vehicle manufacturing by an astonishing 15,000 percent.

Stalin's model worker, Alexei Stakhanov, smiles for a publicity photograph. In a carefully orchestrated campaign to impose higher production targets, the state organized an entire movement around this Ukrainian coal miner who, it was claimed, had cut fifteen times more coal than the norm during a single six-hour night shift. In fact, the feat was a sham. Stakhanov had two helpers, and the race to increase output seriously damaged product quality and worker safety.

While peasants gather the harvest on a Ukrainian collective farm, a truck full of government officials produce a propaganda sheet extolling Stalin's agricultural policies. In reality, the effects of collectivization were disastrous in the Ukraine, where an estimated two million people starved when the harvest failed in 1932 and the central government refused to divert relief supplies of grain earmarked for export.

A REIGN OF TERROR

In December of 1934, the popular and talented Leningrad Communist party chief Sergei Kirov was murdered by unknown assailants. Almost certainly Kirov's assassination had been ordered by Stalin, who used the crime as a pretext to launch his Great Purge of political rivals—real, potential, and by the end of the five-year witch hunt, largely imaginary.

His first targets were close party colleagues. They were arrested on trumped-up charges, forced to confess imaginary crimes at widely publicized show trials, and then either sent to prison camps or executed. Lower-ranking party officials soon shared their fate, often for alleged support of Trotsky, the disgraced organizer of the 1917 Russian Revolution. With political opposition crushed, Stalin turned on the Red Army, liquidating its commander and fourteen of his sixteen generals.

As the purge accelerated, it fed on itself, with citizens denouncing one another for their own advantage, and then being denounced in turn. Even when the accusations were patently absurd, the police and public prosecutors did not dare dismiss them in case they, too, laid themselves open to charges of treason. That did not save them, for in the end, Stalin, realizing that the country was bleeding to death from the wounds he had inflicted, ordered a purge of the purgers themselves.

The doomed Marshal Mikhail Tukhachevsky, seventh from left, lines up with fellow senior Red Army officers at the 1934 Communist Party Congress. Three years later, Tukhachevsky was removed from his post as commander in chief, charged with spying for Germany, and executed with most of his generals. So began a purge that claimed the lives of more senior officers than would die in World War II.

A bowler-hatted symbol of foreign capitalism drives a team of ravening dogs atop a 1930 propaganda float. Behind marches a caricature of Leon Trotsky, Lenin's likely successor until Stalin maneuvered him out of the running, out of the party, and finally, in 1929, out of the country. Trotsky continued his opposition from abroad until 1940, when he was murdered in Mexico by one of Stalin's agents.

Communist officials gather (top) at the fortieth anniversary of the Moscow Arts Theater in 1938. Standing fourth from right is the head of the Soviet secret police, Nikolai Yezhov. That same year, Yezhov was removed from office and sent to an asylum for the criminally insane. When the picture was republished in 1949 (bottom), his image had been removed. Also missing was the theater's director—a victim of clumsy photographic retouching rather than the purge.

Joseph Stalin, champion of world communism, shakes hands with Nazi Germany's foreign minister, Joachim von Ribbentrop, at a reception to celebrate the signing of the Nazi-Soviet nonaggression pact on August 23, 1939. Although the partnership was a marriage of convenience between irreconcilable ideologic enemies, the pact served the short-term interests of both parties. For Hitler, aware that his planned conquest of Poland might lead to conflict with France and Britain, it removed the risk of having to wage war on two fronts. For Stalin, it provided a precious breathing space in which he could rebuild the Soviet Union's military and industrial strength. The agreement also gave him a license to bolster his western defenses by annexing the Baltic states of Estonia, Latvia, and Lithuania, as well as parts of Poland, Finland, and Rumania. Although his interests were entirely cynical, Stalin came to place a misguided and obsessive faith in the pact.

A white-clad Finnish soldier stands over the frozen corpses of Soviet invaders of his country, one of them still in the crouching position in which he died. The Winter War began in November 1940, when the Soviet Union set out to strengthen its northern defenses at the expense of Finland. But the Red Army, incompetently led and poorly equipped for winter warfare, suffered 200,000 casualties in four months before sheer numbers and superior firepower overcame Finnish resistance.

AN OPPORTUNIST ALLIANCE

Throughout the 1920s, Stalin concentrated on domestic policy rather than foreign affairs. Whereas the discredited Trotsky wanted to spread communism around the globe, Stalin's expressed aim was to create "pure" socialism inside the Soviet Union before attempting to export it.

As a result of this introspective attitude, the Soviet Union had become diplomatically isolated and, by 1933, was exposed to threats from two hostile neighbors—Ger-many in the west and Japan in the east.

Stalin therefore instructed Communist agents to form hitherto-discouraged alliances with leftist groups overseas; their efforts helped Communist-backed governments to power in Spain and France. Meanwhile, Stalin's foreign minister, Maxim Litvonov, was winning international support for a policy of unified resistance to German aggression.

The policy came to naught, however, when Britain and France signed the 1938 Munich Agreement with Germany, effectively sanctioning Hitler's seizure of Czechoslovakia. When Hitler, anxious to complete his conquests in Europe before launching his planned invasion of the Soviet Union, offered Stalin a ten-year treaty of nonaggression, the dictator hastily accepted. Stalin also took steps to secure his eastern frontier by concluding a similar pact with Japan.

THE WORLD AT WAR

It was the time of the summer solstice, the longest day of the year. Along the Soviet Union's western borders between the Baltic and the Black Sea, there was barely enough darkness to conceal the German troops massed in their forward positions. But the Soviet commanders turned a blind eye to the menace that confronted them; Stalin himself had ordered them to avoid any posture that Hitler could interpret as a "provocation." None was needed. At 3:15 a.m. on June 22, 1941, while squadrons of Luftwaffe dive bombers were already approaching sleepy Soviet airfields, the armed array—some 150 divisions, more than three million troops with 3,580 armored vehicles—advanced across the border almost unopposed. The twenty-two-month conflict that had transformed the face of Europe was about to assume new dimensions of space and ferocity. Operation Barbarossa, Adolf Hitler's dream made military reality, was under way.

Until that June morning when the Wehrmacht came crashing through the muddled Soviet defenses, the war in Europe had seemed, to all intents and purposes, over, leaving Germany in a position of unassailable dominance. The Third Reich had swallowed half of Poland and controlled Austria, Czechoslovakia, France, Belgium, and the Netherlands, as well as Denmark, Norway, Greece, and Yugoslavia. Fascist Italy was a solid ally, and Hungary, Finland, and Rumania had thrown in their lot with Hitler. Sweden was compliantly neutral, its iron ore feeding the furnaces of the Ruhr's steelworks. Even Stalin, still placing his faith in the nonaggression pact he had signed with the Führer in 1939, was shipping vital supplies of oil and grain to Germany. The United States remained politically hostile to the Nazi regime, but isolationist sentiment—President Franklin D. Roosevelt had won the 1940 elections on a no-war platform—seemed certain to keep the world's greatest industrial power well clear of the conflict in Europe.

Only Britain, battered and almost bankrupt, still stood in arms against the German dictator. The air battles of 1940 had shown Hitler the near-impossibility of launching a successful invasion of his island opponent. It appeared to be equally clear that American aid in the form of the lend-lease arms transfer scheme, which had started in April 1941, would keep Britain in the struggle after its own resources were exhausted. But even under the implacable leadership of Winston Churchill, the British were incapable of causing any serious harm to the superior military power of Germany. It was only a matter of time, it seemed, before Churchill or a less obdurate successor realized the hopelessness of the situation and sued for a peace that Hitler would be more than happy to grant.

There were, to be sure, a few problems—caused less by Hitler's enemies than by his friends. His efforts to save the Italians from their self-inflicted disasters in North Africa and Greece had involved Germany in expensive sideshows: The German

Wives and mothers seek out their dead after a German massacre of Russian partisans during fighting in the Crimea in 1942. Millions would share these women's grief before the first truly global war was over. Of the estimated 100 million men and women mobilized to fight, some 20 million died in battle, but civilian deaths were even higher. About seven million noncombatants perished in the Soviet Union alone, which bore the brunt of conflict in the war's European theater.

By the autumn of 1942, Germany and its allies controlled almost all of Europe—from the Volga, where German troops were fighting in the streets of Stalingrad, to the French Atlantic coast, from which U-boats harried Allied shipping. In North Africa, German and Italian troops had approached within striking distance of the Suez Canal. But the Greater German Reich (colored red on the map), which Hitler had vowed would endure 1,000 years, had less than 1,000 days to run. November 1942 brought a devastating Russian counteroffensive at Stalingrad and an Anglo-American invasion of North Africa. The former marked the beginning of the German army's long westward retreat back to Berlin; the latter would lead to Allied control of the Mediterranean and the seaborne invasion of Europe.

airborne assault on the island of Crete alone had cost some 4,000 German lives. More serious still, the fighting in Greece involved troops earmarked for the attack on Russia, originally scheduled for May. And although the unusually wet spring of 1941 would almost certainly have postponed Barbarossa in any event, the fighting around the Mediterranean was an unwelcome distraction for the German army on the eve of the greatest military operation in history.

Hitler, though, was determined to proceed with what he had always regarded as his true mission in life: an eastward war of conquest and extermination that in time would leave a Germanic population of 250 million people ruling the entire area between the Atlantic and the Urals. Whatever some of his generals might say about the dangers of fighting a war on two fronts, he himself had no doubts that Germany had the might to translate his murderous dream into reality. Two months, he reckoned, would finish the business. "We have only to kick in the door," he declared, "and the whole rotten structure will come crashing down."

As a matter of fact, Hitler had seriously underestimated the real military strength of

the Soviet Union. When he was confronted with reasonably accurate intelligence estimates of the Soviets' ability to manufacture tanks, for example, Hitler simply dismissed most of them out of hand—and considered those that he did believe as all the more reason for an immediate attack, before the Russians reached their full strength. It was the first in a long series of errors that would end with the ruin of Germany—not to mention most of the rest of Europe—and the red flag of the Soviets flying in triumph over the city of Berlin.

In that summer of 1941, though, a Nazi victory seemed a foregone conclusion, for Operation Barbarossa began brilliantly. Three powerful army groups were involved: North, launched through Latvia and Lithuania toward Leningrad; Center, battering past the fortress of Brest Litovsk along the Minsk-Smolensk highway to Moscow; and South, charged with the occupation of the Ukraine. Everywhere, deep armored penetrations not only tore through Soviet border defenses but smashed and surrounded entire armies behind the front. The Red Army's high command, gutted by the purges of the late 1930s, could not match the skill and experience of Germany's

At its largest, in January 1943, Japan's Greater East Asia Co-Prosperity Sphere *(within the yellow line on the map)*, covered most of China and Southeast Asia. Despite its name, it brought little prosperity: Like Nazi Germany, imperial Japan treated its conquests as loot to enrich the homeland. And the new Japanese empire proved as fragile as its German equivalent. On land, the endless defeats the Japanese inflicted upon China were patiently absorbed, bringing victory no nearer. The seaward side of the empire depended on a naval dominance that Japan could not maintain in the face of American industrial strength. Island-hopping counterattacks were followed by aerial bombardment of Japanese cities and, in August 1945, a final, terrible scourging in nuclear fire.

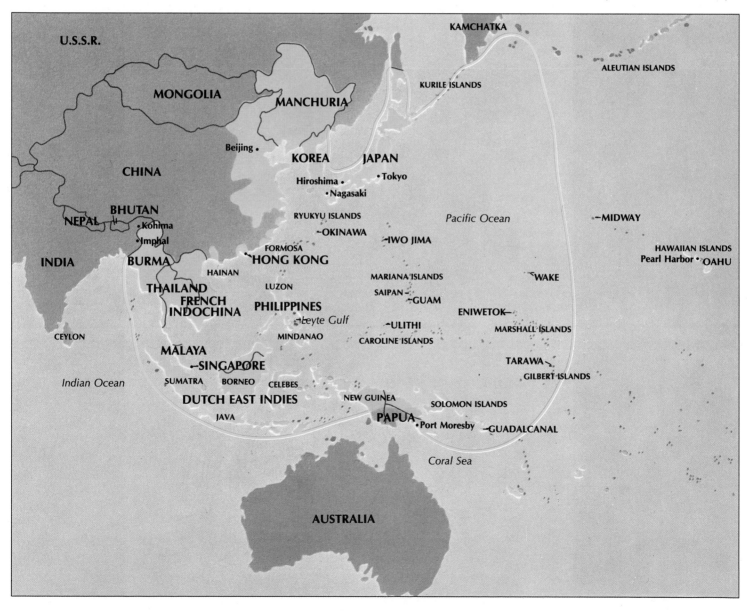

generals and their staffs. Stalin himself, the "Man of Steel," spent the first eleven days of the war in shocked, near-catatonic isolation from his suffering troops and people. Hundreds of thousands of Soviet prisoners shambled westward in the despair of defeat. On July 3, Colonel-General Franz Halder, chief of the German general staff, wrote confidently in his diary: "It is probably no overstatement to say that the Russian campaign has been won in the space of two weeks."

There were some ill omens, though. The invaders had already encountered Russian KV and T-34 tanks, which were more powerfully armed, better armored, and more mobile than their German equivalents. Even Hitler was perturbed by reports of dogged Soviet resistance: He told Mussolini that "the Russians fight with a truly stupid fanatacism. Pillbox crews blow themselves up rather than surrender." The sacrifice of hundreds of thousands of troops gave the Soviets time to dismantle the important industrial facilities in the Germans' path and ship them, lock, stock, and barrel, to new sites beyond the Ural Mountains, where they would resume production by the spring of 1942.

Not all Soviet units, however, were fighting to the last man. The fact was that Stalin's long rule of terror had made him a figure of hate to many of his subjects. In the Baltic provinces of Latvia, Estonia, and Lithuania, which had been independent

states until the Soviet Union virtually annexed them in 1939, and in the western Ukraine, where there was a long tradition of nationalism, the advancing Germans were frequently received as liberators. But Hitler rejected suggestions that anti-Soviet prisoners be reenlisted as German allies: He had no intention of owing any favors to people whose country was no more than a "big cake," as he put it, to be sliced up for Germany's advantage.

In any event, pro-German sentiments generally evaporated quickly. On the heels of the Wehrmacht's combat troops came SS Chief Heinrich Himmler's Einsatzgruppen —"special forces" entrusted with the murder of Jews, Communist officials, and other potential troublemakers; this last category could and did include just about everyone. Indeed, by a colossal irony, the indiscriminate German onslaught achieved something that a generation of Five-Year Plans, secret police, midnight executions, and Siberian labor camps had scarcely accomplished: It was legitimizing Soviet rule in the hearts and minds of the Soviet Union's people.

From the first days of Operation Barbarossa, the war was seen as a murderous affront not to the Bolshevik regime but to the holy soil of Mother Russia. It was a mood quickly sensed by Stalin. On July 3, he broke his long silence with a broadcast to the nation. In a speech that deeply affected his listeners—many of whom had never heard their leader's voice before—he talked not of Marx and Lenin but of a "national patriotic war . . . for the freedom of our Motherland." Churches, long closed for ideological reasons, were reopened, and cities rang with the somber pealing of formerly silenced bells.

Hitler paid no heed to the enemy's new spirit of resistance. Convinced that his eastern campaign was already as good as won, he even ordered a cut in tank production to increase the amount of scarce steel allocated to the U-boat building program. After the capture of Smolensk in late July, he decided to divert the main attack on Moscow southward, to bring the whole of the Ukraine's rich agricultural land under German control. Many of his generals protested, arguing that Moscow was the key to the Soviet Union's overcentralized railroad communications, the seat of political power, and the one clear objective that their troops, as well as the watching world, could understand. Hitler, increasingly obsessed with the economic exploitation of his new territory, overruled them.

The first result of the switch was a colossal battle at Kiev in September, when more than 600,000 prisoners and a vast amount of military booty fell into German hands. Another consequence was that the attack on Moscow could not be resumed until October 2—a day on which the first ominous snowflakes of the coming winter fell. For most of October, however, rain was the greatest obstacle to progress, bogging down the invaders on Russia's unpaved roads. The frost, when it came, actually sped the German armor on its way. But as October turned to November, the steadily dropping temperatures brought misery to the lightly clad German troops and chaos to their supply system. Hitler had been so confident of achieving victory in 1941 that he had not provided for a winter campaign.

The very speed and scale of the German offensive contributed to its undoing. By late November, Hitler's armies had conquered an area more than three times the size of France. Leningrad was locked in a siege that would ultimately cost more than one million civilian lives, and German patrols in the vanguard could see the spires of the Kremlin from the suburbs of Moscow. But the Wehrmacht's supply system could not keep pace with the advance. Even around the great Russian cities there were few

In July 1941, during the initial German onslaught on the Soviet Union, German panzer grenadiers rush from the cover of their armored troop carrier to clear Russian defenders from a burning village near Smolensk. Motorized to keep pace with the tanks that spearheaded the assault, the grenadiers were generally on hand to deal with troublesome enemy positions, while less mobile foot soldiers brought up the rear. The Germans' shrewd combination of troops—infantry, armor, and artillery, backed by Luftwaffe dive bombers—was the main reason for the astonishing speed of their advance through the shocked Soviet Union in the first stages of Operation Barbarossa.

roads, and most of these were no more than dirt tracks. The railroad system was badly damaged, and the Wehrmacht's horse-drawn wagons—the Germans never had enough motor-vehicle transportation to mechanize their infantry units, let alone their supply services—could furnish only a fraction of the fuel and replacement parts needed. Even without the mounting battle casualties inflicted by stubborn Soviet defenders, wear and tear that could not be swiftly made good kept German tank and aircraft strength dangerously low.

Yet the 1941 battles for Moscow were close indeed. In mid-October the city was in the grip of panic, and many senior party officials fled. Stalin, his nerve recovered, stayed behind. By November 7, the twenty-fourth anniversary of the Bolshevik Revolution, when Soviet troops marched straight from the traditional celebration parade to the nearby front line, fear had been replaced by grim determination. As winter closed in and temperatures fell to −20° F., the German forces clawed their way slowly forward against a Soviet defense that inflicted 250,000 casualties for an advance of only 100 miles. Frostbite claimed thousands more victims. At the end of the month, Chief of Staff Halder warned, "We have reached the end of our human and material resources."

Then, on December 6, the Soviets launched a massive offensive of their own. There had been Soviet counterattacks before: Usually ill-timed and badly coordinated, they had simply added to the Red Army's horrifying losses. This time, though, Stalin had twenty fresh divisions of experienced troops. They were tough Siberian units transferred from the Soviet Union's eastern frontier, where they had been standing guard against a possible Japanese attack from Manchuria. Japan had signed the Tripartite Pact with Germany and Italy in September 1940, and although the Japanese foreign minister had concluded a neutrality agreement with Stalin a few months later, it was known that many of his colleagues favored a strategic offensive against the Soviet Union. No such attack would now come, Soviet intelligence chiefs had assured Stalin: The Japanese had laid other plans.

Stalin's judgment would soon be proved right. In the early hours of December 7, far from the icy death struggle on the outskirts of Moscow, two soldiers training on newly installed radar at the U.S. Navy's Pacific Fleet base in Pearl Harbor, Hawaii, reported some puzzling blips upon their screen. "Hell," said a bored officer, "it's probably just a pigeon with a metal band around its legs." Fifty minutes later, hundreds of Japanese strike aircraft caught the huge base off guard. In less than two hours, they sank or damaged eight battleships and three cruisers, destroyed 188 planes, and killed almost 2,500 men. A shocked America found itself at war.

British Prime Minister Churchill, informed of the attack by BBC radio, telephoned Roosevelt. "What's this about Japan?" he demanded. The American president answered that it was true: "We're all in the same boat," he said. "This actually simplifies things," responded Churchill, and he calmly went to bed. Three days later—December 11 by Greenwich mean time—Adolf Hitler "simplified things" still further by declaring war on the United States. The conflict was now global: Not just a continent but an entire planet was locked in combat.

The Second World War stands out in a war-stained century for the unprecedented scale of the fighting—at least 50 million people died as a result of it—as well as for the political upheavals that it set in train. By 1945, German power in Europe, a key political force for seventy years, had been smashed. Europe itself, including victo-

Bomb-bursts garland the U.S. Pacific Fleet's capital ships during the surprise Japanese attack on Pearl Harbor in Hawaii. The stately line *(left),* moored tranquilly in the base's "Battleship Row," made an easy target for Japan's carrier-launched strike pilots, who sank or crippled eight battleships as well as thirteen smaller vessels at the cost of only twenty-nine aircraft. But the raid was not an unmitigated disaster for the United States; the Pacific Fleet's own carriers, far at sea on exercise when the Japanese blow fell, escaped unharmed. And far from shaking American morale, the attack—delivered without declaration of war—united the country in a quest for vengeance. It would be many months before the United States could hit back, however, and in the meantime, the nation's anger vented itself on America's Japanese community. More than 100,000 men, women, and children *(above),* most of them loyal U.S. citizens and many of them from families resident for generations, were bundled into makeshift resettlement camps.

rious Britain, had lost its former supremacy in a world now uneasily divided between the United States and the Soviet Union, forged by the fires of war into superpowers. Japan's attempt to build a "Greater East Asia Co-Prosperity Sphere" collapsed in ruins; but Asians could not forget the defeats that the Japanese had inflicted upon their white colonial overlords. Nationalism and independence were the dominant themes in what, during the postwar years, would become known as the Third World.

World War II brought other huge changes. The war created a massive growth in the manufacturing capacity of heavy industry, which was matched with enormous advances in technology: The atom bomb was the most fearful example, but radar, rocketry, computers, mass-produced antibiotics, and organochlorine insecticides such as DDT were also among the conflict's enduring legacies. For the first time in history, the fate of nations was largely determined by the obscure research of unseen scientists. It was a war fought on the home front as well as on the field of battle. Whole populations were mobilized to work and fight, the routines of their daily lives conditioned by the struggle, their very thinking shaped by the mass propaganda employed by all the belligerents. It was a war without limits in space, morality, courage, or cruelty. There were few true "noncombatants," for death rained from the sky upon civilians—men, women, and children, workers, housewives—and soldiers alike. It was war carried to the extreme: absolute, pitiless, and world-changing.

Vividly pictured in a 1942 Italian poster, a huge Japanese samurai slashes through an Anglo-American fleet. The artist's work reflected Axis enthusiasm for Japan's drive of conquest, but there was little real cooperation between Germany and Italy and their far-off ally. Physical distance was one disadvantage, but politically, too, there was little attempt to act in unison. Thus Japan never declared war on the Soviet Union, and until 1945, American ships flying the Soviet flag sailed unmolested across the Pacific, carrying vital lend-lease supplies to the Russian port of Vladivostok.

Throughout the month of December 1941, the Wehrmacht found itself fighting desperately against Soviet armies that were better motivated than its own. By that time, the Soviets had clear strategic directions and commanders capable of achieving their objectives. In Georgy Zhukov, Stalin had found a general with a will as unshakable—and as ruthless—as his own. A sample order to one of his officers during the Moscow fighting was typical of his style: "If Antonov's division has not reached its position by dawn, I shall shoot you like a traitor." Such "unwarranted abruptness," as a fellow general later called it, was not by itself enough to make a great commander, but when Zhukov ordered a formation to a position, it was usually the right position. And he had plenty of able subordinates, for six months of disaster had brutally winnowed incompetent party hacks from the Soviet command structure. In effect, the "subhuman" Slavs had turned into winter supermen, and German morale would never completely recover from the shock.

On several occasions, the entire central front was near collapse. But when Hitler's commanders pleaded for a general retreat, he was obdurate: "They must dig into the ground where they are," he ordered, "and hold every square foot of land." Most likely the dictator was right. In the snowbound confusion, an organized withdrawal to better positions would have been impossible to coordinate, and total rout might well have followed. Nevertheless, the standfast orders cost troops and equipment that could not easily be replaced, and in any event, the Soviets pushed the German front back more than ninety miles before the deepening winter made conditions impossible even for the well-clad Siberians.

Hard-pressed as he was in the East, Hitler's declaration of war on the United States, by far the world's richest and most industrialized nation, was an incredible act of folly. Certainly, Roosevelt's support for the British war effort had been galling, and Japan was Germany's ally; but Hitler could not take the war to America—he could only wait for America to bring it to him. Throughout its history as a united nation, Germany had feared a war on two fronts. Hitler, by an act of his own megalomaniac will, had gone further: He now had almost the whole world in arms against him.

His Japanese allies made no reciprocal gesture of support, maintaining carefully correct relations with the Soviet Union. But elsewhere, Japan's war plan was even more of a gamble than Nazi Germany's. The war party in Japan's government—a clear majority, since pacifists were frequently assassinated by ultrapatriots—saw conflict with the United States as inevitable sooner or later and urged immediate action. Japan, the party reasoned, had reached a near-peak in military might. Its fleet in 1941 was superior to the U.S. Pacific Fleet, but Japan could not hope to match the shipbuilding effort the Americans had already begun, and Japan's relative strength could only decline. By striking hard at once, Japan could seize almost all of Southeast Asia, including the strategically vital oil fields of the Dutch East Indies, as well as a perimeter fence of islands halfway across the Pacific that would deny the Americans the forward bases they would need for any sort of counterattack.

The Japanese planners were certain that their offensive would be unstoppable for at least six months. Britain, embroiled with Nazi Germany, could offer no serious resistance. As for the United States, it would eventually come to terms with the new situation—or so Japan's warlords thought. However deluded their hopes would prove to be, they were based on more than mere wishful thinking. The U.S. economy was barely out of the doldrums of the Great Depression, and in 1941, few Americans could have predicted the astonishing production levels the war industries would achieve in the course of hostilities. Unemployment and dissatisfaction were rife; President Roosevelt was unpopular with a large segment of the population. Even so, few of his opponents disagreed with the peace-at-any-price policy with which he had barely won the 1940 election. Most significant of all in the minds of the Japanese war leaders, the August 1941 renewal of conscription legislation, in a time of unprecedented world crisis, had been approved in the U.S. House of Representatives by only one vote. The American people, Japan's military believed, would never have the stomach to slog it out at close quarters against Japanese troops who were imbued with the sam-

Hands raised in surrender, British troops captured at Singapore in February 1942 await their fate. The speed with which Japan's bicycle-borne soldiers overran the Malay Peninsula had unnerved British and Australian commanders, and the city, supposedly the impregnable bastion of Britain's Far Eastern empire, fell with little resistance. The jubilant Japanese could scarcely believe their good fortune, for their men had reached Singapore's defenses exhausted by their rapid advance. They were far lower in food, fuel, and ammunition than the defenders, whose generals cited their own shortages to justify the capitulation to an enraged Prime Minister Winston Churchill.

During the battle for Stalingrad in 1942, Soviet infantrymen, quilted against the cold of autumn, find firing positions in the gutted shell of a building. Weeks of fighting reduced the city to little more than rubble, its fallen homes and factories a warren of dugouts for attacker and defender alike. Control of the city was essential for Germany's grand strategy (above), which involved an enormous pincers movement intended to link troops fighting in Russia with their comrades in North Africa. But the Germans could not quite overcome Stalingrad's defenders, and when the snows came in November, it was the Germans who were the victims of a pincers movement—a huge Russian counterattack that encircled and annihilated an entire German army.

urai warrior tradition and fanatically loyal to their emperor and who had been battle-hardened in Manchuria.

These were dangerous assumptions on which to hazard the fate of a nation, for no Japanese leader had the least idea of how Japan could win if the Americans, with their huge advantages in industry, natural resources, and manpower, decided to fight to the finish. In fact, Japan's militarily brilliant surprise attack on Pearl Harbor achieved a political near-impossibility. It united the American people in a way no act of Roosevelt's could have done, and it provided them with a sense of moral outrage that made any aim short of total victory unthinkable. As war-winning weapons, such unity and purpose were well worth the cost of a few battleships. Ironically, the attack's master planner, Admiral Isoroku Yamamoto, suspected as much himself. English speaking and widely traveled in Europe and America, Yamamoto dismissed his fellow officers' congratulations after the Pearl Harbor raid. "I fear," he told them, "that we have only succeeded in awakening a sleeping tiger."

For the time being, it was the Japanese tiger that was on the rampage. As predicted, the Pacific offensive began with six months of unbroken success. In a dazzling sequence of operations, Japanese troops seized the great entrepôt of Hong Kong, the American dependency of the Philippines, British Malaya—source of most of the world's natural rubber—and the fortress of Singapore. The oil-rich Dutch colonies of Indonesia fell by April 1942, while the emperor's warriors were driving the last demoralized British, Indian, and Chinese defenders from Burma and threatening the Indian frontier. To the south, Japanese troops were firmly established in New Guinea; to the east, the strategically important islands of the Solomons and the Gilberts had been swallowed up early in the offensive, along with the luckless American outposts at Guam and Wake Island.

In most places, the Japanese advance was met by the ignominious surrender of Southeast Asia's white overlords. Usually, the victorious troops were given at least a guarded welcome by local populations who were glad to see their colonial masters humiliated by fellow Asians. Asian nationalism stirred even beyond the conquered territories: The British, their prestige never lower, found India almost ungovernable when the Indian Congress party called for a "mass struggle" against them.

But the Japanese were no more liberators than the Germans had been in the Ukraine. Their purpose was exploitation, and they went about it with a brutal thoroughness that made British or Dutch rule seem a pleasant memory. (The region's large Chinese community was treated with special cruelty.) Thus, although Japan's victories gave the local nationalists a healthy dose of pride in Asian accomplishment, within a few months, many of the Greater East Asia Co-Prosperity Sphere's new subjects were involved in clandestine resistance and guerilla warfare—skills that would prove useful for the postcolonial future.

The first check to the Japanese advance came even as Burma was falling. In early May 1942, a Japanese invasion force, covered by three aircraft carriers, was heading for Port Moresby in New Guinea when it encountered an American carrier task force in the Coral Sea. The confused, blundering battle that followed was the first naval engagement in history fought by fleets that were never in sight of one another. Instead, swarms of carrier-borne aircraft searched—and struck. "Scratch one flattop!" radioed a jubilant American pilot: The carrier *Shoho* was the first major Japanese naval loss of the war. One of the other Japanese carriers was seriously hit and had to return to base for repairs. But the Japanese scored, too. Their aircraft destroyed

LIFE ON THE HOME FRONT

As part of their efforts to defeat Hitler, the Allied democracies and their Soviet partner mobilized their populations to an extent that was unmatched by totalitarian Germany until the latter stages of the conflict.

While Germany enjoyed peacetime standards of consumption until 1941, the Allies put their economies on a war footing at the commencement of hostilities, cutting production of consumer goods, increasing industrial output, and imposing rationing. In Britain, a frugal weekly allowance of meat, fat, and sugar actually improved the diet of many citizens.

For Soviet office workers—who received shorter rations than manual laborers—the weekly allotment of foodstuffs was merely one-third the British level, and nonessential items were not available to civilians. Dentists, for example, had to pull teeth without anesthetics, and cigarettes were so scarce that smokers could charge passersby two rubles a puff.

Even in the United States, civilians had to make sacrifices; some twenty previously essential items, ranging from gasoline to tomato ketchup, were rationed.

Welders take a break at the Bethlehem Steel shipyard in Pennsylvania. Working long shifts, women in all areas of the armaments industry were a powerful weapon in Roosevelt's "arsenal of democracy," contributing to a sixfold increase in the tonnage of U.S. shipping and helping to increase aircraft production fivefold between 1939 and 1944.

During the siege of Leningrad, which claimed one million civilian lives, a teacher takes his students outside their shell-

Another difference between Germany and the Allies lay in the extent to which the Allies employed women in the war effort. Fully 51 percent of the Soviet labor force were women, and in the United States, six million additional female workers made it possible to double industrial production during the war.

In Germany, by contrast, only one-third of the potential female workers joined the labor force. Drawing on a tradition of long standing that women should limit their activities to *Kinder, Kirche, und Küche* (Children, Church, and Kitchen), Nazi propaganda chief Joseph Goebbels declared that the most important tasks of a woman were "being beautiful and bringing children into the world."

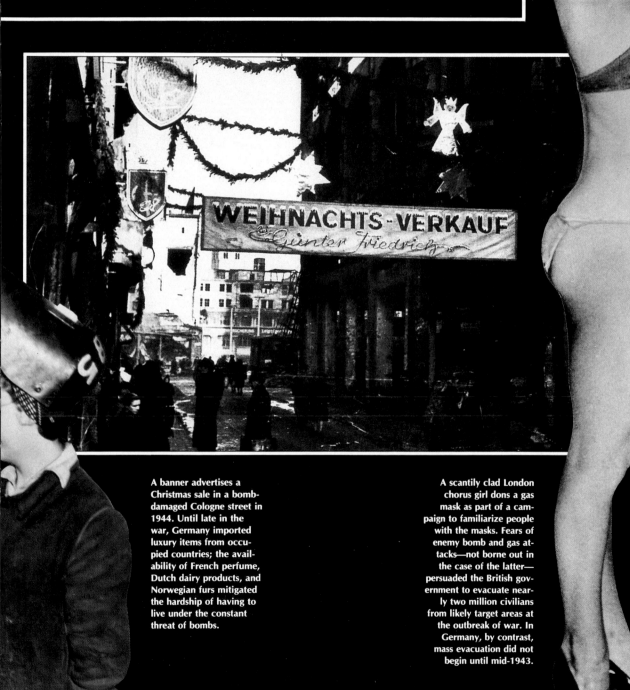

A banner advertises a Christmas sale in a bomb-damaged Cologne street in 1944. Until late in the war, Germany imported luxury items from occupied countries; the availability of French perfume, Dutch dairy products, and Norwegian furs mitigated the hardship of having to live under the constant threat of bombs.

A scantily clad London chorus girl dons a gas mask as part of a campaign to familiarize people with the masks. Fears of enemy bomb and gas attacks—not borne out in the case of the latter—persuaded the British government to evacuate nearly two million civilians from likely target areas at the outbreak of war. In Germany, by contrast, mass evacuation did not begin until mid-1943.

With the tortured bodies of eight hanged comrades dangling behind him as an example of Nazi cruelty, a Soviet partisan commander urges his men to greater efforts. Partisans were active from the early days of the German invasion, and by 1942, Moscow had developed a vast organization to train, supply, and direct them. In large areas of the occupied Soviet Union, German control was confined to towns and the main roads that linked them, and partisan attacks were a constant drain on the German supply system. But the fighting inflicted grievous suffering on the peasant communities that the irregular forces operated among. The partisans were ruthless with collaborators, willing or unwilling, while the Germans responded to their actions with reprisals that were savage even by Nazi standards.

the carrier *Lexington* and so badly damaged her sister ship, the *Yorktown,* that her captain reckoned she would need three months in a dockyard before she could fight again. In terms of losses, the battle was more of a draw than a Japanese defeat, but it gave notice that the season of easy victories was over.

Confirmation came a month later, when Admiral Yamamoto launched a complex assault on the key island outpost of Midway. His plan involved a coordinated attack by eight carriers, eleven battleships, twenty cruisers, and scores of lesser craft. He would first seize the island, then use his massive striking power to destroy the U.S. Pacific Fleet when it steamed to the rescue. As far as he knew, after the Coral Sea fighting, the Americans had only two intact carriers left, and Japanese intelligence placed them far from Midway.

In fact, the United States had three carriers, because the damaged *Yorktown* had been made combat-ready in seventy-two frenzied hours at Pearl Harbor. And all three were moving to intercept the Japanese main carrier force. They already knew its course and general whereabouts—information supplied by American cryptanalysts, who had broken the main Japanese naval code in April. The Americans found the Japanese first and, at heavy cost in aircraft, left four carriers sinking in flames. Japanese counterstrikes finally put paid to the *Yorktown,* but the outcome was a decisive American victory. Not only was Midway safe from invasion but Japan would make no more conquests of significance in the Pacific theater. Thenceforth, the Japanese fleet would fight on the defensive, in an increasingly desperate attempt to hold on to its early gains.

The two battles did much to disabuse the Japanese of their illusion of U.S. weakness. American pilots had pressed home their attacks through murderously effective antiaircraft defenses—they lost 150 planes—with near-suicidal courage. A Japanese admiral who watched the fliers die was moved to say, in troubled admiration, "These men are samurai." Back in the United States, a huge training program was producing more such aviators, but the 150 or so strike pilots lost by the Japanese could not be so easily replaced. As for the machines they flew, American factories were turning them out at least five times as fast as the Japanese, and production was increasing. The achievement of the damaged *Yorktown*'s resurrection was another indication of the technological disparity between the two sides: Japan's injured carriers lingered far longer in port before they were battle-ready again.

The Pacific war, in fact, would be a war of high technology, where relatively small groups of trained troops with expensive, complicated machines were worth infinitely more than ordinary soldiers. In other words, it was precisely the kind of war that Japan was least able to wage effectively. Japan's formidable foot soldiers, scattered throughout the Pacific conquests, would eventually be a liability—immobile mouths to be fed at the end of long supply lines in a huge new short-lived empire that would prove far harder to defend than it had been to conquer.

While American forces recovered confidence and strength in the Pacific, the Allies were planning strategies for the war in Europe. As early as December 1940, the United States had identified Germany as potentially the most dangerous enemy; and despite the sting of the Pearl Harbor raid, Roosevelt reaffirmed that the destruction of Germany should receive the highest priority. The Soviet Union, of course, was still at peace with Japan. In many ways, the "United Nations"—Roosevelt's name for the grand coalition against Germany—was an uncomfortable alliance: The two democracies had found a strange bedfellow in Stalin's totalitarian Soviet Union.

Britain and the United States began combined planning sessions in December 1941. For the remainder of the war, Anglo-American coordination of policy and resources was remarkably close, although it was not without friction. Relations with the Soviet Union were more difficult. Essentially, Stalin wanted a "second front"—an Anglo-American invasion of Europe—and he wanted it immediately, to take pressure off the Red Army. Although the Americans broadly supported him, the British, frankly appalled at the likely cost of a premature assault on Hitler's home ground, demurred. With the reluctant consent of the Americans, more modest invasion plans, aimed at North Africa and the Mediterranean, were put into effect, and a decisive landing in France was postponed until 1943 or 1944. But there was no doubt of the primary objective of the so-called Big Three, and at a conference at Casablanca in January of 1943, Roosevelt spelled it out: unconditional surrender from Germany and the other Axis powers.

In early 1942, however, any sort of German surrender remained a distant dream. The year began as grimly in Europe as in Asia. Elated by the Red Army's December triumph before Moscow, Stalin ordered an additional series of winter offensives— against the advice of his best commanders. As Zhukov wrote later, with politic tact, "Stalin was very attentive to advice but, regrettably, sometimes took decisions not in accord with the situation." The Soviets were short of equipment and munitions, and they suffered heavy losses with very little to show for the price that had been paid. At Vyazma on the Moscow front, most of one attacking army was surrounded and destroyed; an attempt to cut through to Leningrad left the Second Shock Army isolated, though still fighting; in the south, an amphibious assault aimed at relieving the besieged fortress-city of Sevastopol in the Crimea ended in bloody disaster. Yet in March and April, Stalin attacked again, both in the north and in the south—with even worse results. A massive effort to save the Second Shock Army failed at the cost

The Atlantic sea lanes were the Allies' most vital supply artery; if German submarines could close them to Allied merchant shipping, the industrial power of the United States would be of no help in Europe.

For the first few years, the Germans seemed near to achieving their aim, but by 1943, the vulnerable merchant fleet was sailing in convoys protected by specially built submarine hunter-killers as well as by close escorts. The ships were carefully deployed to provide minimum exposure to attack; because they presented a bigger target from bow to stern than head-on, they sailed only five deep over a wide front (sometimes with a rescue ship in the rear to pick up survivors). Long-range aircraft and aircraft carriers were soon added to the convoys' defenses, and more and more U-boats littered the seabed, fulfilling the nickname—iron coffin—bestowed upon the submarines by their own crews.

A merchant officer, a few feet from a life raft, surveys the slow-moving columns of a 1942 Atlantic convoy. Since most U-boat attacks were pressed home in the hours of darkness, counting surviving ships at dawn became an obsession with many convoy sailors during the three or four weeks of their voyage.

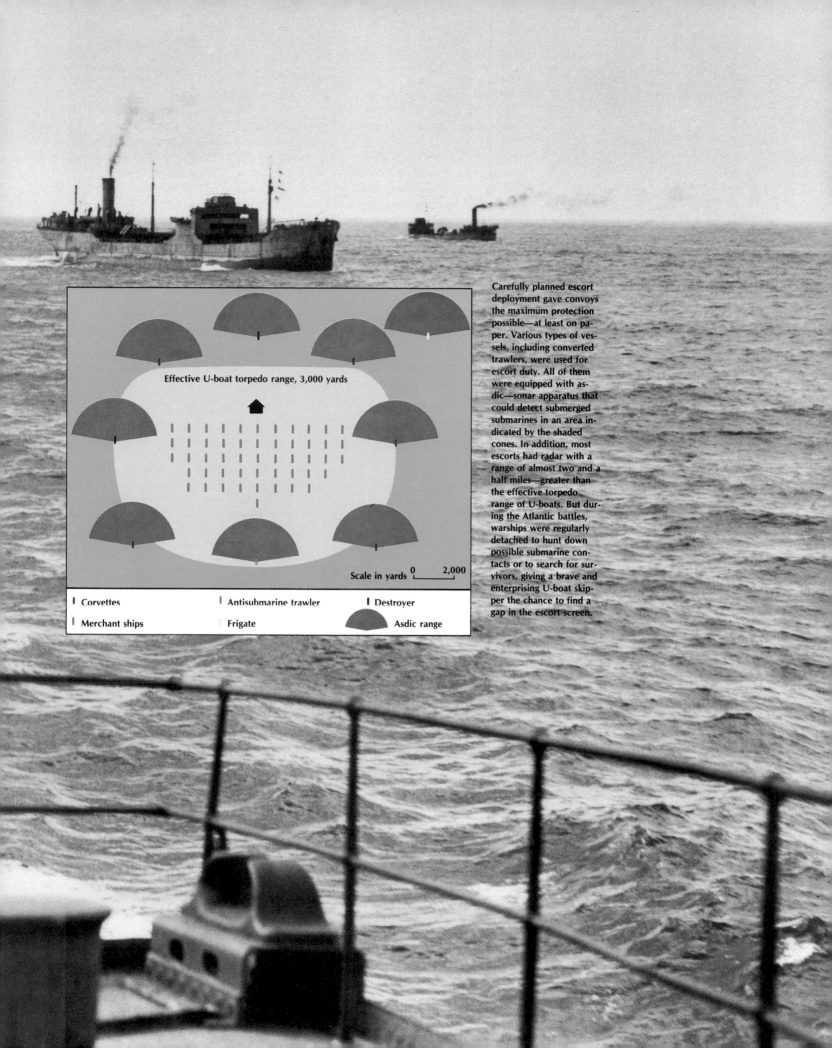

Effective U-boat torpedo range, 3,000 yards

Scale in yards 0   2,000

| Corvettes | Antisubmarine trawler | Destroyer |
| Merchant ships | Frigate | Asdic range |

Carefully planned escort deployment gave convoys the maximum protection possible—at least on paper. Various types of vessels, including converted trawlers, were used for escort duty. All of them were equipped with asdic—sonar apparatus that could detect submerged submarines in an area indicated by the shaded cones. In addition, most escorts had radar with a range of almost two and a half miles—greater than the effective torpedo range of U-boats. But during the Atlantic battles, warships were regularly detached to hunt down possible submarine contacts or to search for survivors, giving a brave and enterprising U-boat skipper the chance to find a gap in the escort screen.

of 100,000 lives. On the southern front, a drive to recapture the industrial city of Kharkov drove deep into German-held territory, only to be annihilated by a German pincers attack. This time the losses amounted to 200,000 troops, as well as most of the Red Army's tanks. An April assault in the Crimea also failed. Since January, Stalin's offensives had cost, on all fronts, almost 500,000 prisoners and nearly as many dead and wounded. Not even the Soviets, with their huge reserves of manpower, could continue to sustain casualties at such a rate.

Now it was the Germans' turn to go on the attack. Hitler had taken personal charge of the grand offensive planned for 1942: Operation Blue. For the time being, Moscow and its enormously reinforced defenses were to be left alone. Instead, the blow would fall in the south.

The plan was ambitious in the extreme. German troops would first smash through the heavily industrialized basin of the Don River. Then, while the attack's northernmost element seized the city of Stalingrad as a bastion, the main force would swing southward into the oil fields of the Caucasus, all the way to the Turkish border. Even that was only part of the gigantic pincers movement Hitler had planned. If all went well, German and Italian troops would drive the British out of Egypt and capture the oil fields of the Middle East. In such circumstances, Turkey would surely enter the war as a German ally, as it had done in 1914. When the operation was over, a gigantic

As shellbursts fountain on the horizon, Soviet infantry advances behind T-34 tanks during the 1943 battle for the Kursk salient, in central Russia. The fighting, waged over open steppe country, began with a German attack that was fiercely resisted by the massed Red Army defenders. It ended with victory salutes fired in Moscow and a Soviet advance along much of the Eastern Front.

East Wall would seal off the remnants of the Soviet Union, which in any case would have nothing left to wage war with. The British and Americans, deprived of Soviet support, would soon come to terms; and Nazi Germany, like a well-fed beast of prey, would quietly digest its conquests.

The big question was whether the nation had the resources to achieve such grandiose objectives. Considering the magnitude of the task before it, the German army in the East was woefully undermanned and underequipped. Its 1941 strength had already proved insufficient, and it began 1942 with 625,000 fewer soldiers. The manpower problem was partly eased by trimming unit sizes to create more divisions, by paring home-based reserves to the bone, and by enlisting major aid from allies. Between them, the Hungarians, Rumanians, Slovakians, Finns, and Italians provided fifty-one divisions. But the new, smaller divisions were weaker than the 1941 versions, and the allied troops were rarely as reliable as German units and seldom had anything close to a full quota of tanks and artillery.

The Germans themselves were dangerously short of equipment. Their factories had been able to replace only 10 percent of the vehicles lost so far, and the supply of tanks and aircraft was not much better. Even in horses and mules, the mainstay of German army transport, there was a shortfall of 160,000 beasts.

The sluggishness of German industrial production was largely a self-inflicted wound, for the machines and skills existed to do much better. But in a curious way, Hitler had failed to understand the nature of the total war that he himself had unleashed. While Britain, the Soviet Union, and the United States had all put their economies on an emergency war footing, German factories operated much as they had in peacetime, often with only one shift per day. Consumer goods, impossible to obtain in Britain and Russia and growing scarce even in the United States, were widely available in the Reich. Women, by now a large part of the Allies' work force, stayed at home with their children in Germany—in accordance with Nazi ideology but not with the needs of the hour.

The truth was that Hitler, who expected his troops to lay down their lives for him without a murmur, was reluctant to ask for even modest sacrifices on the home front. The Nazis' prewar popularity had depended more on the prosperity they had brought than on torchlit parades and racial ranting, and Hitler knew it. He did not choose, until much too late, to impose upon his people the kind of tightly directed economy that Britain and America, as well as the Soviet Union, had come to take for granted.

Nazi ideology was the cause of many difficulties, and not just because it relegated German women to the home. Throughout the war, Germany was plagued with a chronic personnel problem: The army was always trying to snatch workers from the factories, where they were needed just as much as in the front line. To fill the gaps, millions of workers from the occupied territories were conscripted into the Reich, but their productivity was dismally low, and the bolder spirits regularly resorted to sabotage. These workers would have contributed more to the Nazi war effort if they had been left at home—or could have, if the Nazis had not systematically looted factories throughout the occupied lands of their machinery, much of which spent the rest of the war, abandoned and forgotten, in railroad sidings.

The hordes of Soviet prisoners were another squandered resource. A high proportion of them were simply allowed to die, by starvation and neglect, because respect for human life certainly did not hinder Nazi Germany. By mid-1942, there were

Armed with thirteen machine guns and protected by a liberal provision of armor plate, the American B-17 Flying Fortress seemed to live up to its name. U.S. planners were convinced that its interlocking fields of fire would make the bomber almost invulnerable to enemy fighter attack. But Luftwaffe pilots soon found the bomber's weak point. Ball and upper turrets were barely able to respond to a head-on attack, and the other forward-firing guns were rubber-mounted weapons manned by the bombardier and the engineer, whose gunnery training was skimpy.

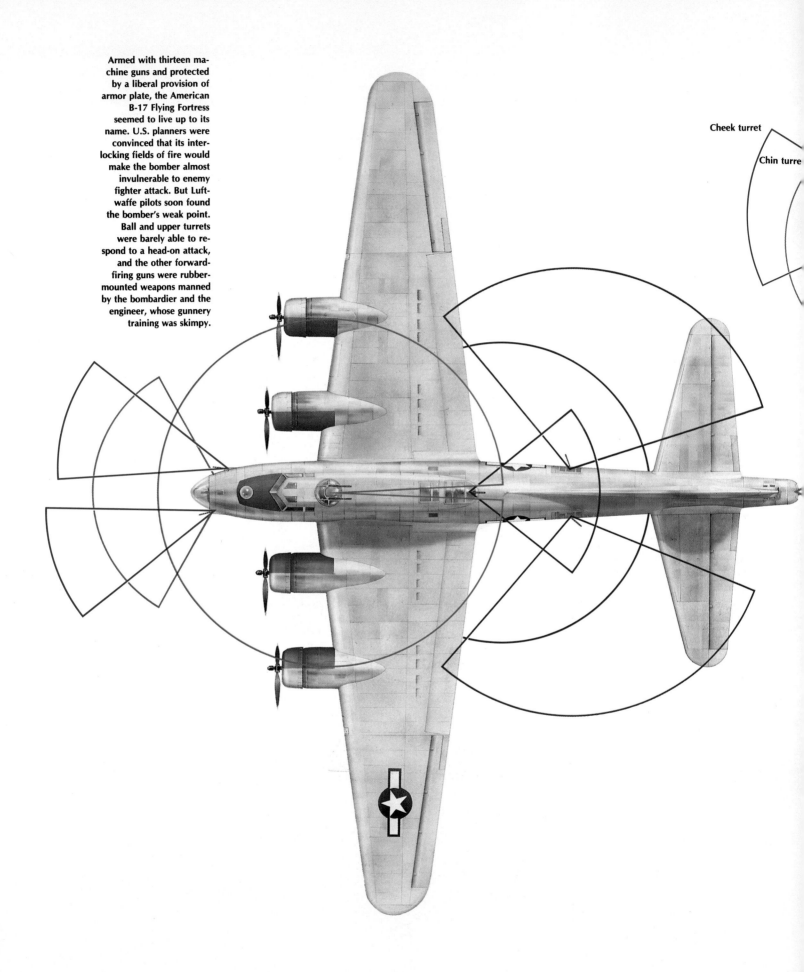

Cheek turret

Chin turret

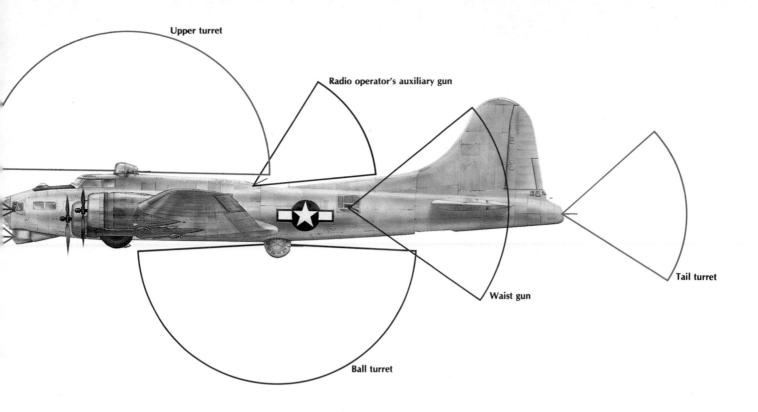

Upper turret

Radio operator's auxiliary gun

Tail turret

Waist gun

Ball turret

In the air war against Germany, the British pursued a strategy of area bombing by night, while the Americans favored precision daylight bombing. They were sure that their heavily armed B-17 Flying Fortresses and B-24 Liberators would be able to defend themselves against enemy fighters, and they believed that their Norden bombsights would enable them to hit targets with pinpoint accuracy. Although the B-17s were excellent bombers, they were no match for fast enemy interceptors, and it was not until long-range escort fighters became available near the end of 1943 that daylight bombing became possible without intolerable losses. Even then, the difficulty of sighting targets in bad weather meant that, on the average, less than one-third of the bombs dropped fell within 1,000 feet of the specific target.

FLYING FIREPOWER

A B-17 ball-turret gunner shows how to squeeze into his cramped station. On a mission, he might spend ten hours there, encumbered by forty-five pounds of protective clothing and oxygen equipment. The B-17 carried four full-time gunners, plus the pilot, copilot, navigator, bombardier, flight engineer, and radio operator.

American troops wade chest-deep into heavy German fire at Omaha Beach, one of the five landing areas on the coast of Normandy chosen for the great Allied invasion on D-Day—June 6, 1944. In the greatest amphibious operation in history, 176,000 men were set ashore in a twenty-four-hour period, supported by 600 warships and more than 10,000 aircraft. The devastating firepower they provided numbed most of the defenders, and D-Day casualties were lower than Allied commanders had feared—except at Omaha, where a fiercely held sea-front embankment *(background)* kept the issue in doubt until evening.

already huge slave labor camps—Auschwitz, for example—whose purpose was unashamedly to work their inmates to death; those too old, too young, or unfit to work were killed immediately on arrival. But the German economy gained little from the suffering of its victims. The nadir of the Nazi madness came in late 1942 and 1943, when the so-called Final Solution—the mass murder of Europe's Jews, along with gypsies and other "undesirables"—got into full swing. Scarce transport resources were tied up for months in order to carry millions of able-bodied and often highly skilled people not to German workshops, where they were desperately needed, but to German gas ovens. Their only economic contribution to the glory of the "1,000-year" Reich was to be bundles of shoes and soiled clothing, human hair for mattresses, and the gold fillings from their teeth.

Nazi organizational methods were another war loser. Hitler had always believed in the principle of "divide and rule." High party officials were given overlapping responsibilities; both mutual suspicion and bureaucratic empire building were encouraged. Himmler's SS, for example, was virtually a state within a state, running its own factories and scientific research programs, which guaranteed duplication—and waste—of effort. Major decisions were made for reasons of internal politics, sometimes merely on Hitler's whim. There was none of the careful committee work that marked the planning of the United States, Britain, and the Soviet Union. It was a nice irony that Hitler the dictator exercised no real central control over his economy—far less than Churchill or Roosevelt. Matters improved somewhat after mid-1942, when Albert Speer, a young architect and gifted amateur economist, was appointed chief of German production. But with an effective time-lag of eighteen months between production decisions and their deployment upon the battlefield, Speer's reforms came too late to turn the tide.

On the Eastern Front, Operation Blue ended in disaster. The offensive got off to a good start in late June. Within days, the key Don city of Rostov was in German hands, and Army Group B was driving steadily onward toward Stalingrad on the Volga, while Army Group A swung southward into the Caucasus. In late August and early September, General Friedrich Paulus's Sixth Army broke through to the Volga both north and south of Stalingrad, and the battle for the city—it was built almost entirely on the west bank of the river—began. It was a fearful struggle, in which every ruined building was a strongpoint to be captured and recaptured at a terrible cost of the best troops on both sides. Inch by inch, the Sixth Army gained ground.

But General Zhukov had devised a plan to break the German stranglehold on Stalingrad and trap the entire Sixth Army. If the Soviets kept their nerve, he explained to Stalin, the dictator's namesake city could be held with minimum reinforcements, while powerful reserve forces were assembled well north and south of the battlefront. Then, when all was ready, a great pincers movement would pull a double ring of steel around the Germans. Stalin agreed; the plan proceeded.

Throughout September, the fighting in the city continued. Hitler had become obsessed with the place, as much for its name as for its strategic importance. In October, he ordered troops moved from Army Group B's vulnerable flanks to take part in a final push that would surely leave the Germans in possession of Stalingrad's rubble. The flank guards were replaced by Rumanian and Italian divisions, low in tanks, guns, and in many cases, morale. By early November, only a few Soviet bridgeheads remained on the west bank, but the Germans were too exhausted to shift them.

Then, on the 19th of November, the great blow fell—precisely on the second-grade formations of the Germans' northern and southern flanks. Within a period of only four days, the two arms of the Soviet pincers, scattering or annihilating everything before them, joined together. Twenty-two Axis divisions were trapped—250,000 troops, along with all their armor and artillery. A rapid attempt at a breakout might have succeeded, but Hitler was adamant that Stalingrad should be held. Besides, Hermann Göring had promised that his Luftwaffe could keep supplies flowing to the Sixth Army until the spring.

In December, troops from a force commanded by Field Marshal Manstein came close to cutting an escape corridor through the encirclement. But a new Soviet attack in the middle Don area put even the relief force in jeopardy, and although Manstein succeeded in pulling his own troops back more or less intact, Paulus's Sixth Army was doomed. All through January 1943, the soldiers endured agonies of cold, hunger, and disease. When the army finally surrendered in February, there were only 90,000 men left alive. And the Soviets were attacking elsewhere, too. Before the winter was over, they had regained Kursk and Kharkov and partly broken the siege of Leningrad. All told, the fighting had cost Hitler almost one-quarter of his troops in Russia. Stalin, promoting himself as marshal of the Soviet Union, declared, "The mass expulsion of the enemy from the Soviet Union has begun."

In fact, there was precious little good news for Germany in 1942.

Wearing an armband to mark him as a legitimate combatant, a resistance fighter of the French Forces of the Interior (FFI) takes cover behind a truck during the Allied advance on Paris in August of 1944. FFI volunteers appeared by the thousand to offer aid to Allied units, and their efforts gave their nominal leader, General de Gaulle, a valuable political stake in Allied councils. But the liberation of Paris itself was entrusted to the more orthodox soldiers of Free France's only armored division, built around a core of émigrés who had fought in Allied ranks since 1940.

Shortage of matériel hampered German efforts everywhere—not just on the vital Eastern Front. In the North African desert, the Afrika Korps, commanded by Field Marshal Erwin "The Desert Fox" Rommel, was always short of tanks, although German tactical skill and British blundering brought Rommel close to triumph in May. But the Afrika Korps was painfully difficult to supply. The overextended Luftwaffe—scarcely 15,000 aircraft were produced in 1942, compared with 23,672 in Britain, 25,436 in the Soviet Union, and 47,836 in the United States—could no longer maintain its previous air superiority over the Mediterranean; by late 1942, the British were sinking up to 70 percent of the Axis freighters that attempted the crossing, while their own buildup in Egypt continued almost unmolested.

The result was that Rommel's 1942 desert offensives were not capable of packing enough punch to rout the British. After his failure to break through at El Alamein in Egypt during July 1942, Rommel had little choice but to wait until Britain's Eighth Army, with a new commander—General Bernard Law Montgomery—and a carefully assembled advantage of 600 tanks, was ready to attack. The second battle of El Alamein, which lasted for twelve days in late October and November, drove the Afrika Korps into headlong retreat.

A few days later, with Operation Torch, a huge Anglo-American armada landed an army in Algeria and Morocco. Rather than staging an immediate evacuation, Hitler reinforced: The thought of the whole North African coast in Allied hands made him fear for the security of what he was already beginning to call Fortress Europe.

The Germans at first made some headway against the raw American invaders: The rapid expansion of the U.S. Army from 185,000 strong in 1938 to three million only four years later had inevitably meant sketchy training and an acute shortage of experienced officers. But the Germans—including Rommel—were awestruck at the quantity and quality of U.S. equipment; as for training and experience, these would

General Charles de Gaulle, who appointed himself leader of Free France in 1940, is greeted by ecstatic crowds in the French town of Laval in August 1944. De Gaulle was not always so popular with his compatriots; after the fall of France, many of them regarded his broadcasts from exile in London as provocations from an officer acting without authority. But de Gaulle was a consummate politician, with a sense not only of his own destiny but also of his country's. From a small group of supporters—and with the sometimes-reluctant aid of his allies, Churchill and later Roosevelt—he built up a military and political organization that made him the most respected figure in post-Liberation France and went a long way to restoring the pride his nation had lost in the 1940 debacle.

be provided in the hard school of battle by the Germans themselves. Although the campaign dragged on until May 1943, the outcome was inevitable: The Axis lost 300,000 soldiers, including 215,000 prisoners.

In addition to the defeats in Russia and North Africa, the Germans had to fight on a new front—the skies above the Reich. The Royal Air Force's Bomber Command had begun its strategic offensive as early as July 1940, but for almost two years its achievements had been negligible. Daylight raids had proved suicidal, and Britain lacked both suitable aircraft and the navigational equipment necessary to find targets at night. Churchill had authorized the attacks more to bolster British morale than to inflict decisive damage.

But Churchill allowed himself to be persuaded by air-power theorists that strategic bombing, properly directed, could bring Germany to its knees without the heavy land fighting and consequent casualties that he and most senior British officers remembered with horror from the First World War. Britain chose to invest immense resources in the construction of heavy four-engined bombers, which by the end of 1942 formed the backbone of the attacking force. British scientists developed new target-finding techniques, and in Air Marshal Arthur Harris, Churchill found an aggressive and single-minded exponent of stategic bombing. The new weapons would be used not for precision raids—Harris considered that a waste of effort, and results so far largely bore him out—but for area attacks against cities. The German population would be "de-housed."

A concentrated attack on the old Baltic seaport of Lübeck demonstrated the kind of damage that could now be done. The place was of no particular importance, but it was easy to find and its wooden buildings were quick to burn. In March 1942, the RAF Bomber Command flattened half the city. Two months later, by using every crew and aircraft he could muster, including training units, Harris sent more than 1,000 bombers—by far the largest air raid of the war so far—to Cologne. The next morning, the flames of the burning city were brighter than the rising sun. The Terror Fliers, as the Germans nicknamed the bomber crews, were bringing the horrors of war to the German homeland.

Such concentrated attacks were difficult to organize and, even with the new electronic navigation gear, required clear weather for success. There were no more thousand-bomber raids in 1942. But nights in an air-raid shelter became a depressingly regular experience for a large part of Germany's population. And before the year was out, American day bombers, heavily armed and armored against fighters and flak, were joining the campaign. After "practice" missions against relatively undefended targets in the occupied territories, they launched their first raid on Germany in January 1943. The air defense of the Reich would make yet another claim on Germany's limited resources.

Aged by defeat and scarcely recognizable as Italy's once-triumphant Duce (above), Mussolini gives a last interview in April 1945. A few days later, he was captured by Italian Communist partisans. Fearing the political consequences of a drawn-out trial, their leaders summarily shot the ex-dictator, along with his mistress, Clara Petacci. Their bodies (right), together with that of a Fascist official, were later strung up in a Milan square. Standing before the firing squad, Mussolini apparently recovered some of his old style. "Shoot me here," he reportedly said, tapping his chest. "Do not spoil my profile." And he could still inspire loyalty: Although Petacci could have escaped arrest, she chose to accompany her lover to the end.

Strategic bombing was high-technology war par excellence. The attacker's gadgets were met by countergadgets as each side's scientists tried to outguess and thwart their opponents. Target-finding beams and radar would be jammed, jamming would be counterjammed, and the cycle would begin again at a higher and usually much more expensive level. Germany, the best-educated nation in Europe, should have acquitted itself well in such a contest, but given the general muddle that marked Nazi scientific planning, it was not surprising that the Anglo-American system, in which information and ideas were freely exchanged between combat units and research stations, usually managed to stay ahead.

With the improving weather of spring and summer 1943, the Anglo-American strategic bombing campaign steadily intensified. In what the publicity-minded Harris referred to as the Battle of the Ruhr, hundreds of British bombers belabored the industrial heartland of Germany night after night, while the Americans launched what

As the Red Army closes in on Berlin during April 1945, Adolf Hitler inspects his last Storm Troopers: boys of the Hitler Youth, whom the Führer expected to die for him in the coming street-fighting. The annihilation of Germany's next generation meant little to Hitler, who felt that the nation had somehow betrayed him and should go down with him in utter ruin. He issued orders for the destruction of such industry and communications as remained. If carried out, they would have meant inevitable starvation for the survivors of the Third Reich, but this time, Hitler's deputies—even SS chief Heinrich Himmler—ignored their master. And army officers in the last, doomed battles did what they could to send the militarily useless Hitler Youth home—many of these child-fanatics were killed nonetheless.

they hoped were pinpoint raids on targets on the fringe of the Reich. The climax came in July, when a succession of massive air raids came close to destroying the historic port city of Hamburg. The unending showers of incendiary bombs created a firestorm in the center of the city: Temperatures reached almost 2,000° F., and at least 40,000 civilians were killed.

The bomber campaign took a heavy toll of Allied aircrews, too. American long-distance penetrations later in the year brought insupportable losses at the hands of the Luftwaffe, and when Harris attempted to use the same tactics for a so-called Battle of Berlin during the winter of 1943-1944, German night fighters slaughtered his crews. There was some controversy as to the effectiveness of the bombing campaign. German production was almost always less badly disrupted than the Allies imagined, for it was much easier to hit the centers of towns, where people lived, than the outskirts, where heavy industries were generally located. Besides, the incendiaries favored by the Allies for city wrecking did little harm to machinery, and the Germans proved adept at patching up damaged war factories.

The destruction of nonessential plants often freed bombed-out workers for the labor-hungry arms industry, and the skillful way the Nazi party made itself responsible for relief work in the scarred cities kept the population remarkably loyal. In any case, indiscriminate bombing of civilian targets was a poor advertisement for the Allied cause and provided the Germans with a rich source of propaganda. The costs, too, were staggering: In 1942, a B-17 cost more than $250,000. Moreover, the pilots usually represented the cream of Allied manpower; as a result of the bombing offensive's demands, Britain and the United States would later find themselves seriously short of junior infantry officers. But if the bombing campaign was hurting the resource-rich Allies, it was hurting the Germans more. The necessity for home air defense put an intolerable strain upon the Luftwaffe, and for the rest of the war, German soldiers on every front could expect little or no air support.

There was one Western campaign that still seemed to hold some hope for Hitler, if not of outright victory then at least of stalemate: the long-drawn-out Battle of the Atlantic. Since 1939, German U-boats had been trying to block the sea lanes on which first British survival and later the American buildup depended. But here, too, Allied superiority in production and technology eventually swung the balance. Germany had begun the war with too few U-boats to force a decision, even against Britain's slender force of unpracticed antisubmarine escorts, equipped with primitive sonar—equipment for detecting underwater objects by means of reflected sonic waves. By the time U-boat numbers had reached a dangerous level, there were more escorts, equipped with increasingly sophisticated technology, including radar, improved sonar and depth charges, and a radio-location system that could pinpoint a submarine's position from its brief, coded signals to headquarters.

There were still some bad moments for the Allies. In November 1942, for instance, they lost almost 800,000 tons of shipping, and in the first three months of 1943, the U-boats did enough damage to cause real fears that the planned invasion of Europe would have to be delayed. But most U-boat successes were against unescorted merchantmen. As more escorts became available, fewer ships traveled alone, and attacks on convoys imposed a steady attrition on U-boat strength. By 1943, American industry was turning out freighters far faster than the U-boats could sink them: One of these so-called Liberty Ships, a standardized design prefabricated for speed of manufacture, was actually built in eighty hours and thirty minutes.

Finally, after April 1943, the Allies possessed a fleet of long-range aircraft capable of patrolling the entire North Atlantic. It was the last straw for Germany. By then it often cost more than one submarine for every merchantman destroyed. The U-boat campaign was reduced to nuisance level, at high cost to Admiral Dönitz's German navy: Of every eight men who served in his submarines, seven failed to return.

There was one other important sea lane: the North Cape route to Russia. In the face of strong air, sea, and surface attack, the Western Allies had been sending aid to the embattled Soviet Union since 1941. In the beginning, it was not much more than token assistance, which was of more value politically than militarily. Even when the volume of aid increased, shipments of war matériel were never of the highest importance: Tanks manufacured by the Soviet Union, for example, were far better than anything Britain or the United States produced throughout the war. But vast quantities of foodstuffs eased the problems of war-stricken Soviet agriculture, and from late 1942 onward, a steady supply of jeeps and trucks gave the Red Army a degree of

Skeletal corpses of Jewish prisoners litter the ground at Bergen-Belsen concentration camp in western Germany. The British, who liberated the camp in April 1945, found 10,000 dead and 40,000 inmates barely alive; their SS guards were still shooting them even as the British arrived—to keep order, they claimed. Reports of German murder camps had circulated for years but had generally been dismissed as propaganda-inspired atrocity stories. The fall of the Third Reich brought incontrovertible evidence of massacre and cruelty on an unimaginable scale. Although a few of its perpetrators were shot out of hand by liberating troops, and others were prosecuted by War Crimes Tribunals in later years, most merged quietly back into civilian life.

mobility that it would put to devastating effect in the campaigns of 1943 and 1944.

And if the Allies' technical superiority were not enough, they also had huge advantages in military intelligence. Stalin could rely on reports from loyal Communists throughout the world—in London and Washington as well as Berlin—to keep him informed; such sources had warned him repeatedly of Barbarossa, and it was not their fault that the dictator had failed to act on their reports.

The British had another kind of access to Axis secrets. In 1940, a group of their cryptanalysts succeeded in cracking the supposedly unbreakable German cipher system, which was based on a complex encoding machine called Enigma. So confident were the Germans of Enigma's security that they used it for almost all their radio transmissions. With the help of one of the world's first computers, Allied intelligence officers could often read vital enemy signals within hours of their interception.

Another aspect of the secret war was the underground movements scattered throughout occupied Europe. In the Soviet Union and the Balkans, partisan forces were of major military importance; in Yugoslavia, for example, the leader nicknamed Tito had 150,000 men and women under arms. Elsewhere, resistance activity was less overt. Despite harsh German punishments, there was a constant trickle of sabotage, and Allied fliers shot down in occupied Europe had a fair chance of finding an "underground railroad" that would get them safely home through neutral Spain or Switzerland. Just as useful, the forced laborers on whom Germany's factories had come to depend were a valuable source of information for Allied planners. In time, and as an Allied victory became more certain, men and women of the resistance would increase both in numbers and in daring.

The events of 1943 left no doubt as to who was winning in Europe. In the Soviet Union, the Red Army had learned its lessons well. After Stalingrad, it had pushed the Germans back along most of the Eastern Front. And almost all of its offensives were well calculated; seldom again would Soviet troops push forward recklessly only to be encircled and destroyed by canny German commanders. From now on, they themselves would do the encircling—with just one exception. A vigorous German attack in March 1943 recaptured the city of Kharkov, taken by the Soviets only days before. The Kharkov battle, modest by the standards of the gargantuan Eastern Front, would be the German army's last victory.

There were still four million Axis soldiers in the Soviet Union—only slightly fewer

than the number fielded by the Red Army. In tanks, artillery, and aircraft, though, they could no longer match their opponents. But Hitler was determined to stage one more offensive, if only to avoid passing the initiative completely to the Soviets: Operation Citadel would pinch out the great Soviet-held salient around Kursk, destroying the best of the Red Army's troops and equipment. Even Hitler recognized the risks. "Whenever I think of this attack," he told one of his generals, "my stomach turns."

Originally, Citadel had been scheduled for May, when it might have stood some chance of success; but Hitler decided to postpone the offensive to give his panzer divisions a chance to reequip themselves with new and more deadly machines—the Panther and Tiger tanks. In the meantime, a Soviet spy ring based in Switzerland had passed details of Citadel to Moscow. The Soviets, who had been considering an offensive of their own in the same area, massively reinforced the salient. When the German attack was finally launched on July 5, it stormed into the strongest position on the front.

The Battle of Kursk, fought over steppe- and farmland, was the greatest armored clash of all time. Almost two million troops, with 6,000 tanks, took part. The Red Air Force, rebuilt almost from scratch after its 1941 humiliation, flew 28,000 sorties, and even the battered Luftwaffe managed to put together 140 squadrons. Within a few days, the German attack began to falter. Despite their powerful new tanks—and these, untried upon the battlefield, had plenty of technical problems—they could make no real headway against the deeply layered Soviet defenses.

But the contest was not pushed to a final resolution. On July 10, Anglo-American

Against a backdrop of desolation, Russian tanks and guns grind their way across Berlin's Spree River. Even before the Russian onslaught, Anglo-American air attacks had left much of the city in ruins. The Red Army's battle with Berlin's last-ditch defenders accounted for most of the rest and cost the Soviets some 300,000 casualties. The Western Allies lost about 800,000 during the campaign that took them from Normandy into the heart of Germany.

armies invaded Sicily. Three days later, Hitler summoned his commanders to tell them that he would have to transfer his Kursk forces to protect his European southern flank. In fact, the Germans released only one division for the fighting in Sicily, and Citadel dragged on until the end of July. When the Germans did finally withdraw, disengaging themselves as best they could, it was in response less to the Sicilian landings than to Soviet offensives aimed at cities north and south of Kursk.

The Sicily invasion was nonetheless a decisive event, for it opened a new theater of war. On July 21, Mussolini was deposed by members of his own Grand Council who wanted to pull Italy out of the war. Not one of the Fascist party's four million members raised a finger to save him, and some of his captors proposed that he should be handed over to the British and the Americans as proof of Italy's intention to abandon its German ally. But the surrender negotiations were mishandled, and within days of the Allied landing on the mainland in September, at Salerno, just south of Naples, the Germans had rescued Mussolini, disarmed most of the war-weary Italian army, and seized the country's strategic strongpoints.

Churchill had once called Italy and the Balkans "the soft underbelly of Europe." Politically, the British prime minister had a point. Militarily, though, the mountainous Italian peninsula with its succession of rivers and ridgelines was perfect defensive country, and the Germans made the most of it, fighting with skill and tenacity.

The key to Italy was its long coastline. Thanks to superior seapower, the Allies could land troops almost anywhere along it. But a shortage of landing craft—the Pacific war was using far more than had been anticipated, and others were being hoarded for the invasion of France—delayed an additional Allied landing until January 1944, at Anzio, just south of Rome. The landing achieved complete surprise, but once safely ashore, the Allied commanders moved too slowly, giving the Germans time to mount an assault that bottled up the invaders on their beachhead—"the largest self-supporting prison camp in the world," as German propaganda boasted. It was not until May of 1944 that there was a successful breakout, and by the time the Anzio force joined up with other Allied units advancing from the south, most of the Germans had escaped northward with their equipment. Rome fell on June 4, but the Italian campaign would drag on for almost another year before German resistance at last collapsed.

Meanwhile, in Russia the German defense was less successful. After Kursk, the Red Army thrust westward on a wide front. German casualties and transfers had reduced their forces to around three and a half million troops, against whom the Soviets could field six million, with another million in reserve. The Red Army still could not match the Germans in small-scale tactics, and its advances cost heavily in blood, but Soviet lives were seldom spent pointlessly. The Red Army persistently sought and found the weak points in the shaky German line, for the Soviet commanders who had learned to outfight the Germans at Stalingrad were fast learning how to outthink them, too. The list of liberated towns grew steadily longer.

The Soviet advance gave a new urgency to the most horrific Nazi policy of all: the annihilation of the Jews. Hitler, his dreams of conquest collapsing, was determined to succeed in this objective, at least. His regime had been murdering Jews since 1939, but generally by the messy, uneconomic means of a bullet in the head. In 1942 and 1943, the Nazis began to use mass-extermination methods, including poison gas. By early 1945, Hitler had killed almost six million Jews—three out of every four in his crumbling empire.

Less than two miles long, the key islet of Betio in the Tarawa atoll *(left)* saw some of the fiercest fighting in the Pacific campaign. The well-entrenched Japanese defenders inflicted 3,000 casualties on an inexperienced U.S. invasion force before they themselves were killed. The Americans learned quickly from their mistakes, building replicas of Betio's blockhouses in Hawaii to test new and more effective demolition techniques. Their ambitious, two-pronged attack on Japan's conquests, under General Douglas MacArthur in the south and Admiral Chester W. Nimitz in the north, went ahead as planned *(below)* with minimal losses—at least to the Americans. Japanese soldiers died by the thousand in their pulverized bunkers, often without even seeing their enemies.

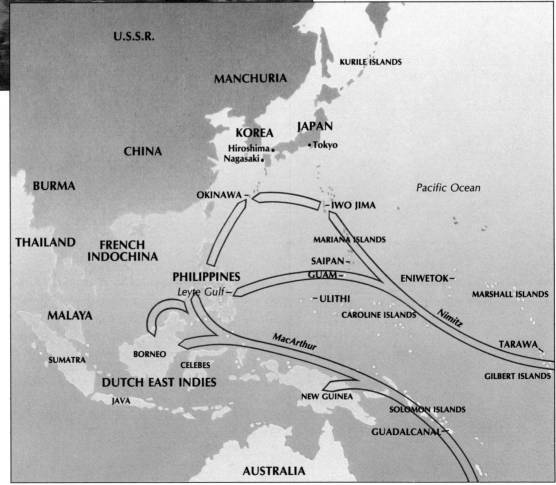

At only a fraction of the 90 to 100 aircraft she could accommodate belowdecks, the 29,700-ton carrier USS *Essex* steams across the Pacific in May 1943. Fast carriers of the Essex class, capable of making thirty-three knots, formed the core of the hard-hitting strike forces with which the U.S. Navy dominated the Pacific after mid-1943. Sailing at the center of a battle group bristling with antiaircraft guns, the carriers inflicted devastating damage on Japanese fleets, shore installations, and merchant shipping.

Not even Hitler believed that slaughtering Jews would help him win the war. For that he placed his hopes on either a great falling-out between the Western Allies and the Soviet Union, or on the secret weapons his scientists were developing. There was little chance of the former. Relations between Stalin and his Anglo-American allies would become distinctly uneasy as the Red Army pushed past the old Russian frontier and it became clear that the countries of eastern Europe were destined for a future inside a new, totalitarian Soviet sphere; but the desire for the complete destruction of Nazi Germany proved a powerful cement, and the alliance held until the end.

Secret weapons were almost as much of a pipe dream. Of scores of German projects—including a long-range bomber capable of attacking New York and a gun powered by liquid explosives—only two came to fruition. The first, the so-called V-1, was a small, pilotless plane that could carry more than 2,000 pounds of explosives from France or Belgium to London. It was an ingenious device, cheap to make and requiring no scarce materials. When it was first used in 1944, it greatly alarmed the

British, who had to resort to highly expensive countermeasures. The second weapon, though, was the one that most appealed to Hitler. The V-2, a liquid-fuel rocket with a range of about 220 miles—a longer-range version was on the drawing board—was the forerunner of the intercontinental ballistic missile. Since it rose out of the atmosphere on firing and descended at more than 3,000 miles per hour, there was no defense against it. But its cost was huge—fifty times that of a V-1, which carried roughly the same payload—and it absorbed resources that were in short supply, including a high proportion of Germany's best technicians.

To make the V-2 a war-winning weapon, something more powerful than conventional explosives would have been needed. Since 1939, a number of British and

American scientists had feared that Hitler might be developing just such a weapon. Even before the war, the theoretical possibility of an atomic bomb had been explored—and Germany had been a world leader in atomic research. To Western physicists, including large numbers of German-Jewish exiles, it was imperative that the Allies develop such a fearful weapon first. By 1941, the British had done the theoretical groundwork; when the United States entered the war and British research was made available to U.S. scientists, President Roosevelt authorized the start-up of the Manhattan Project: an enterprise that was considered to be the greatest scientific and engineering project of the first half of the twentieth century.

The Americans spent lavishly and well, their research teams driven by the fear that Hitler's scientists would beat them to their goal. In fact, the Manhattan Project was a one-horse race, because Germany's nuclear program never received any kind of priority, and research was dilatory. But not even the prodigal expenditures and industrial skills of the Americans would have the bomb ready before 1945. Germany would have to be defeated the hard way.

A deck officer on the USS *Enterprise* clambers onto the wing of a burning Hellcat fighter to drag its injured pilot to safety from his cockpit. Carrier-borne planes frequently crashed attempting to land on rolling and pitching flight decks little more than 800 feet long.

Since 1941, Stalin had been demanding from his allies a second front, a full-scale invasion of Europe, but 1942 came and went without it. A raid on the French port of Dieppe, ostensibly to test German reactions, ended in disaster. As 1943 passed without an invasion, Stalin grew noisily suspicious of Anglo-American intentions, but the Allies' obligation would soon be fulfilled. North Africa, Sicily, and Italy—not to mention the Pacific—had taught the Western Allies, sometimes painfully, the art of seaborne landing. American industry had built enough of the specialized craft that were required. By the spring of 1944, the British Isles creaked under the weight of the troops, tanks, and aircraft massed for the great assault.

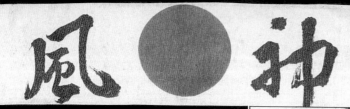

In the minutes before taking off on his mission, a suicide pilot (*right*) calmly waits while a smiling comrade ties his headband—formerly worn by samurai warriors as symbols of courage in the face of death. The example above carries the Japanese legend Divine Wind.

A burning Kamikaze plane falls like a meteor into the sea between two U.S. aircraft carriers in July of 1945. The knowledge that they were under attack from suicide pilots greatly improved the reaction time and accuracy of American gunners.

KAMIKAZE

In the heat of combat, pilots of all the warring nations had occasionally been known to use suicidal ramming tactics against their enemies. Only the Japanese, though, went so far as to organize squadrons of fliers formally sworn to die—the Kamikazes. Named after the "Divine Wind" that saved thirteenth-century Japan from a Mongol invasion, the corps was formed in an hour of equal peril, on the eve of the 1944 U.S. attack on the Philippines. There was certainly cold logic behind the plan: With pilots flying deliberate, one-way missions, even the obsolete aircraft that Japan had available might inflict devastating blows.

But there was nothing cold about the response. In a mood of exaltation, young men flocked to volunteer, for courage and patriotic devotion were among the few resources the Japanese did not lack. Those selected were usually the inexperienced; battle-seasoned pilots were too valuable to lose. The volunteers spent their last days quietly awaiting the summons to their final flight. Many sent moving letters home: "I have been given a splendid opportunity to die," wrote one Kamikaze. "Let my death be as sudden and clean as the shattering of crystal."

When the time came, they drank a last glass of sake with their comrades, then sought their end in fiery collision with the biggest American ship they could find. Although their leaders exhorted them to return and wait for another opportunity if there was no suitably valuable target, few pilots ever did.

In the end, their effect on the war was negligible. Between the Kamikazes' foundation in October 1944 and Japan's surrender, 1,228 died to sink 34 U.S. ships—only three of them larger than destroyers—and to damage 288 others.

Operation Overlord, the campaign to vanquish Hitler's Germany, was launched on June 6, 1944, when American, British, and Canadian troops landed on five beaches in Normandy. Massive air superiority made it difficult for the Germans to counterattack in force; besides, a skillful Allied deception scheme convinced the Germans that a second invasion was likely in the Calais area, and Hitler refused to transfer all the reserves available to him. A stubborn German defense kept the Allies within a confined area for almost two months, but the fighting cost them irreplaceable equipment. When German resistance finally collapsed in August, there was nothing between the Allies and the Seine River.

A crushing defeat of the long-expected Allied invasion had been Hitler's last hope of wresting something other than total ruin from the war. Now that hope was gone. And while the German forces in Normandy bled to death, the Soviets launched a series of attacks that led to the complete destruction of the German Army Group Center. By August, the Red Army was on the banks of the Vistula in Poland.

Between the hammer of the Soviets and the anvil of the Western Allies, Germany could expect no mercy. Recognizing the imminence of disaster, a group of senior German officers attempted to assassinate Hitler on July 20. The attempt failed—a matter of little importance to the Allies, who were determined to enforce an unconditional surrender on the Reich and had no intention of negotiating terms with a military junta. Hitler, convinced that his life had been saved by divine providence, was equally determined to fight to the death.

In a bold gamble aimed at ending the war in 1944, Anglo-American forces risked a huge airborne operation to capture the Rhine bridges in the Netherlands. But the attack was smashed, and in December, Hitler even managed a daring offensive of his own. Against the advice of his commanders, he sent some of his carefully hoarded panzers through the snow-covered and thickly forested Ardennes in an effort to slice between the British and the Americans and recapture Antwerp. Although the attack caused panic initially, it had no real chance of triumph: Even on the first day, there were Allied commanders who welcomed the chance to draw German armor forward in order to crush it. Hitler succeeded only in wasting German reserves that might otherwise have prolonged the war for a few months.

Germany's cities were spared the ultimate agony of nuclear attack, but they were exempted from very little else. The year 1944 saw an intensification of the Allied air offensive, which reached its destructive height on February 13 and 14, 1945, when great raids on the baroque city of Dresden reduced it to a scorched necropolis. The Luftwaffe could offer only feeble resistance. Many of its planes had been shot from the sky by the long-range fighter escorts the Americans had used throughout 1944; more still were immobilized by lack of fuel.

With the end of the war in sight, the Allies set about planning the division of the spoils. Roosevelt, Churchill, and Stalin met early in 1945 at Yalta in the Crimea; although their "Declaration on Liberated Europe" was filled with high-sounding rhetoric about free elections and the rights of all peoples to choose their own governments, the future Soviet domination of Poland and other Eastern European countries was tacitly recognized. There could be no arguing with the huge Soviet forces that were already in occupation.

The Red Army entered Germany in January 1945, driving toward Berlin and inflicting a savage revenge on the German population. Soon millions of German refugees were fleeing westward. Anglo-American forces crossed the Rhine in March.

Mushrooming high above the Japanese city of Hiroshima, a colossal cloud marks the death of 80,000 of its people—victims of the world's first nuclear attack, on August 6, 1945. The bomb, one of only two in the U.S. arsenal, was dropped in the hope that its awesome power would force the Japanese to surrender without the need for a bloody invasion of their home islands. When no immediate answer was forthcoming, the Americans dropped their remaining "device" on Nagasaki, and the Russians launched a promised invasion of Manchuria. Within a week, the Japanese government had agreed to the terms of surrender, and a formal capitulation was signed on September 2.

In early April the final Soviet assault on Berlin began, and on April 25 the Red Army and the Americans met on the Elbe River. In what was left of the Third Reich, squads of Nazi fanatics shot and hanged "defeatists" by the score, while Hitler raved in his Berlin bunker, ordering nonexistent units into impossible counterattacks. "Afterward," he said on one of those last days, "you rue the fact you have been so kind." On April 30, as the Russians were fighting their way through Berlin's streets, the Führer committed suicide.

For another week, remnants of the German army kept fighting, buying time to allow as many refugees as possible to reach zones under Anglo-American control. The final, unconditional surrender came on May 8. From Moscow to Normandy most of the

Continent lay in ruins, and the dead would never be accurately counted. But the war in Europe was over.

The last message received by Berlin's telegraph office as the Red Army closed in was brief: "Good luck to you all." The message came from Tokyo. Whatever happened in the Western world, Japan was still fighting with the courage of despair against ever-lengthening odds.

After Midway in June 1942, the initiative had passed firmly to the Americans. In their first offensive action of the war, they landed on Guadalcanal in the Solomons, where the Japanese had been building an airfield to threaten communications between the United States and Australia. The savage struggle for the island lasted nearly six months and cost the Japanese two-thirds of their 36,000-strong force. The Japanese navy did better in the sea battles around the island, inflicting more damage than it suffered, but unlike the Americans, it could not make good its losses. At the same time, a largely Australian force halted the Japanese in New Guinea and began to claw back lost territory.

The pattern for the next three years was set, as the Americans, with increasing air and naval superiority, island-hopped their way toward Japan. While U.S. submarines

The razed center of Hiroshima shows what lay beneath the nuclear mushroom's terrible beauty. Although the bombing undoubtedly shortened the war, even the American military planners were shocked by the devastation their weapon had caused. There were other, unseen effects, too. As at Nagasaki, Hiroshima's survivors were stricken by a numb, helpless lethargy that remained with them for weeks. In the months and years that followed, many apparently uninjured by the blast would die of radiation-induced ailments.

waged a highly successful campaign against Japanese supply lines, a twofold offensive moved into gear. Southwest Pacific Area Command, based in Australia under General Douglas MacArthur, took the route through New Guinea and the Philippines; Central Pacific Command, led by Admiral Nimitz from his headquarters in Hawaii, took the direct westerly route through the Marshalls, Marianas, and Iwo Jima and Okinawa. Whenever possible, Japanese garrisons were bypassed and left to "wither on the vine," as Nimitz put it; but the campaign still required more than 100 island invasions, 68 of them involving heavy fighting.

Guadalcanal, Tarawa, Eniwetok, Saipan, Ulithi—tiny places with names no one had heard of—became graveyards for Japan's army in the Pacific. American casualties, though painful enough for an unmilitary democracy, were comparatively light; American firepower and technology saw to that. The capture of the little atoll of Tarawa in the Gilberts chain, for example, cost almost 1,100 U.S. lives; a few months later, the Americans took the whole Marshalls group with losses of fewer than 600. The Japanese, in both cases, fought almost to the last man. At Tarawa, there were only 17 prisoners taken from almost 5,000 defenders.

As the ring closed around Japan, it was forced into desperate expedients. The invasion of the Philippines in late 1944 brought the Japanese navy to all-out action. Since an American success would cut them off from their East Indies oil supply, the Japanese risked everything on the disastrous Battle of Leyte Gulf—after which they had neither oil nor fleet. Short of experienced pilots, they introduced a new kind of air warfare: the suicide attack, named after the legendary Kamikaze, or "Divine Wind," that had saved Japan from a Mongol invasion in the thirteenth century. In the Philippines, more than 400 Kamikazes set out on one-way missions that sank 16 ships and damaged 80 more, but a scarcity of planes—there were plenty of volunteer pilots—ensured that the suicide air corps could never turn back the tide of invasion.

Direct air attacks on Japan began in June 1944, from China. With the capture of the Mariana Islands and Iwo Jima, bases for the gigantic new American B-29 bombers were even closer. Systematic firebombing reduced most Japanese cities to ashes: One raid on Tokyo, in March 1945, killed more than 80,000 of its citizens.

The Japanese fared no better on mainland Asia. A rash 1944 attack on Imphal on the Burma-India frontier—at a time when Japan had barely enough resources to sustain a coherent defense—ended in a crushing defeat at the hands of the British and their Indian Army. In 1945, British and Indian troops advanced to destroy the hard core of Japanese resistance in central Burma.

The Japanese continued fighting, however—with no hope of victory but with no fear of death. The Americans were now faced with the appalling prospect of an invasion of Japan itself. The Soviet Union had agreed to declare war within three months of Germany's defeat, and a Soviet attack on Japanese-held Manchuria was considered essential to the final and total defeat of Japan. Even so, realistic estimates for U.S. casualties were as high as 250,000; and

In this well-known photograph, a U.S. sailor snatches a kiss from a passing woman in New York's Times Square. The date was August 15, 1945—V-J Day, the end of World War II. The war's conclusion provoked euphoria in the victorious nations, at least for a brief moment, and even for the defeated, there was as much relief as anger and humiliation.

no one tried to count how many Japanese would die in a suicidal defense of their homeland. But there was another way to force Japan to admit defeat.

The Manhattan Project had at last borne its dark fruit. On July 16, 1945, as plans were being made for the invasion of Japan, a nuclear "device" was successfully detonated in the desert of New Mexico. Harry Truman, who had become president upon Roosevelt's death in April, was convinced that the monstrous weapon his scientists had created would end the war at far less cost in human lives than a conventional invasion. On August 6, a solitary B-29 dropped an atomic bomb, as powerful as 22,000 tons of TNT, over the hitherto undamaged city of Hiroshima. Almost 80,000 civilians died in seconds; many more were hideously injured. On August 9, the day after the Soviet Union made its declaration of war on Japan, a second bomb fell on Nagasaki.

It was enough, more than enough. A few more days passed before the Japanese government, racked in the hour of its dissolution by assassinations and suicides, could come to its decision, but on August 15, Japan announced its surrender, which was formally accepted on September 2. The world was at peace, six years and one day from the moment that Adolf Hitler had ordered his legions across the Polish border. By 1945, that first attack was ancient history. As victors and vanquished alike were coming to understand, the world they shared in smoldering, sullen peace was no longer the same world that had gone to war.

A refugee sobs amid the shattered bricks of the home she had left behind. It was a scene repeated in countless villages, towns, and cities throughout the world in 1945. In Germany and the Soviet Union alone, at least 7.5 million dwellings were destroyed, and even the photographer could not later recall where he had taken this shot. Although grief would always remain, reconstruction—of nations and moral values as well as of houses and municipal edifices—could now begin.

Israel was conceived in oppression and born in war. It was Hitler's Final Solution—the wholesale massacre of the Jewish population—that convinced European Jewry that any hope of a secure and peaceful future must lie within the borders of their own independent state. As victims of nazism their cause attracted widespread sympathy, but tragically, the high ideals on which Israel was founded were soon to be eroded by bitter sectarian violence.

Jewish nationalism found its political expression in late-nineteenth-century czarist Russia, where violent anti-Semitism inspired in many Jews a longing, after 1,800 years of Diaspora, to return to their homeland of Israel and its ancient capital, Zion, part of Jerusalem. A Zionist movement, founded by Viennese journalist Theodor Herzl in 1897, encouraged Jews to emigrate to Palestine, then part of the moribund Ottoman Empire. There was already a long-established Jewish community of 25,000 in Palestine, consisting primarily of pious men and women who had come to the land of the Bible to study their religion. By 1914 they had been joined by some 60,000 immigrants fired by nationalist rather than religious ideals. Thus, by the outbreak of World War I, there were 85,000 Jews living in Palestine, compared with about 650,000 non-Jews—predominantly Arabic-speaking Muslims.

During World War I, the Zionists won from Britain a promise of extraordinary significance. Hoping to attract the support of American and Russian Jewry for the Allies, the foreign secretary, Arthur Balfour, de-

clared British approval for "the establishment in Palestine of a national home for the Jewish people." Since Britain also supported the local Arabs in their desire to throw off Turkish rule, there was no mention of statehood. And there was a qualification: "Nothing shall be done which may prejudice the civil and religious rights of existing non-Jewish communities in Palestine." At the time, very few people regarded the two ideals as contradictory.

The Balfour Declaration of 1917 was given international sanction in 1922, when the newly founded League of Nations granted Britain a mandate, or temporary trust, over Palestine, which was to be encouraged toward independence. The Balfour pledge was incorporated in the terms of the mandate, and the Zionist movement was recognized as the appropriate "Jewish agency" for assisting the British in building the national home.

At once, there was a violent outcry from the Palestinian Arabs. This was their land; they, too, had political aspirations within an Arab world of newly independent nations emerging from the now-defunct Ottoman Empire; and Jerusalem was as holy to Muslims as it was to Jews and Christians. That year, clashes between Jews and Arabs left some fifty dead on each side.

Despite additional trouble in the ensuing years, Jewish immigration into Palestine increased with Adolf Hitler's accession to power in 1933. From 1929 to 1932, European emigration had averaged about 5,000 a year; as the menace of nazism became apparent, however, the figures increased

rapidly, from 30,000 in 1933 to more than 60,000 in 1935, by which time Jews formed 25 percent of Palestine's population. In 1936, when the British authorities refused to halt immigration, Arab insurgents called a strike and began to attack Jews, British officials, and fellow Arabs who declined to join the rebellion.

To counter such attacks, the Zionist organization set about building a national defense force, the Haganah, inspired by the semiofficial Jewish Special Night Squads, which had been established with British help to protect scattered settlements. Some Jews prepared for more savage measures by founding a terrorist group, the National Military Organization, or Irgun. Among its ranks was an ultranationalist called Abraham Stern, who would later set up his own terrorist force.

By now, it was clear that Balfour's ideals were irreconcilable and that no solution would work for both sides. The outbreak of World War II further complicated the picture. The British authorities—dependent on Arab oil to sustain the war effort—adopted a policy of limiting Jewish immigration; when the quotas were filled, additional immigrants were turned away. It was a harsh policy, and when the first authenticated reports of the Final Solution reached the outside world in 1942, it could be seen as downright murderous. Certainly extremists viewed it in that light and acted accordingly. On November 4, 1944, Lord Moyne, British minister of state in the Middle East, was shot dead by two members of the Stern Gang.

The following month, Britain's opposition Labour party made a rash commitment to allow unlimited Jewish immigration to Palestine. In the meantime, however, the foreign secretary, Anthony Eden, had assured the Arab world that the British government would "give their full support" to an Arab union. The hope was that a coalition of Arab states would regard a Jewish national home in their midst as a minor matter; in fact, the seven-nation Arab League that was established in March 1945 was united on very few issues except anti-Zionism. When the Labour party leader Clement Attlee became prime minister a few months later, he found the league determined to oppose Jewish immigration no matter what the cost.

By now, however, the British were increasingly losing control of the situation. Every action the British took to suppress disorder merely served to escalate the violence. In June 1946, the Haganah blew up all bridges across the Jordan River. Jewish leaders were arrested. On July 22, the Irgun retaliated for the arrests by blowing up a wing of the King David Hotel, the British army's headquarters in Jerusalem, killing

Two small ships crammed with 1,300 illegal Jewish refugees lie tantalizingly close to the coast of Palestine, on August 12, 1946. Refused permission to land by Palestine's British authorities, who had promised the country's Arab majority that they would restrict Jewish immigration from Europe, the refugees were eventually put on board a British freighter and sent to internment on the island of Cyprus. In a vain attempt to prevent their deportation, Jewish sympathizers attached mines to the ship's hull and blew a hole in its side.

Finally, Prime Minister Attlee decided—as he did at roughly the same time with regard to India—to pull out. Foreign Secretary Ernest Bevin announced in February 1947 that Britain would hand over its mandate of Palestine to the United Nations, the successor to the League of Nations. A UN Special Committee arrived in June to study the issue of partition. Its inquiries were conducted under the threat of yet more violence: Three Irgun terrorists were under penalty of death by hanging, and two British soldiers were being held hostage to force the terrorists' release. In addition, many shiploads of illegal Jewish refugees were heading for Palestine.

One boat, the *President Warfield,* soon to be renamed the *Exodus,* was carrying 4,500 German Jews, survivors of the Bergen-Belsen concentration camp, who had embarked at Marseilles. The vessel was intercepted off Haifa by British warships. As the destroyers closed in, the immigrants on board kept up a continuous radio commentary to the outside world. Finally, with its siren wailing—"a wounded cow bellowing through the night"—the *Exodus* surrendered. Sent back to Marseilles, the refugees were refused sanctuary in France and were eventually landed in Hamburg, which was a grim irony not lost on the public.

On the same day that the *Exodus* returned to Marseilles, the three condemned Irgun terrorists were hanged; the two British hostages were killed by the Irgun the next day and their bodies booby-trapped with mines. "We repaid our enemy in

kind," said the Irgun leader and future prime minister, Menachem Begin. "He forced us to answer gallows with gallows." The news of the killings aroused anti-Semitic feeling in Britain, where there were anti-Jewish riots in several cities.

On November 29, 1947, the United Nations proposed its own solution: an end to the British mandate and a partition of Palestine into an Arab state and a Jewish state; the city of Jerusalem was to come under international administration. The Zionists accepted the UN plan with alacrity. The Arabs rejected it and began to make preparations for war.

Both the United States and the Soviet Union—which saw a Jewish state in Palestine as an anti-imperialist wedge in the Middle East—voted for the UN resolution. Britain voted against, but it was no longer willing or able to control events. In December, as riots raged unchecked, the British announced that they would withdraw from Palestine by May 15, 1948.

Fierce fighting broke out even while the British mandate still ran, and by the end of March 1948, Jews and Arabs had suffered more than 1,000 casualties. On the morning of May 14, a day before the mandate was due to end, the Union Jack was lowered at Government House, Jerusalem, as Jews and Arabs were seizing positions in and around the city. At 4:00 p.m., 200 Jewish leaders gathered in the Tel Aviv Museum of Modern Art to hear David Ben-Gurion, the country's first prime minister, read a short declaration proclaiming the establishment of the state of Israel.

Within hours, the new state was recognized by the United States and the Soviet Union. Early the next morning, the neighboring Arab League nations—Lebanon, Syria, Iraq, Jordan, and Egypt—invaded.

In numbers, the opposing forces were evenly matched—some 35,000 Israeli troops against approximately 40,000 Arab soldiers. In terms of military equipment, however, the Israelis were at a disadvantage, and Arab firepower soon told. In the first month of the war, the Syrians advanced into Upper Galilee, the Iraqis drove westward to reach a point less than ten miles from the Mediterranean, and the Jordanian Arab Legion besieged Jerusalem, capturing the Old City with its Jewish quarter. The Egyptian army threatened the rest of Jerusalem from the south.

At this point, a UN mediator, Count Folke Bernadotte of Sweden, arranged a month's truce. The Israelis used the time well, flying in arms bought from France and Czechoslovakia, and then, in a vital ten-day period in mid-July, putting into action several well-planned offensives. On July 18, a second truce came into effect.

Bernadotte was keen to arrange for the return of the many Arab refugees who had fled Palestine. On September 17, members of the Stern Gang, which actively tried to terrorize Arabs into fleeing the country, murdered him. Shocked at such an act, which could only alienate world opinion, Ben-Gurion ordered the dissolution of both the Stern Gang and the Irgun.

By this time, the Israelis were better armed and beginning to take the ofensive. The Arab military effort broke down in disunity over political and military goals. Feeling that they had done enough, the Syrians and Iraqis withdrew across their borders. The Jordanians had taken Old Jerusalem, which was all they had set out to do, and they were willing to arrange a cease-fire with Israel, which then retook the south from the Egyptians. On December 29, the UN Security Council ordered a cease-fire, and Israel's war of independence came to an end early in 1949 in a series of armistice agreements.

When the smoke had settled, Israel found itself in possession of 21 percent more land than it had been assigned under the 1947 partition plan. More than half a million Arab refugees had sought sanctuary in the enclaves of the Egyptian Gaza Strip and the Jordanian West Bank, including Old Jerusalem, as well as in Lebanon. One million Jews now had a home of their own and had demonstrated their willingness and ability to defend it. The politics of the Middle East had a new and volatile element; its stored resentments and unconcealed passions were to break out in three more wars in the next four decades.

On May 14, 1948, one day before the British mandate in Palestine expired, Jewish leaders gather in a Tel Aviv museum to hear the state of Israel proclaimed by David Ben-Gurion, soon to be elected its first prime minister. Above him is a portrait of Theodor Herzl, the founder of modern Zionism, who in the late nineteenth century championed the cause of a Jewish national home. Although Israel was immediately recognized by the United States and the Soviet Union, Ben-Gurion's announcement was the signal for a concerted attack on Israel by its Arab neighbors.

INDEPENDENCE FOR INDIA

3

On April 13, 1919, in the city of Amritsar in the Indian province of Punjab, a crowd of more than 10,000 men, women, and children filed down a narrow street that led into an expanse of open ground enclosed by high walls that was known as the Jallianwala Bagh. Many of them had come to attend a political meeting, but there were also many who were visiting the city for the annual horse fair and had followed the crowd out of curiosity. Few of those who came from outside the city were aware that the meeting was illegal.

For three days, Amritsar had been the scene of violent demonstrations against British residents and property. The town hall, the telegraph office, an Anglican church, a mission school, and a railway freight yard had been set alight. Five British officials had been killed by angry mobs, and a female missionary had been attacked. Brigadier General Reginald Dyer, commander of the nearest army units, had been called in to restore order. On April 12, he had forbidden public meetings, and on the following morning, he had gone through the city with a drummer announcing that all mobs would be fired on.

But Dyer's threat was not sufficient to deter the citizens of Amritsar. Their quarrel with the British was based upon the reluctance of the British government—which had ruled India directly for more than sixty years—to grant the degree of independence demanded by Indian nationalist leaders, whose patience was running short. A British promise that India would become self-governing on the conclusion of the Great War had not been fulfilled; instead, in March 1919, the British Parliament had passed laws designed to suppress nationalist agitators. Known as the Rowlatt Acts after the judge who had been appointed to advise the British government on security, this legislation provided for the internment without trial of those suspected of subversive activity and for the trial of certain political offenders by judges without juries. The riots in Amritsar had developed after the leaders of a peaceful protest against these repressive measures had been arrested.

When General Dyer heard that his orders had not been followed, he immediately set out for the Jallianwala Bagh with two armored cars and fifty riflemen. The vehicles were left outside the compound, because they were too wide to negotiate the narrow passageway through which the crowds had filed. The soldiers took up kneeling positions on the rising ground just inside the entrance and released the safety catches on their rifles.

Without giving any warning, Dyer gave the order to open fire. In the moments before horror dawned, many of the Indians believed that the soldiers were firing blanks; but when bodies began to fall, an uproar broke out. The crowd panicked, some seeking desperately to escape by climbing the walls, others crawling for shelter behind the bodies of their comrades, still others trampling the wounded as they fled

The Indian nationalist leaders Jawaharlal Nehru and Mahatma Gandhi share a moment of relaxation during a political meeting in Bombay in 1946. Gandhi, a devout Hindu, believed that India's vast rural population could be provided with food, clothing, and health care without recourse to Western technology; to symbolize his views, he habitually wore the villager's traditional clothing, a homespun dhoti, or loincloth. Nehru, who was to become free India's first prime minister in 1947, was an agnostic socialist committed to wholesale modernization. Both men, however, were united in their conviction that India must be liberated from British rule, and together they led a massive campaign of nonviolent resistance to achieve that goal.

to the farthest reaches of the compound. A few jumped into a well and were drowned by those who fell on top of them. In just ten minutes, the soldiers fired 1,650 rounds of ammunition, very few of which were wasted. According to the official reports, 379 people were killed and 1,208 wounded.

While the screams of the wounded still filled the air, Dyer ordered his troops to rise, shoulder arms, and leave the compound. "I fired and continued to fire until the crowd dispersed," he told a subsequent inquiry, "and I consider this is the least amount of firing which would produce the necessary moral and widespread effect it was my duty to produce if I was to justify my action." During the two months of martial law that followed the massacre, he continued to carry out what he perceived to be his duty with the same thoroughness. Water and electricity supplies to the Indian quarters of Amritsar were cut off, and six men who contravened the curfew were publicly flogged. Any Indian passing along the street where the female missionary had been

The campaign for Indian independence culminated in the creation of not one but two nations: Hindu India *(shaded yellow)* and Muslim Pakistan *(shaded green)*. As the map shows, the latter originally consisted of two separate enclaves that were 1,000 miles apart. Muslim leaders, fearing that their coreligionists would have few political rights in a country dominated by a Hindu majority, had begun to demand their own homeland during the 1930s, but agreement was not reached until shortly before the British left India. Subsequently, civil war was to lead to the secession of East Pakistan, which in 1971 became the independent nation of Bangladesh.

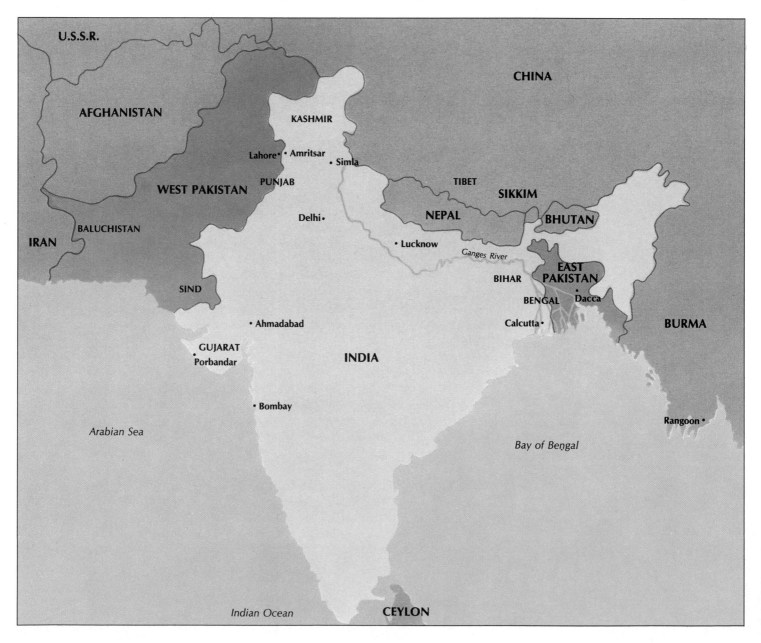

attacked was forced to crawl along the ground for more than 150 yards, spurred on by the heavy boots of British soldiers.

After the inquiry, Dyer was forced to retire. His actions were condemned by the secretary of state for India. In a speech to the House of Commons, Winston Churchill, the secretary of state for war, borrowed a phrase from the historian and writer Lord Macaulay to describe the massacre as "the most frightful of all spectacles, the strength of civilization without its mercy. We have to make it clear," he continued, "some way or other, that this is not the British way of doing business."

But Dyer's actions were approved by the House of Lords, by many individual members of Parliament, and by large sections of the British press. In India, money was collected for him by members of the exclusive clubs that were the center of the social life of the European residents. This widespread failure of the British to denounce General Dyer rubbed salt into the Indian wounds and gave symbolic significance to the massacre itself, which was seen as an example of the capricious use of force by a tyrannical overlord.

Since 1858, when India had been declared a Crown possession, the key decisions affecting the lives of a population of more than 350 million had been made by no more than a thousand senior British bureaucrats. Trust and a degree of goodwill had played as much a part in the working of this system as military force. After the atrocity at Amritsar, that trust no longer existed; many of the Indian leaders who had been prepared to cooperate with the British while seeking increased political rights for their own people now became ardent nationalists, and India was set irrevocably on the road to independence.

Britain had a closer relationship with India than with any other part of its empire. Although the British raj—so called from a Hindi term for government—was not formally established until 1858, British interests in India extended back as far the early seventeenth century, when the first merchants had arrived and trading settlements had been founded. By the beginning of the twentieth century, many British military and administrative officers who served in India came from families whose links with the country dated back for generations. In addition, many Indians had firsthand experience of life in England, having traveled there to study at universities. To the British and to many Indians as well—in particular the several hundred Indian princes who were allowed to continue governing their states under British patronage—the destinies of the two countries appeared to be tightly interwoven.

But although the feelings of pride and of affection for the people of India expressed by the British were often deep and sincere, their actual familiarity with the country was very limited. Most were handicapped by prejudicial beliefs in their own racial superiority. Few learned to speak any of India's almost 200 native languages or sought to understand its culture. To the majority of the British, the beliefs and customs of the people who lived outside the walls of their comfortable compounds remained a baffling mystery. One British officer likened himself to "a man wandering about with a dim lantern in the dark."

In every province, adherents of different religious faiths lived side by side, often indistinguishable to European eyes but in fact following very different traditions. The largest community was made up of Hindus, who comprised well over half of the population; the most conspicuous aspects of their 4,000-year-old religion were its pantheon of many gods and the caste system, which divided its adherents irreversibly

Seated in a gold-embossed howdah on an elaborately adorned elephant, the viceroy of India, Lord Curzon, and his consort proceed at a stately pace through the streets of the capital city of Delhi. Following the tradition of the Indian durbar, at which a prince assembled all the members of his court, the British held ceremonial processions to mark occasions such as the coronation of a new monarch or a royal visit to India. These displays—which also served to impress the watching crowds with the majesty of the British raj—were considered politically valuable in a country whose 350 million people were ruled by just a few thousand British administrators and army officers.

into different hereditary classes. A prominent minority of the population—more than 50 million in all—were Muslims, descendants of the conquerors from central Asia who had ruled in India for 700 years before the British arrived and of the people who had converted to Islam during this period. In addition, there were large numbers of Sikhs, members of a reformed Hindu sect who were especially prevalent in Punjab, as well as Parsees, Jains, Christians, and Jews.

These various communities followed different religious leaders and different observances. But they had in common the experience of being subjects of the British empire and, as such, second-class citizens in their own country. While the British hunted, danced, played polo or cricket, lived in spacious bungalows, and traveled in luxurious first-class compartments, Indians stood by to serve their every need. To the Hindus, who took pride in the achievements of their ancient civilization and whose caste system made them acutely sensitive to matters of social status, this situation was especially irksome.

Many of the early leaders of the Indian independence movement emerged from the ranks of the middle-class professionals—lawyers, journalists, businessmen, and teachers. They had been educated in the schools and colleges that were established during the early years of the raj to train Indians for jobs in the middle and lower ranks of the civil service. The acquisition of English for these practical purposes also enabled them to read books about Western political philosophy and history, brought them into contact with new concepts of nationalism, liberalism, and democracy, and gave them the intellectual tools with which to analyze the injustices of colonial rule.

One particular cause of resentment was Britain's economic exploitation. Raw Indian cotton, cheaply purchased, was used in British mills to manufacture textiles that were then sold back to India at a profit. Money from the Indian economy was sent back to London to run the India Office and to pay interest on British loans. Unemployment in India rose steadily, both among the ancient class of skilled artisans and —since the universities turned out more graduates than the civil service could accommodate—among the the new class of educated Indians.

In 1885, the British condoned the creation of the Indian National Congress, an assembly of seventy-three Indian representatives that, although it wielded no power, at least provided a forum for debate on nationalist issues. Year by year, the Congress leaders grew more radical in their demands. To begin with, most of them accepted British dominance and sought to obtain reforms simply by submitting petitions to the British viceroy; soon after the turn of the century, certain members of the Congress— at that time still a predominantly middle-class movement—set out to campaign for the support of the masses, and extremist factions began to resort to terrorist activity. As support for the Congress increased, however, divisions between the Hindu and Muslim communities—each wary of being subjugated by the other—threatened to cripple the nationalist cause. The Indian National Congress was dominated by the Hindus. In 1906, the Muslims founded the All-India Muslim League to promote their own political interests.

During the First World War, more than 1.3 million Indian soldiers fought alongside British troops, and the vast majority of the Indian people supported the British cause. But political activity—and also isolated acts of terrorism—continued. In 1916, Congress leaders surprised everyone by concluding the Lucknow Pact with the Muslims, by which the latter agreed to support Congress's demand for self-government in return for a promise to accept separate Muslim constituencies—with representation greater than their numerical proportion of the population justified—in any new constitution. In answer to widespread agitation, the British announced that, as soon as the war was over, India would become a dominion within the empire; this status would give India its own government under a British governor general.

Expectations were consequently high at the end of the war, but the Government of India Act, which was passed by the British Parliament in 1919, fell far short of what was hoped for. The creation of new legislative assemblies in which a percentage of the members would be elected by a limited franchise was considered insufficient reward for a nation that had suffered more than 100,000 casualties. When the United States had entered the war in 1917, many Indians had taken to heart President Wilson's definition of the Allies' goals as ''freedom and justice and self-government amongst all the nations of the world.'' The British still regarded self-government as a privilege to be bestowed upon a subject people; the Indians, however, were demanding it as an inalienable right.

The passing of the Rowlatt Acts in March 1919, which removed two of the precious legal rights that were among the few undeniable benefits of British rule, added insult to injury. Mass protest meetings were called in many Indian cities. The massacre at Amritsar and other sternly repressive actions taken by the British only served to swell the ranks of the nationalists and strengthen their resolve. And in the following year, a leader emerged who possessed such charisma and such an intuitive gift for dramatic gestures that he would extend support for the Indian National Congress among the illiterate millions of India's population.

Mohandas Karamchand Gandhi was born on October 2, 1869, at Porbandar in western India, where his Hindu father was hereditary chief minister of a small state. Gandhi was brought up as a pacifist and a vegetarian, and he was married as a boy to a child bride. At the age of eighteen, he was sent to London to study law, and in 1891, he returned to India as a qualified barrister. But success eluded him in his own country. Two years later, he set out to practice law in South Africa instead, and during the twenty-two years that he remained there, he developed the personal philosophy that was to lie at the heart of his actions for the rest of his life.

Drawing upon a variety of sources—including Hinduism, Christianity, and the works of the Russian novelist Leo Tolstoy, with whom he exchanged letters—Gandhi came to believe that the prime objective of life was the pursuit of truth, and that the two most vital allies in this task were nonviolence and self-discipline; later in his life, the specially trained followers who shared his ambitions and methods styled themselves "truth fighters." Suffering assaults and imprisonment in the course of his work for the political rights of Indians who had settled in South Africa, Gandhi remained always courteous and restrained toward his opponents. His faith in the moral power of passive resistance never wavered, and his persistence was rewarded by the repeal of several repressive laws. When he finally returned to India in 1915, the poet Rabindranath Tagore gave him the name Mahatma—"Great Soul"—in recognition of his work and teaching.

A thin, genial, self-effacing man in spectacles, the forty-six-year-old Gandhi did not look like a man of action, but his demeanor disguised an iron will and boundless energy. For all his idealism, he was an astute politician, and he had a talent for directing the energies of the various nationalist factions—Hindus and Muslims, moderates and radicals, urban intellectuals and rural peasants—toward a common goal.

On his return to India, Gandhi spent several years studying the political situation, taking part in industrial disputes, and setting up a community on the outskirts of Ahmadabad where he gathered and trained his truth fighters with the help of subsidies from Hindu merchant princes. (As one of his followers cynically remarked: "It cost a great deal of money to keep Gandhi in poverty.") He made his own judgments of people and causes and acted accordingly. A relentless enemy of the British empire, he numbered many English men and women among his friends. A champion of Hinduism, he was yet a stern critic of the system that had allowed the poorest and lowest-ranking Hindus to become known as "untouchables" because the higher ranks were forbidden even to touch them.

To symbolize his empathy with the humblest people of India, Gandhi gave up wearing European clothes in 1921 and wore instead a dhoti, a peasant's homespun cotton loincloth. He also endeared himself to the rural masses—and convinced them that, among all the politicians who claimed to speak for their cause, he alone could be wholly trusted—by his observance of rigid codes of conduct. In 1906, he took a vow of chastity, and although he believed that families should have no more than three or four children, the only form of birth control he countenanced was sexual abstinence. He refused to make use of any medication other than natural herbal remedies; so strict was his adherence to this principle that in 1944, when his wife was

Smartly dressed in European-style clothes, Gandhi faces the camera with his staff outside his Johannesburg legal practice in 1913. Following his arrival in South Africa in 1893 as a newly trained lawyer, Gandhi built up a prosperous business that specialized in safeguarding the political rights of his compatriots. During the course of this work, he advocated civil disobedience as a means of combating repressive laws. Despite suffering imprisonment and often the loss of their livelihoods, thousands of Indians followed Gandhi, and the success of such tactics encouraged him to employ them on a wider scale after his return to India in 1915.

Believing that only if he renounced all worldly needs and desires could he proceed toward spiritual truth, Gandhi limited his personal possessions to the bare minimum. Shown above is a selection of his belongings: two small food bowls, which had been issued to him in prison and which he retained as souvenirs; a wooden fork and spoon; his diary, watch, and spectacles; a copy of the Hindu sacred text Bhagavad-Gita; a spittoon; a pencil case; one pair of leather sandals; and one pair of wooden shower clogs. The Mahatma's only object of purely sentimental value was the ivory statuette of the three monkeys who "speak no evil, see no evil, hear no evil." These items accompanied Gandhi on all his travels, along with a simple spinning wheel that he made time to use every day.

Violence and excess were equally abhorrent to Gandhi. He lived on a vegetarian diet and never ate more than he required; his sandals were made from the hides of cows that had died naturally. Millions revered Gandhi as a saint, his ascetic lifestyle according with those of a long tradition of Indian spiritual leaders.

THE MAHATMA'S ASCETIC LIFESTYLE

dying of acute bronchitis, he refused to allow her to be injected with the penicillin that might have saved her life.

Gandhi was at first prepared to cooperate with the British, but after the massacre at Amritsar, he declared: "Cooperation in any shape or form with this satanic government is sinful." Now committed to open opposition to the raj, he sought two immediate objectives. The first was to present a united front by cementing an alliance between Hindus and Muslims; the second was to persuade the Congress to adopt a policy of widespread passive resistance.

The first goal was achieved in early 1920 when, after Gandhi himself had joined a Muslim protest organization, Hindus and Muslims demonstrated together throughout India. To attain the second, Gandhi outlined his doctrine of "progressive nonviolent noncooperation" to a special session of the Congress in Calcutta in September 1920. The simple but revolutionary aim was to make India ungovernable. He called on Indians to boycott everything that was British—not just British goods but also the raj's courts, the legislative assemblies, and the schools and colleges.

Among those who opposed this program was Muhammad Ali Jinnah, a lawyer and former leader of the Muslim League. Jinnah, a reserved and dignified man who dressed in immaculate English suits, suspected the populism of Gandhi's approach and described his supporters as "inexperienced youths and the ignorant and illiterate." But the great majority of the Congress ratified Gandhi's proposal and proceeded to define its objective as self-government "by all peaceful and legitimate means."

The response to the noncooperation program was enthusiastic. Imported cloth was burned in public. Teachers abandoned their profession, students their studies. Many eminent lawyers relinquished lucrative practices. From Gandhi's point of view, the only cause for misgiving was the lack of self-discipline evident in many of the demonstrations. In November 1921, riots broke out in Bombay that lasted for five days and caused the deaths of fifty-three people. A month later, while Gandhi was preparing a program of civil disobedience that was to include nonpayment of taxes, twenty-two police officers were attacked and killed after firing on a political procession. As soon as he heard the news, Gandhi called off the entire campaign. Reluctantly, his followers obeyed.

By then, many of the demonstrators were in prison. After the Bombay rioting, the government had declared all Congress and Muslim protest organizations illegal. But instead of acting as a deterrent, this decree raised the morale of the Congress supporters and gave them a sense of suffering for a cause. The jails were crowded with as many as 30,000 political prisoners; and after the campaign had been called off and the violence had calmed down, Gandhi himself became one of them, arrested and sentenced to six years' imprisonment for sedition.

By 1924, when Gandhi was released early from prison after an appendectomy, the accord between Hindus and Muslims had broken down, and it seemed to many that his policies had achieved almost nothing. But attitudes had changed; the resignation of old was gone. Among the industrial workers of Bombay and Ahmadabad in particular, labor unrest and union organizations spread rapidly. Terrorists robbed post offices and railway stations.

The British were forced to make concessions. The Rowlatt Acts were repealed. A royal commission proposed that 50 percent of India's civil servants should be Indian, and eight army units were set aside to be commanded entirely by Indian officers. In November 1927, the government appointed a commission to look into the workings of the administration and to recommend the next steps toward self-government.

The announcement of the names of the commissioners set off a fresh blaze of nationalist protest. They were all British, with not a single Indian among them. The Congress voted to boycott the commission at every stage; and when Sir John Simon and his seven commissioners arrived early the next year, they were met everywhere by demonstrators bearing banners inscribed with the words "Simon go back!"

At the same time, in a more positive vein, nationalists decided to draft their own constitution for India. Representatives of the Congress, the Muslim League, the Central Sikh League, and every other political group met at the end of February 1928 and appointed a committee to take on the task under the chairmanship of Motilal Nehru, a lawyer from the highest Hindu caste, the Brahmans, who had given up a successful practice as part of the boycott. In August, Nehru submitted the committee's conclusions: He proposed a democratic federation of states with a two-chamber parliament for which the vote would be given to all men and women. In order to make the plan more acceptable to the British, he also indicated that India would step back from the goal of total independence and accept dominion status with a governor general as representative of the Crown.

This proposal was accepted by the majority of the Congress, but it was opposed by certain young radical members and by Muhammad Ali Jinnah. The latter was concerned that the proposed new constitution did not safeguard the rights of Muslims.

Mounted police armed with batons and revolvers send Indian demonstrators fleeing for safety in Calcutta in January 1931. A year before, the Indian National Congress had pledged itself to the goal of complete independence; throughout the 1930s, breakdowns in negotiations between the British government and nationalist leaders led to renewed campaigns of civil disobedience, and clashes between protest marchers and the authorities became increasingly violent.

In 1940, a detachment of Indian soldiers march in step with their Scottish comrades in arms, the kilted Cameron Highlanders, past the Egyptian pyramids. Later that year, Indian contingents led a successful Allied attack against the Italian army at Sidi Barrani, on the country's northwest coast. Despite continuing opposition to British rule in India, the majority of Indians supported Britain's stand against nazism during the Second World War and supplied both men and equipment to support the Allied armies.

The former insisted that India should demand nothing less than complete independence from Great Britain.

The most forceful radical leaders within Congress were two graduates of Cambridge University in England: a zealous judge's son from Bengal, Subhas Chandra Bose, and Motilal Nehru's son Jawaharlal. While he was in England, the urbane young Jawaharlal Nehru had been entertained by some of Britain's noblest families; returning to India, he had been repeatedly snubbed by white, middle-class colonials. After meeting Gandhi in 1916 and being impressed by his emphasis on action rather than speeches as a means of combating injustice, Nehru had been arrested and imprisoned for demonstrating; and in his cell, he had studied Karl Marx and added

socialism to his philosophy. His radical education had been completed one night when he traveled on the same train as General Dyer, who was returning from the inquiry into the massacre at Amritsar. From the next sleeping compartment, Jawaharlal Nehru heard Dyer tell other officers that he had wanted to reduce Amritsar to "a heap of ashes" and had only held back because he "took pity on it." Nehru was deeply shocked, as he was by the approval of Dyer's action expressed by the House of Lords and most of the British elite in India. "I realized then," Nehru later wrote, "how brutal and immoral imperialism was and how it had eaten into the souls of the British upper classes."

When the Congress met at Calcutta in December 1928, the moderates and radicals were still implacably opposed. But it was at this moment that Gandhi returned to center stage, by persuading a majority of the Congress members to accept dominion status, provided the British agreed to the new constitution within a year. If they did not, he promised a fresh campaign of civil disobedience.

The viceroy, Lord Irwin, went to London to report the ultimatum. But the Labour government, which had only a tiny majority over its opponents in Parliament, was in no position to rush through legislation. A year passed. At the stroke of midnight on December 31, 1929, the newly elected president of the Congress, Jawaharlal Nehru, led a procession to the banks of the Ravi River and raised the national flag to shouts of "Long live the revolution!" Shortly afterward, a declaration written by Gandhi was read throughout India, in which the objective of the Congress was proclaimed as *Purna swaraj,* "complete independence."

Gandhi began the new campaign of civil disobedience with a gesture that won him the renewed enthusiasm of the masses and the attention of the entire world. He announced that he was going to march to the sea and make a cake of salt from the deposits on the shoreline. In so doing he would be breaking the law, which gave the government a monopoly on the manufacture and sale of salt.

On March 12, Gandhi left his home near Ahmadabad and set out with a bamboo pole in his hand to walk nearly 250 miles to the village of Dandi on the west coast. He was accompanied by seventy-eight of his truth fighters and followed by representatives of the world's press. Every day for twenty-four days, the peasants in the surrounding countryside lined the roads to greet him as he passed, cooling and softening the path beneath his feet by spraying it with water and strewing it with leaves. On April 6, he reached Dandi and spent the entire night in prayer. The next day, he went down to the beach and picked up some of the salt that had dried on the sand after the tide went out. Holding it above his head, he announced that he had manufactured salt.

This gesture was the signal for nationwide demonstrations to begin. The campaign spread rapidly from the cities to the countryside; even middle-class Hindu women abandoned their traditional seclusion and participated in political meetings. But while there were many millions who adhered to the principle of peaceful protest, the hundreds who believed in violence also increased their activities, bombing buildings, raiding armories, and assassinating senior British officials. By the time the demonstrations were over, 60,000 people—including Gandhi and other Congress leaders—had been imprisoned.

While the frustrated authorities in India struggled to suppress the relentless civil disobedience, the Simon Commission published its report in England. Invitations to attend a conference in London in November 1930 were accepted by all interested

The haggard features of Muhammad Ali Jinnah, seated in front of the national flag of Pakistan, betray the ravages of the cancer from which he was to die in September 1948, just one year after becoming Pakistan's first governor general. Trained as a lawyer in England, Jinnah was not strict in his observance of Islamic traditions: He ate pork, attended prayers in a mosque only rarely, and addressed meetings in English rather than Urdu, the chief Muslim language of India. But the creation of an independent Muslim state was largely due to his fierce ambition and his refusal to compromise with either the British or other nationalist leaders.

parties and organizations except the Congress. When the conference ended, the representatives had agreed in principle to a constitution that made India a federation of states and a British dominion like Australia or Canada. But this agreement was worthless without the consent of Gandhi and the Congress, and the British government knew it. Lord Irwin released Gandhi from prison and invited him to the vice-regal palace in Delhi to discuss a compromise.

After long and wary negotiations, Gandhi and Irwin made a pact. In return for a promise by Irwin to release all political prisoners, Gandhi persuaded the Congress to call off the civil-disobedience campaign and send a representative to a second round-table conference in London. Several Congress leaders were appalled; Jawaharlal Nehru wavered in his loyalty and Subhas Chandra Bose came out in opposition. But Gandhi had been won over by the viceroy's sincerity. "I submitted," he said, "not to Lord Irwin, but to the honesty in him." The viceroy was not quite so complimentary in his description of Gandhi: "a most baffling enemy, generous, irrational, and elusive, and as hard to pin down on a point of logic as a butterfly on the plains of his native Gujarat."

Inevitably, Gandhi was chosen as the Congress representative at the second round-table conference. But he was not among friends. The government was unsympathetic to his demand for complete independence; and his efforts were hindered both by Muslim leaders—who wanted assurances that in any future constitution, Muslims would be treated as a separate community with separate representation—and by representatives of the low-caste Hindus, who demanded the same rights for themselves. The situation was described aptly by one of the Muslim leaders, who told the British: "It is the old maxim of divide and rule. But there is a division of labor here. We divide and you rule." Before the conference concluded, Gandhi left in disgust and returned to India.

The civil-disobedience campaign began again, and Gandhi was soon back in jail. This time, however, the Indian people had lost their enthusiasm. As Jawaharlal Nehru wrote later, "The initial push of inspiration was far less than in 1930. It was as if we entered unwillingly into battle." Many moderate Congress leaders began to drift back into cooperation with the British. Eventually, in May 1933, Gandhi gave orders from his prison cell to suspend the campaign.

Meanwhile, the British government had been enacting legislation to fulfill some of the agreements reached at the second conference in London. In August 1932, the prime minister announced that low-caste Hindus would be granted their own electorates. Gandhi, who was opposed to any system that kept the "untouchables" separate from the rest of the Hindu community, declared that he would fight the proposal with a "perpetual fast unto death." Shortly before noon on September 20, he took a last meal of honey and lemon juice and then prepared himself to refuse all food and drink except water. He was sixty-two years old and his frail, skinny body had no reserves of fat. Fearing that his death was imminent, leaders of both the high-caste Hindus and the "untouchables" gathered around the bed in his prison cell, and within six days, they had reached a compromise. Low-caste Hindus would vote with other Hindus in joint constituencies, but for a period of years to come, until their lot had improved, a large number of places would be reserved for them in the legislatures. Gandhi had effectively prevented the emergence of a third major political force of more than 50 million people that might compete with the Congress and the Muslim League.

Vultures pick over the remains of corpses littering a Calcutta alley in August 1946. Jinnah had organized a day of peaceful demonstrations in support of Muslim demands for a separate homeland, but agitators spread rumors of a Hindu plot to murder Muslims, and violence erupted. Since only Hindu shops were open on the day of the demonstrations, the mobs easily identified their quarry. The Hindus retaliated, and 6,000 people died in the ensuing bloodbath, more than in all previous communal riots in India under British rule.

In 1935, the Government of India Act, which provided for a new constitution, was at last approved by the British government after long delays caused by right-wing Conservative opposition. The longest statute ever passed by the British Parliament, the act proposed a federation of provinces that would elect their own governments, with a central administration of Indian politicians to be overseen by a British governor general. The compromise pleased nobody. Nehru denounced it as a ''charter of

slavery." Nevertheless, to the surprise of the British, all the Indian political parties took part in the election held at the beginning of 1937 as a first step toward implementing the constitution. When the votes were counted, the Congress was in a position to form governments in seven of the eleven provinces.

Flushed with victory, the Congress representatives failed to recognize the dangers of not being magnanimous. In forming their cabinets, they refused to appoint any Muslim ministers unless they dissociated themselves from the Muslim League and joined the Congress. Jinnah, to whom increasing numbers of Muslims looked to save them from Hindu dominance, now widened still further the divisions between the Congress and the league by arguing for the creation of a separate homeland for the Muslims. "The majority community have clearly shown their hand," he said. "Hindustan is for the Hindu."

In 1930, the Muslim poet Sir Muhammad Iqbal had suggested to a meeting of the league that a state of their own in northwest India "must be the final destiny of Muslims." He did not suggest that it should be independent of India, but soon afterward, a group of young Muslim students took up his idea and proposed an entirely separate country. Their name for it was derived from the first letters of most of the provinces and communities it would comprise—*P* for Punjab, *A* for the Afghans in the North-West Frontier region, *K* for Kashmir, *S* for Sind—and the last part of Baluchistan. The acronym so formed was Pakistan, a word that means "Land of the

Pure." In 1940, although opinions still differed as to the precise status of the intended homeland, the creation of Pakistan became the official policy of the Muslim League.

On the outbreak of the Second World War in September 1939, the British governor general, Lord Linlithgow, tactlessly announced that India was at war with Germany without consulting anybody. The Congress party responded by directing all of its ministries in the provinces to resign. But the Muslim ministries in Bengal, Punjab, and Sind refused to do so, and as a result, the Muslim League rose steadily both in prestige and in influence. By the end of the war, the league had become too powerful to be denied its demands.

Meanwhile, the Congress leaders were not fundamentally opposed to the British war effort: "In a conflict between democracy and freedom on the one side and fascism and aggression on the other, our sympathies must be inevitably on the side of democracy," declared Nehru. But he and his colleagues were determined to exact concessions and asked that they should be allowed to form a national government in return for their cooperation. Predictably, the governor general refused to hand over authority to a body that would not be recognized by the Muslims. The attitude of the British government changed, however, when Japanese forces advanced into Southeast Asia in early 1942; on March 8, the Japanese reached Rangoon in Burma, from where they threatened to invade India, and three days later, the British prime minister, Winston Churchill, sent Sir Stafford Cripps to India with a proposal for compromise.

Cripps promised that, in return for military support, the British would allow the Indians to draw up their own constitution and would introduce dominion status as soon as the war was over. But the Muslims would not accept a proposal that did not concede the creation of a separate Pakistan, and the Congress was holding out for immediate self-government. To Gandhi, a promise from a country that looked as though it was about to lose a war was no better than "a postdated check on a crashing bank." When no better offer was made, his attitude hardened still more: "I used to say that my moral support was entirely with Britain. I am very sorry to confess that today my mind refused to give that moral support. British behavior toward India has filled me with great pain."

Building on the momentum of an anti-British uprising in the east of the country, Gandhi persuaded the Congress to authorize a new nonviolent campaign against the British under the slogan Quit India! The Muslims campaigned under a slogan of their own: Divide and Quit! But the British were at war, and they were in no mood to be conciliatory. Gandhi and the majority of the Congress leaders were arrested. Popular demonstrations were quelled by baton charges and bullets. By the end of 1943, the British had gained firm control over the people of India, and the voice of the Congress was silent.

Outside the borders of their country, however, the continuing opposition of Indians to British rule was more dramatic. Unlike Gandhi and Nehru, Subhas Chandra Bose—whose favorite slogan was Give Me Blood and I Promise You Freedom!—had no qualms about collaborating with Britain's enemies. Early in 1941, Bose escaped from house arrest in Calcutta and made his way via Afghanistan and Moscow to Germany, where he married a German and became infatuated with nazism. He broadcast on behalf of the Axis powers and induced about 2,000 Indian prisoners, taken in North Africa, to join the German Indian Legion. In 1943, an organization called the Indian Independence League invited him to visit the Japanese-occupied

A tide of rejoicing Indians surges around the carriage of Lord and Lady Mountbatten on Independence Day in Delhi. Mountbatten, the last viceroy of India and a great-grandson of Queen Victoria—in whose reign the British raj had commenced—had won the respect of Indian leaders for the decisive manner in which he had organized the transfer of power, but he was unprepared for such popular acclamation. When his passage to the official platform was blocked, Mountbatten had to stand up in his coach and salute the new flag of India over the heads of the densely packed crowds.

121

In the panic caused by the partition of India, a train overladen with Muslim refugees prepares to leave Delhi for Pakistan. In all, around 14 million people crossed the borders between the two nations, but many who began the journey never completed it. Trains destined for Pakistan were frequently attacked en route by Hindus and Sikhs and arrived with all their passengers slaughtered; similar atrocities were carried out by Muslims on trains traveling in the opposite direction. Many thousands of Hindus in Pakistan and Muslims in India who feared to risk the journey, or who delayed for too long the decision to leave, were also butchered.

territories in the Far East, where Indian soldiers who had been captured at Singapore were being used to form the basis of a much larger Indian National Army. Traveling in German and Japanese submarines, he went first to Tokyo and then to Singapore, where he was elected president of the league and announced the establishment of the Provisional Government of Free India.

Early in 1944, the soldiers of the Indian National Army advanced more than 150 miles into their own country as allies of the Japanese. They were eventually driven back with the loss of 4,000 troops; and when the British and loyal Indian forces counterattacked and took Rangoon, 20,000 of them surrendered. Although Subhas Chandra Bose escaped, the plane that was carrying him to Tokyo crashed near Taiwan, and he died a few days later in a Japanese hospital.

Despite continuing nationalist opposition to the British, India's contribution to the cause of the Allies was substantial. By the end of the war, the Indian army comprised more than two million troops, of whom 700,000 were engaged in the final defeat of the Japanese in Burma. Total Indian casualties in the fighting numbered around 180,000. In addition, new steelworks were built, textile and cement industries expanded, and shipbuilding revived in aid of the war effort.

The war drained Britain of both the will and the economic power to hold onto India, and a general election in 1945 brought to power a Labour government that was eager to see the country self-governing as soon as possible. But there were still many obstacles to autonomy, chief of which were the irreconcilable demands of the Congress leaders—who insisted on a united India—and the Muslim League, which demanded a separate state. A conference was convened by Lord Wavell—a quiet, intellectual soldier who had been appointed to the reinstated role of viceroy in 1943—to discuss the formation of a transitional government; this broke down when Jinnah insisted that the league should be the sole representative of all Muslims, in spite of the fact that Congress had the support of many Muslims in Punjab and Bengal. In early 1946, a compromise scheme seemed at first to have satisfied both parties, but then Nehru held a press conference in which he appeared to say that once the proposed new constitution was in operation, members of the Congress would be no longer bound to accept its original terms. From that moment, the tension mounted rapidly, and the British, who had already begun to demobilize their army, were in no position to keep the peace for long.

In his demand for a Muslim country composed of the states where Muslims were in a majority, Jinnah was supported by Muslims from all over India, one-third of whom actually lived in states where Hindus were in a majority. At the Muslim League's annual meeting at Lahore in 1940, where it had adopted the resolution calling for the creation of an independent homeland, it had recognized the problem by requiring "adequate, effective, and mandatory safeguards" for the protection of Muslim minorities. But this was a demand that nobody could guarantee to fulfill.

On July 28, 1946, Jinnah proclaimed his opposition to both the Congress and the British government, and he called on all Muslims to demonstrate their solidarity by observing August 16 as Direct Action Day. When the day came, many thousands demonstrated peacefully, but there were other Muslims whose passions could not be so safely contained.

At dawn, small groups of Muslim thugs entered the city of Calcutta armed with sticks, iron bars, knives, bottles, and shovels. As the city awakened, they began their attacks, looting shops, burning buildings, and hacking to death every Hindu man and woman who stood in their way. Muslim onlookers joined their frenzy. By afternoon, Hindus and Sikhs had started to retaliate. By the time soldiers arrived on the second day in sufficient numbers to quell the rioting, the streets were strewn with casualties. The gutters were clogged with blood and hacked corpses; bloated bodies floated in the river, and mutilated coolies (a pejorative term for unskilled laborers) still hung between the poles of their rickshaws. In twenty-four hours of appalling ferocity, almost 6,000 people had been killed. Jinnah's words suddenly seemed ominous: "We shall have India divided, or we shall have India destroyed."

India was heading for civil war. The violence spread to other cities and then to the countryside, especially in East Bengal, Bihar, and Punjab. For most of the winter, the seventy-seven-year-old Gandhi walked barefoot through the three provinces, resting in humble Hindu and Muslim villages, pleading with the different majorities to help the minorities to rebuild their homes, urging the minorities to forget their fears, and reminding them all that they were "leaves of the same tree." As always, the villagers responded to his sincerity and humility. But their leaders were not listening.

Returned to London, Lord Wavell advised the prime minister, Clement Attlee, that the only way to make the Muslim League and the Congress come to an agreement would be to prepare for immediate British withdrawal. Attlee disagreed and accepted Wavell's resignation. But the man appointed in his place—the forceful extrovert Lord Mountbatten of Burma, who had been supreme Allied commander in Southeast Asia during the war—insisted that a deadline for withdrawal must be set, and Attlee announced that the British would leave India not later than June 1948.

Faced with a deadline, continuing violence, and the intransigence of Jinnah, Nehru and the other Congress leaders accepted that they would have to concede the

The billowing flames of a funeral pyre consume the body of Mahatma Gandhi, assassinated on the day before by a Hindu extremist opposed to his conciliatory policies toward Muslims. The procession accompanying Gandhi's coffin had taken five hours to travel five miles along streets strewn with rose petals. One million mourners had gathered at the site of the cremation, on the banks of Delhi's Jumna River. Among them was Prime Minister Nehru *(opposite)*, who grieved for both a national hero and a personal mentor. In a radio address to the people of India the previous evening, he had declared: "The light has gone out of our lives."

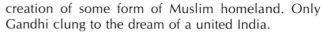

creation of some form of Muslim homeland. Only Gandhi clung to the dream of a united India.

When the new viceroy reached India in March 1947, the violence and atrocities were reaching new heights in Punjab and the North-West Frontier provinces. By the end of the following month, he had seen horrifying evidence for himself. In Punjab, he was shown the ruined village of Kahuta, where more than 2,000 Hindus and Sikhs had been burned to death by a Muslim mob. Many had died in the flames of their homes; those who escaped into the streets were tied together and soaked in gasoline before being set alight. "Until I went to Kahuta," said Mountbatten, "I had not appreciated the magnitude of the horrors that are going on."

Mountbatten was convinced that an independent Pakistan could not survive for long, but he also believed that the only way to prevent a cataclysmic bloodbath, and at the same time save Britain from the blame of having let it happen, would be to accept partition and grant independence to two nations as soon as possible. With advice from Nehru, who had quickly become his friend and confidant, he drew up a plan that seemed to have a chance of being accepted. Then he met Jinnah and warned him that partition would mean the division of Bengal and Punjab, where there were large populations of both Hindus and Muslims. "I do not care how little you give me," replied Jinnah, "so long as you give it to me completely."

Mountbatten moved up the deadline for independence to August 15, 1947, and on June 2, his plan was accepted by the Indian leaders. On the appointed day, Britain would hand over power to two countries, India and Pakistan; each would be a member of the British Commonwealth, with the right to secede if it wanted, and would elect its own government and appoint its own governor general. It was assumed that the provinces that had elected Congress ministries would wish to be part of India; the people of the Muslim provinces would be allowed to choose which country they joined, and the princely states could do the same or else remain independent. New boundaries would be drawn, and the army, the civil service, and all resources would be divided.

When the time came to choose, the provinces split as expected, with Muslim East Bengal and West Punjab choosing Pakistan and Hindu East Punjab and West Bengal choosing India. The princes were less predictable, but Mountbatten persuaded almost all of them that it was in their own interests to decide before it was too late and to surrender their authority in return for compensation.

Deftly, resolutely, and just in time, the British raj had been brought to an end. On August 14, Mountbatten inaugurated the independent Muslim Dominion of Pakistan and installed Jinnah—who was dying of cancer—as governor general. Leaving him to spend his last months as ruler of the country he had devoted his life to create, Mountbatten flew back to Delhi in time to hear Nehru's address to the nation. "Long years ago we made a tryst with destiny, and now the time comes when we shall redeem our pledge, not wholly or in full measure, but very substantially. At the stroke of the midnight hour, while the world sleeps, India will awake. . . ."

At midnight, Mountbatten transferred sovereignty to the Indian Constituent Assembly. Moments later, in a supreme compliment, the assembly invited him to become free India's first governor general, and as his first official duty, he administered the oath of office to his friend Prime Minister Nehru.

However, while messages of goodwill were exchanged between Indian and British leaders and joyous crowds thronged the public places of Delhi in a mood of festive celebration, ominous reports began to emerge from the divided Punjab. On the afternoon of August 15, a group of Muslim women in a town in East Punjab were raped by a Sikh mob and paraded naked in the streets before they were killed and incinerated. Across the border on the same day, a Sikh temple was burned to the ground by Muslims, all the worshipers inside dying in the flames.

As more than 14 million people crossed the new borders of East and West Pakistan, neighbors found themselves divided by nationality as well as religion, and in that division, old friends became enemies. Throughout the provinces, majorities turned on minorities. More than half a million people were killed in Punjab alone. Train-loads of refugees traveling in both directions were slaughtered before they could reach safety. The Hindu quarters of Lahore were left as flat and bloodstained as the Muslim quarters of Amritsar. At a textile factory in Lyallpur, Muslim workers massacred all the Sikhs who had been working beside them for years. Desperate men on both sides shot and stabbed their wives and daughters to keep them from defilement.

The Boundary Force that had been formed to oversee the peaceable transfer of population proved hopelessly inadequate. British officers entered the ruins of countless villages to be met by sights more terrible than anything they had seen in seven years of war. On an afternoon in late August, one officer was traveling toward the town of Hasilpur in Pakistan, just south of Punjab. In a relaxed and confident mood, feeling pleased to be well away from the scenes of the worst violence, he noted what appeared to be heaps of manure scattered near the road. Coming nearer, he realized they were piles of bodies: "Men, women, and children, there they were all jumbled up together, their arms and legs akimbo in all sorts of attitudes and postures, some of them so lifelike that one could hardly believe they were really dead."

Gandhi, meanwhile, was in Calcutta, having stayed away from the official ceremonies inaugurating the divided nations. He believed that the violence had brought dishonor upon India, and that penance, fasting, and prayer were the only appropriate methods of celebrating independence. But his personal influence was still powerful: When Hindus began to attack Muslims in Calcutta, he went on a fast, and within five days, the city was at peace again. Muslims feared that if he died, they would suffer a new and even more terrible onslaught from the Hindus; Hindus did not want to be held guilty of causing his death.

He then moved to Delhi, where riots, arson, and looting had broken out in September, and for the next four months, he worked ceaselessly to quell the constant violence. Slowly, as the flow of refugees dried up, the atrocities and retaliations became fewer. At last the antagonisms subsided and the two suspicious new nations stepped back from the brink of suicidal war.

In January 1948, Gandhi went on another successful fast to persuade the government to pay a disputed sum to Pakistan and to urge the Hindu citizens of Delhi to allow Muslims to return to their homes. Always the champion of the deprived and the oppressed, Gandhi was proving to be as much an irritant to intolerant Hindus as he had been to the British; and secretly, among a disparate group of men that included

Before the massive basalt arch on Bombay's quayside known as the Gateway to India, a guard of Indian soldiers and sailors prepares to salute the departure of the last British troops from India in February 1948. The gateway had been built to commemorate the visit of King George V and Queen Mary in 1911; once the troops had passed through it to embark for England, it became a monument to a dead empire.

a doctor, a municipal councilor, and an illiterate youth, a conspiracy began to take shape that aimed to silence Gandhi's voice by means more effective than the British had ever attempted.

On the afternoon of January 30, Gandhi was making his way through a crowd of people toward his daily prayer meeting when a young man stepped up to him and bowed low as if in obeisance. As Gandhi raised his hands in greeting, the young man drew a pistol and shot him three times in the chest at point-blank range. The last word the Mahatma uttered was the name of God.

The assassin was immediately seized by horrified onlookers, and Gandhi's body was carried into a nearby building. Shocked and scarcely believing the news, Nehru and Mountbatten soon arrived to see for themselves. As the latter forced his way through the crowd, he heard someone shout that the assassin was a Muslim. Mountbatten at once responded, "You fool, don't you know it was a Hindu?" Quietly, the press secretary accompanying him asked how he could possibly know this was true. "I don't," said Mountbatten. "But if it really was a Muslim, India is going to have one of the most ghastly massacres the world has ever seen."

It was a Hindu. He was the editor of an extremist Hindu newspaper, an educated man who respected Gandhi's sincerity but who believed that by preaching nonviolence and toleration of Muslims, Gandhi was undermining both Hinduism and India. Four months later, he was brought to trial along with seven other conspirators; he and his chief accomplice were sentenced to death, five received life imprisonment, and one was acquitted for lack of evidence.

Gandhi had died as he had wished, with the name of God on his lips, but the nation upon which his eyes had closed was far from what he had desired it to be. India was free, but at a price—the separation of Pakistan—that he had considered too high. Having sought all his life to inculcate in his compatriots the ideals of peaceful cooperation, he had witnessed during his last years India's worst-ever internecine massacres. And having preached humility and self-sacrifice by personal example, he had seen many of the Congress leaders—as soon as independence became a reality—begin jockeying for power and prestige.

But none of the discrepancies between Gandhi's ideals and his actual achievements diminished the force of his legacy to India and to the wider world. To the often bitter and brutal struggle between Indian subjects and British overlords, he had imparted a moral perspective in which the injustices of colonialism were fully exposed. His beliefs also did much to shape the goals toward which his friend and disciple, Jawaharlal Nehru, led India in the decade and a half following independence. By a revised constitution inaugurated in 1950, India became a full-fledged republic dedicated to socialist principles; and despite overwhelming problems—beginning with vast numbers of refugees and boundary disputes with Pakistan in the early years, and continuing with the frequent domestic conflicts inherent in this vast nation of many religions and many languages—Nehru maintained a system of parliamentary democracy that made the government directly responsible to the people.

Outside India, Gandhi's ideals and methods became an inspiration to many other nationalist movements. The independence of India marked the beginning of the end for all the colonial empires. The victory of the Indian people taught other subject peoples that history was on their side.

A DOMESTIC REVOLUTION

Electricity," claimed a utility company in a 1925 pamphlet, "provides the modern housewife with the perfect servant—clean, silent, economical." And the "modern" housewife seemed to agree. For in the twenty years between the two world wars, middle-class homes throughout the United States (and later, Western Europe) were transformed by a flood of home appliances—refrigerators, stoves, irons, clothes washers, and many more—made possible by the availability of electric power.

This revolution in domestic technology did not happen overnight, nonetheless. Most of the so-called new products had been invented decades before. But early models of electric appliances were unwieldy, temperamental, and expensive, and at a time when electricity was still a rather frightening novelty and domestic labor was cheap, they had made little commercial impact. After World War I, however, the public's fears of the new technology were allayed by the introduction of electric lighting in streets and homes, and by the advent of home radios, which proved to be an instant success. With domestic help becoming harder to find as workers opted for better-paying jobs in industry, the market for laborsaving devices grew.

Led by the electric utilities themselves, industry stepped in to satisfy the increased demand. Huge sums were invested in research and development, and improved techniques—borrowed from the burgeoning automobile industry—allowed effective mass production and more elegant design.

In the United States, manufacturers of household appliances quickly began to use the recently popular medium of commercial radio to sell their products; elsewhere, advertisements and door-to-door salespeople soon left the customer in little doubt that the laborsaving devices really were indispensable—and, since they were still beyond the reach of most working-class households, such devices became coveted status symbols.

Ironically, the amount of time spent on housework by women actually increased between 1930 and 1950. Although the new technology undoubtedly took the drudgery out of many daily household chores, it also set higher standards of domestic hygiene. In this respect, the "perfect servant" turned out to be a demanding taskmaster.

An American family listens to the radio together in Hood County, Oregon, in 1925. Radio attracted huge audiences throughout the United States, and its commercials helped to promote other household appliances far beyond the metropolitan areas.

The cover of a 1929 issue of Italy's *Radiorario* magazine illustrates how radio provides entertainment for all tastes and puts its listeners in touch with events not only in their own land but across the globe. In many countries, governments were quick to latch onto the persuasive power of the medium.

The young Orson Welles broadcasts to the country in 1938. That same year, Welles unwittingly demonstrated the power of radio when his adaptation of H. G. Wells's novel *The War of the Worlds,* with its story of a Martian invasion updated to twentieth-century New Jersey and told in a series of "news flashes," spread panic across the nation.

Dutch manufacturer Philips had sales of more than 200,000 in the early thirties with their Model 930A Local Station Receiver.

Advertisements present contrasting images to promote the benefits of vacuum cleaners. A 1924 German publicity photo for the AEG Vampyr *(left)* implies that housework could be highly sophisticated. Western Electric chose a more domestic image for their Sweeper Vac in 1930 *(below)*, and a 1928 Austrian poster compares life before and after the vacuum cleaner.

British-made under license, this mid-thirties Hoover Model 541 carries the giant U.S. company's distinctive slogan.

"I tell you we don't *want* an electric cleaner!" cries the harassed housewife in this Fougasse cartoon from a 1936 issue of London's *Punch* magazine. The persistence of vacuum-cleaner salesmen was legendary and a constant source of humor. But their effectiveness as a sales force could not be doubted.

This American Kelvinator K.60 refrigerator of the early thirties was soon superseded by more "streamlined" designs.

Although early refrigerators came in a variety of colors, a glossy white-enamel finish was soon adopted by almost all manufacturers to give an impression of scrupulous cleanliness—a quality stressed in this 1934 poster for the Santo Junior refrigerator, made by German manufacturer AEG.

SANTO
Junior

Der elektrische
AEG Kühlschrank

By the standards of the late 1930s, Premier's "Accident-Proof" electric kettle was sophisticated, boasting a shut-off mechanism activated when the appliance boiled dry. Universal's "Automatic Oven" toaster was similarly advanced in that it had a built-in timer.

Using an electric washing machine outside her Tennessee farmhouse in 1940, this woman would certainly have been envied by her predecessors. Her task was, nevertheless, time-consuming: Although electricity powered the agitator and wringer, it did not heat up the water, and rinsing had to be carried out in a separate tub. Early machines tended to be temperamental, too, and had to be painstakingly oiled before each use.

Despite shortcomings, clothes washers such as the Beatty Model F were popular in the thirties.

Small, straightforward, and therefore cheap, electric irons were immediately popular. As an Austrian poster of 1928 (above) suggests, they were far less unwieldy than the old flatirons, which had to be heated over fire or on the stove and which cooled quickly. Dating from the same period, this "Traveling Iron" exemplifies the virtues of the electric appliances—compact, portable, and elegant.

THE STRUGGLE FOR CHINA

When the Chinese Nationalist leader Dr. Sun Zhongshan died in March 1925, he was given a funeral fit for an emperor—with two important differences. First, as a member of the Methodist church, he was accorded a Christian funeral as well as a state ceremony; and second, as the inspiration of the movement to rid China of its foreign Manchu rulers, the Qing dynasty, his death aroused more heartfelt grief than had been shown for any recent emperor of China.

Yet Sun Zhongshan—better known to Westerners as Sun Yat-sen—left behind a nation on the brink of dissolution. At the time of his death, China was divided between a military government in Beijing trying vainly to impose its will on powerful local warlords, and his own, Canton-based regime, which enshrined the values of the Guomindang, the revolutionary party he had founded in 1912. Out of the ensuing chaos two other charismatic figures would emerge: Jiang Jieshi (Chiang Kai-shek), Sun's successor as head of the Guomindang and the future president of the Republic of China; and the Communist leader Mao Zedong, later chairman of the People's Republic of China. The struggle between these two men would last for nearly a quarter of a century, to end in Communist victory in 1949.

For thirty years, Sun had dedicated his life to the "overthrow of the Manchus, the restoration of China to the Chinese, and the establishment of a republican government." During the last 100 years of Qing rule, which had been established in the mid-seventeenth century, China had been brought to ruin. Corruption was rife at every level of an administration that was inadequate at managing the nation.

The population had grown so fast that the economy could not cope. The peasants—the overwhelming mass of the population—were crippled by oppressive land rents, paid to the landlord gentry. Land was generally measured not by area, but by the weight of food that it was deemed capable of producing, and rent was levied at an average of 50 percent of the crop, often more. Since the rent was the same in a bad year as it was in a good, the Chinese peasants were never more than one harvest away from destitution or outright famine. Not surprisingly, autumn riots were commonplace and major rebellions frequent. These internal crises coincided with the arrival on the scene of foreign imperialists. Under pressure from overseas powers, the world's most enduring civilization had been reduced to semicolonial status—in Sun's words, "not the colony of one nation, but of all."

By the so-called unequal treaties, signed by China under the threat of force, foreign powers possessed nearly 100 treaty "ports"—many of them hundreds of miles inland—where their nationals could reside, own property, and do business outside Chinese jurisdiction. In sixteen of these treaty ports, specific areas—called concessions—were set aside exclusively for foreign residents. Shanghai, which had about

Mounted on horseback, Mao Zedong, chairman of the Chinese Communist party, leaves his northern China base in 1947 to lead an offensive during the civil war between the Communists and the Nationalist forces of Jiang Jieshi (Chiang Kai-shek). At the beginning of the civil war a year earlier, the Communists were outnumbered three to one by their better-equipped enemy, but by 1948, the relative strengths of the two sides had been reversed. The next year, following the military defeat of the Nationalists, Mao announced the establishment of the People's Republic of China—the first government to effectively unite the country since the overthrow of China's imperial rulers in 1912.

From 1931 to the end of World War II, the struggle between Nationalists and Communists for control of China was complicated by the presence of Japanese occupation forces. At its greatest extent early in 1945, the Japanese zone (*shaded yellow*) covered much of the country, from Manchuria to Canton. But the invaders never succeeded in destroying the Guomindang, which established its wartime capital at Chongqing in Sichuan province. And even in the areas nominally under Japanese control, the invaders were harassed by Communist guerrillas operating out of rural bases (*red*).

fourteen square miles of concessions by 1915, was virtually a European city, complete with fine boulevards, a golf course, and a racetrack.

The treaty ports were an affront to national pride, but they were also a powerful influence on modernists such as Sun Zhongshan, who could not help but contrast the stability and wealth of the foreign enclaves with the chaotic conditions prevalent in most of China. They also contained almost the only modern industries and financial institutions in the country—not just foreign concerns, but Chinese-owned enterprises operating under the protection of alien law. Without the treaty ports, in fact, the modernization of China would have been set back many years.

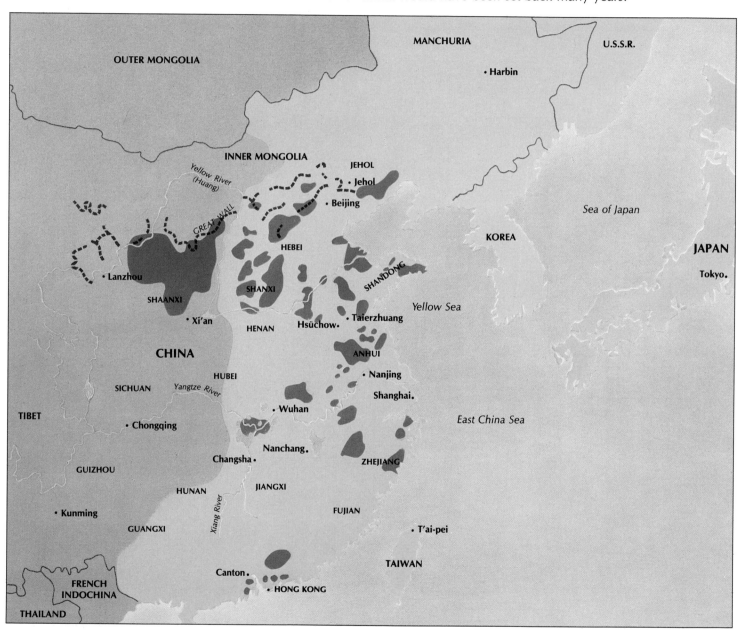

Sun himself came from a region between the southern ports of Canton and Macao where the foreign presence was particularly strong. He was born in 1866 and acquired a Western-style education in Hawaii (where his prosperous elder brother had settled); Sun then studied medicine in Hong Kong. Politically active from an early age, he fled abroad in 1895 after organizing the first of ten unsuccessful revolts against the Manchus. For the next sixteen years, he traveled the world as a political exile, seeking support for the cause of Chinese nationalism.

He found his strongest backing in Japan, a country that many progressive Chinese regarded as a model for the kind of nation that they wanted to create. Only a generation before, Japan had been as apparently backward and inward-looking as China, but by wholesale borrowing of techniques of government and warfare from the West, it had transformed itself into the strongest and most advanced country in the Far East. Impressed by the country's dynamism, many Chinese reformers turned a blind eye to the fact that Japan had recently inflicted a humiliating military defeat on their country in the Sino-Japanese War of 1894 to 1895, and that some influential Japanese, conscious of their country's limited resources and work force, had designs on the vast lands and population of their Asian neighbor.

Despite this fact, it was in Tokyo in 1905 that the various competing Chinese dissident groups came together in the Revolutionary Alliance, the forerunner of the Guomindang. Sun Zhongshan was recognized as leader of the alliance, but internal divisions prevented him from exploiting the growing weakness of the Qing regime. When the Japanese, concerned by the growing radicalization of his supporters, expelled him in 1907, he resumed his globetrotting activities, keeping in touch with events in China through a network of spies. In 1911, while he was on a fund-raising mission in the United States, he heard that the Qing dynasty had finally been toppled by a revolutionary uprising backed by the imperial army. When Sun returned to China at the end of the year, his unflagging opposition to the Manchus earned him election as provisional president of the new Chinese Republic.

His tenure of power was short-lived. Sun's party simply lacked the strength to overcome the problems confronting the nation. Taken unawares by the collapse of the Qing regime, Sun and his colleagues had had no time to work out how they would handle the reins of power; all they had was a vague formula for China's regeneration based on Sun's "Three People's Principles"—nationalism, democracy, and "people's livelihood." Their revolutionary movement had few members in China itself; the party's main backers were Chinese merchants on the Pacific rim. The foreign powers refused to support them, dismissing them as futile visionaries. Worse, they did not command any military force. After only forty-seven days, Sun resigned his post in favor of Yuan Shikai, the former war minister of the Qing regime, who by virtue of the control he exercised over the old imperial army, was regarded as the only leader who could make the new republic work.

It soon became apparent that Yuan's commitment to Sun's Three Principles was nonexistent. When the Guomindang achieved a majority in the 1913 elections, he had its leader assassinated and forced Sun into exile in Japan. Abandoning plans for a constitutional government, Yuan set himself up as a military dictator and embarked on a campaign to have himself crowned emperor. But the bonds that tenuously linked the nation had been broken, and he found that his authority extended only to those places where troops loyal to him could impose his will. Elsewhere in the country, power passed to local military commanders. The warlord era had begun.

A uniformed Jiang Jieshi stands respectfully beside his mentor, Dr. Sun Zhongshan (Sun Yat-sen), a leading force in the republican revolution that ended imperial rule in China. After serving briefly as the new republic's acting president, Sun was forced into exile in Japan, where he befriended Jiang, a professionally trained soldier and a supporter of Sun's Guomindang, or Nationalist party. In 1923, when Sun succeeded in establishing a government in the southern port of Canton, Jiang was put in charge of the Guomindang army's reorganization. After Sun died in 1925, leaving no successor, Jiang exploited his friendship with the late president to enhance his standing as a potential leader of the party, a position he finally attained in 1928.

Until his death in 1916, Yuan was fully occupied trying to control these freebooters; but the warlords invariably combined against any of their number who looked as if he might gain supremacy, including Yuan himself. While he was alive, foreign powers preserved the fiction that he represented an effective central government, if only because they needed someone with whom they could negotiate treaty rights and debt repayments. But when they became embroiled in what one Chinese called the European Civil War—World War I—one of the interested powers grabbed the chance to extend its influence in China: In 1915, Japan seized the German concessions in Shandong province and presented a set of demands that would have made China a Japanese protectorate. Yuan temporized, eventually making concessions that gave Japan a sphere of influence in Manchuria. At the Versailles Peace Conference after the war, the victorious Allies confirmed Japan's holdings in China.

This example of European jobbery inflamed anti-imperialist sentiment, producing a wave of patriotic fervor in all sections of Chinese society, especially among the young. On May 4, 1919, some 3,000 students demonstrated in Beijing. "China's territory may be conquered," they declared, "but it cannot be given away. The Chinese people may be massacred, but they will not surrender. Our country is about to be annihilated. Rise up, brethren!" One-third of the demonstrators were jailed after wrecking the house of the Chinese minister they blamed for the humiliation, but under the pressure of public opinion, the warlords who controlled the capital were forced to release them.

Short-lived as the incident was, its impact was enormous. In addition to forcing the government to reject the Treaty of Versailles, the demonstration triggered a reformist movement whose objectives, besides resisting imperialism, included the replacement of Confucian ethics by more modern concepts and the use of phonetic spelling for written Chinese. Among the exponents of reform were China's handful of Communists.

Sun Zhongshan was too busy struggling to retain a place in the political arena and participate in the reformist movement. After Yuan's death, he made several comebacks, establishing two temporary revolutionary governments in Canton with the help of local warlords. On each occasion, he squabbled with his backers and was ousted; but he refused to give up the cause of national unification, and in January 1923, after militarists loyal to him expelled rival warlords from Canton, he returned to install himself as leader of a new regime dedicated to the reconstruction of China.

This time, however, he determined to approach his goal by a different path. Trying

The commander of a warlord's execution squad signals that his men have performed their macabre duty. Taking advantage of the anarchic conditions that followed the collapse of imperial rule in 1912, local military leaders established personal power bases over immense tracts of China. Taxes levied to support their petty conflicts caused severe hardship and deprived the national government of vital revenues. In the turmoil of the warlord era, millions of peasants fled, leaving flood-control and irrigation works in decay. Although Jiang Jieshi's first mission as military leader of the Guomindang was to destroy the warlords, the last of them were not deposed until the civil war ended in 1949.

to make an accommodation with local warlords had proved disastrous. The foreign democracies he so much admired had consistently turned down his pleas for assistance. Nevertheless, in February 1923, he made another desperate attempt to enlist Western aid, going so far as to invite the United States to lead an international occupation force with authority over the Chinese army and police and the right to appoint key administrators. Rebuffed yet again, he announced that he had lost "hope of help from America, Britain, and France . . . the only country that showed signs of helping us is Soviet Russia."

In fact, Sun Zhongshan had been in contact with the Soviet government almost from the beginning of its existence in November 1917. He also had meetings with members of the Chinese Communist party (CCP), which had been officially founded in July 1921 by twelve Chinese officials and a Dutch and Soviet representative of Communist International (Comintern). A pledge by the Soviets to renounce their concessions in China (a promise that was not to be fulfilled) helped transform Sun's view of the Soviet Union from that of a menacing foreign aggressor to that of a fellow Asiatic power also struggling to throw off the chains of imperialist domination. Late in 1922, Sun engaged in talks with a Soviet emissary that culminated in a joint manifesto designed to pave the way for collaboration between the Guomindang and the Chinese Communist party.

Many members on both sides disliked the idea of an alliance, but Sun dragooned his party into accepting it, and the CCP, under pressure from Moscow, reluctantly conceded that "the Guomindang must be the central force of the revolution and assume the leadership of it." The fact was, the Communists' Soviet backers did not believe that the CCP—which had only 432 members by June 1923—could bring about a true socialist revolution in an agrarian society. The peasants, according to orthodox Communists, were too scattered, too innately conservative, and too wedded to the ambition of becoming landlords themselves. In Marxist-Leninist theory, the revolution could be achieved only by an uprising of the disaffected urban working classes—or, in Lenin's words, "as the number of Shanghais increases." But as a first step along this revolutionary path, the Soviet theorists insisted, left-wing and "bourgeois democratic" elements must form a united front to liberate China from imperialists and their warlord lackeys.

Sun reaped the first benefits of the alliance in August, when a Guomindang delegation visited Moscow on a mission to obtain Soviet military aid. Two months later, Moscow sent an experienced Comintern revolutionary, Mikhail Borodin, to reorganize the Guomindang along the lines of a centralized party dictatorship. The veteran of a dozen Comintern missions, this Latvian-born, Russian-trained, former Chicago language-school owner soon became one of Sun's most-trusted advisers. Over the next few months, he turned his considerable organizing talents to restructuring the party, developing labor unions, carrying propaganda to the peasants, and constructing a reliable army.

On Borodin's recommendation, Russian funds were used to establish a military academy on the island of Huang Pu, off Canton. Its first director was the thirty-seven-year-old leader of the delegation recently returned from Moscow, Jiang Jieshi. An austere man with gray eyes, unusual in a Chinese, Jiang held himself with the formal rigidity he had learned at a Japanese military academy. During the 1911 revolutionary period, he had led a regiment partly financed by a Japanese secret society that gave backing to Sun Zhongshan. The two became friends when Jiang, an opponent of Yuan Shikai, was forced to flee to Japan. After the president's death, Jiang returned to Shanghai, where he enriched himself by speculating on the Shanghai stock exchange. He also formed strong links with the city's criminal underworld, possibly joining the inner circle of the notorious Green Gang, which controlled much of Shanghai's opium trade, gambling, prostitution, and protection rackets. In the jockeying for power that followed Yuan's death, Jiang risked his life by allying himself with Sun; his steadfast support enhanced his standing in the Guomindang when Sun finally came to power. Jiang Jieshi's wealth and influence would be increased in 1927, when he married a sister of the wealthiest banker in China, T. V. Soong (another sister was the widow of Sun Zhongshan), converting to Methodism on his wife's account.

These were not the credentials of a committed socialist, and in truth, Jiang nurtured a pathological hatred of his Communist colleagues. But at this stage of his career, he still cultivated the image of a revolutionary nationalist, and he was highly respected by Borodin and the Soviet military adviser, General Blücher, a hero of the Russian Revolution. Among Jiang's closest associates at Huang Pu was his elegant and cultivated senior political commissar, Zhou Enlai, who had recently returned from Paris, where he had helped establish the European headquarters of the CCP. Only twenty-six years old in 1924, Zhou was destined to play a leading role in the foundation of the People's Republic of China, as was his deputy, Chen Yi.

A poster bearing idealized likenesses of Sun Zhongshan *(top)* and Jiang Jieshi *(bottom, on a white horse)* commemorates Guomindang victories over warlords during the Northern Expedition of 1926 to 1928. In the first year of this campaign, a united front of Nationalist and Communist forces defeated some thirty separate warlord armies. Jiang, who commanded the joint forces, subsequently emerged as the most powerful figure in China. The military was backed by an organized propaganda machine staffed by more than 3,000 student volunteers. Covering large parts of the country in trains equipped with printing presses, they were successful in broadcasting the Guomindang goal of a republican China unified under the Nationalist flag.

During this period of cooperation between Right and Left, Jiang's apparent support for the revolutionary union was reciprocated by Mao Zedong, a diligent member of the Guomindang's Central Committee. Mao, who was thirty in 1924, was the son of a grasping peasant in Hunan province, which he had represented at the formal establishment of the CCP. His revolutionary consciousness had been developed during a spell as a librarian at Beijing University, where he met the first of his three wives, the daughter of a radical professor. Mao was tall and thin, with dark good looks in early adulthood, and he became an accomplished poet and pamphleteer whose political ideology was inspired as much by the Chinese classics as by the textbooks of Karl Marx. Although he was not an orthodox Communist, his rural upbringing had given him an understanding of the Chinese peasantry unrivaled by his colleagues. His combination of romantic idealism and practical knowledge would prove vital to the Communists' survival in the years after the death of Sun Zhongshan.

Jiang had no illusions about the CCP's aims—to use the Guomindang as a tool for a Marxist revolution. But he was obliged to maintain a facade of cooperation because he needed Soviet aid to build a strong army around Huang Pu's graduate officers. Once this had been formed, his intention was to break the northern warlords and take Beijing. International recognition would be his reward, along with control of all customs revenue and access to the foreign monies required for China's modernization. Only then would he be in a position to crush his Communist colleagues.

With these aims in mind, Jiang Jieshi set about cultivating allies, embarking on a masterly campaign to make himself indispensable to all factions. For the benefit of Sun Zhongshan's admirers, he presented an attitude of filial veneration, the better to demonstrate his right to inherit the mantle of leadership. From the Russians he received aid to counter the Japanese, who were developing Manchuria as a major source of food and raw materials. For their part, the Japanese offered assistance in return for a pledge to limit Soviet influence in the region. Shanghai's business community promised financial support on condition that he eradicate the left-wing organizers of the new unions in the rapidly industrializing city. At the same time, Jiang continued to encourage the Communists in the task of building up the Guomindang. To the warlords, Jiang promised rank or money provided that they joined his side.

By the spring of 1925, Jiang was confident that he had assembled enough support to launch the much-heralded Northern Expedition against the warlords. The ultimate aim was to take Beijing and unify the whole country, first consolidating Guomindang control in the south. On June 5, the Guomindang government named Jiang commander in chief of the National Revolutionary Army (NRA); its first, and only, revolutionary campaign began the following month.

Though outnumbered by the opposing forces, the NRA—advancing north from

A Nationalist picket searches a man suspected of carrying left-wing pamphlets during the Shanghai Purge of April 1927, which ended the fragile union of conservative and Communist elements in the Guomindang. Jiang Jieshi's army had entered Shanghai a few days earlier, after pro-Communist labor unions had seized control of the city. With the help of underworld thugs and right-wing unionists, Jiang crushed the opposition. About 5,000 Communists and their sympathizers—including this suspect—were killed, and their leaders were forced to go underground.

Canton—was able to exploit the chronic disunity of the warlords. And it was well led by graduates of Huang Pu and their Soviet military advisers. Moreover, it reaped the benefits of a massive campaign of propaganda and subversion. A new labor organization called strikes at strategic times and places to stop the movement of warlord troops and their supplies. Members of the recently formed farmers' unions impeded the passage of enemy forces while helping the NRA with supplies and information. Bribes brought many warlords and their generals over to the Nationalist side. By the end of the year, the Guomindang controlled the seven southern provinces and almost 50 percent of the population of China. During the advance, membership in the Guomindang and its unions had soared. Most of the unions were under the leadership of the Chinese Communist party, which saw its membership rise to 70,000 by the beginning of 1927.

But even as the army was rolling north, another battle was raging within the Guomindang itself. A majority, which included the left wing, wanted to set up a new capital at Wuhan, a Communist stronghold in the central province of Hubei; Jiang and his right-wing supporters favored Nanchang, provincial capital of neighboring Jiangxi, as the new seat. The leftists acted first, proclaiming Wuhan the capital on

In 1933, two years after Japan occupied and set up a puppet state in Manchuria, Japanese soldiers advance to take the northern Chinese province of Jehol. Japanese expansionist fervor had swelled at the end of the 1920s, when the Great Depression impoverished the country by crippling its export markets. An authoritarian philosophy took hold among Japan's military, who disregarded civil government in their determination both to check Soviet influence in eastern Asia and to acquire territory that would provide resources and living space for the large Japanese population. China, embroiled in conflicts between Nationalists, Communists, and warlords, could put up only limited resistance to Japan's imperialist designs.

January 1. Conscious of the threat to his position, Jiang abandoned his revolutionary goals as well as his drive to the north. Instead, while stressing the need for the continuance of the Guomindang-CCP alliance, he turned his attention to Shanghai.

Several factors influenced his decision. Having established excellent relations with Shanghai's business community and gangs, he could count on them to give him the financial support that would make him independent of the Wuhan government and Soviet aid. Equally important, Shanghai was China's window on the world, and therefore it was the best place to demonstrate to foreign powers that the kind of Guomindang government he envisaged posed no threat to their interests. Shanghai, however, was also China's biggest industrial city and the stronghold of the Chinese labor movement; it was the workers, organized by Zhou Enlai among others, who took control on March 21, 1927. Five days later, Jiang entered the city.

Now he fulfilled the bargain he had made with the city's merchants and bankers; even while Stalin and other Communist leaders were hailing Jiang's military successes, the general was plotting a purge of the Left. To that end, the first person he received was the boss of the Green Gang. On April 12, Green Gang bands attacked the headquarters of the Shanghai Trade Union Federation and other union offices, massacring many of their members. Protesters taking part in a demonstration on the next day were machine-gunned by Jiang's army, and during the following week, an estimated 5,000 leftists were hunted down and killed, their dripping heads displayed on bamboo poles or platters.

In other cities held by the Guomindang, fierce fighting broke out between Jiang's supporters and the Communists. It was the right wing that had the initiative, and it was the right wing that generally proved successful. On April 18, at a banquet attended by his Soviet advisers, Jiang ended a long speech by raising his glass and shouting: "Down with the Communist party."

At this point, Stalin reversed his policy and ordered the CCP to take power by force. But party membership had fallen drastically as a result of persecution, and many of its leaders were dead or in hiding. A Communist uprising in Canton was easily and brutally suppressed with the destruction of much of the city. In Wuhan, the left wing of the Guomindang decided to break with their CCP colleagues, leaving them defenseless against Jiang's forces, which slaughtered some 100,000 party members and their sympathizers in a massacre that raged until the summer of 1928. Borodin and Blücher managed to escape to Moscow, where both eventually fell victim to Stalin's purges. The few survivors of the Central Committee of the CCP went underground in Shanghai. By 1928, when the party held its Sixth Congress in a Moscow suburb, it had fewer than 10,000 members.

Meanwhile, the Nationalists had continued the Northern Expedition, capturing Beijing from the warlords and establishing a national government in Nanjing headed by Jiang Jieshi, who also retained his position as commander in chief of the national army. As he had anticipated, foreign countries accorded China a new degree of respect. Although Japan remained determined to retain its influence in Manchuria, Britain, which had the largest interests in China, relinquished two of its treaty ports, and the United States, which had a strong missionary presence in China, was sympathetic to the new government and its Christian leader. It was a period of optimism and idealism for the Chinese. "Something new has come to China," declared a Guomindang commander, "the birth of patriotism and public spirit."

And yet the country's basic problems had not changed. The Guomindang was a

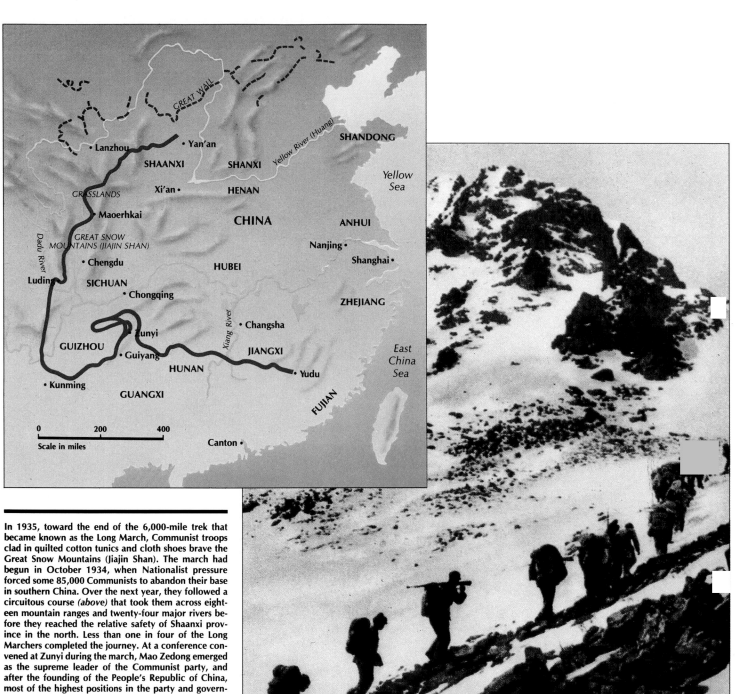

In 1935, toward the end of the 6,000-mile trek that became known as the Long March, Communist troops clad in quilted cotton tunics and cloth shoes brave the Great Snow Mountains (Jiajin Shan). The march had begun in October 1934, when Nationalist pressure forced some 85,000 Communists to abandon their base in southern China. Over the next year, they followed a circuitous course *(above)* that took them across eighteen mountain ranges and twenty-four major rivers before they reached the relative safety of Shaanxi province in the north. Less than one in four of the Long Marchers completed the journey. At a conference convened at Zunyi during the march, Mao Zedong emerged as the supreme leader of the Communist party, and after the founding of the People's Republic of China, most of the highest positions in the party and government were held by survivors of the odyssey.

collection of competing factions whose allegiance to Jiang was uncertain. The war-lords had been tamed rather than defeated, and Jiang's sphere of control was still confined to the lower Yangtze valley; in the rest of the country, the writ of the Nanjing government ran only on sufferance. The lives of the peasants were still subject to the vicissitudes of the weather and the greed of their landlords. Between 1929 and 1930, an estimated six million Chinese died in a famine that went virtually unreported by the world press. Sun's widow left the Guomindang and went into exile, accusing her husband's successors of organizing the party as "a tool for the rich to get still richer and suck the blood of the starving millions." During the early 1930s, Jiang made efforts to stem the corruption within his party. Disillusioned with democracy, he flirted with fascism and established the Blue Shirts, a body devoted to building him up as a dictator and to promoting his semireligious New Life Movement for the moral regeneration of the nation. And all the time, he continued his efforts to eradicate communism from China.

Tied to Communist orthodoxy and bound to obey the Comintern, the surviving remnants of the CCP continued to pin their hopes on the urban proletariat; but cities were few in China, and even the warlord armies were better trained and equipped than the workers' militias. Mao, however, was beginning to move away from Marxist-Leninist doctrine. After spending much of 1925 organizing peasant associations in his native Hunan, he had written a report in which he identified the revolutionary potential of the rural masses. Oppressed by heavy rents and interest rates as high as 80 percent, and exploited by corrupt officials, they were ripe for revolution, he claimed. He also believed they could provide what the CCP lacked, a large and effective military force.

Although his theories were rejected out of hand by the CCP's political office, or politburo, he had been given a chance to test them in Hunan as one of the leaders of a movement called the Autumn Harvest Uprising, staged in 1927. It was a disaster. The peasants responded with apathy to his calls for insurrection, and the few who did join the rising were poorly armed and badly coordinated. They were brutally sup-pressed, and Mao himself narrowly escaped with his life after being captured by Nationalist troops.

For this failure, Mao was dismissed from the politburo. Unaware of this, he re-treated with the remnants of his force, finding refuge in the notorious bandit lair of Jinggangshan, on the Hunan-Jiangxi border. There he was joined in April 1928 by a professional officer, Zhu De, and 600 survivors of a Communist uprising in Nan-chang. Among them was Chen Yi, the former deputy of Zhou Enlai (who remained in Shanghai), and a brilliant twenty-one-year-old soldier called Lin Biao, who would eventually become Mao's heir apparent.

In defiance of his Shanghai colleagues, who accused him of being a military adventurer and of deviating from the party line, Mao began the long procedure of building up a guerrilla army, gaining the support of the peasants by taking action against what he described as "local bullies and bad gentry, corrupt officials, milita-rists, and all counterrevolutionary elements."

While Zhu and Lin directed their efforts to turning peasants into soldiers, Mao concentrated on their political training, using sets of slogans easily learned by the mainly illiterate recruits. The Communists' Three Principles summed up the behavior demanded of the troops: Obey orders at all times; do not take even a needle or a

MAO'S SOCIAL EXPERIMENT

In 1936, Mao established a Communist capital at the small town of Yan'an, in Shaanxi province. Poor and remote, alternately suffering through flood and drought, it seemed an unpromising place to test Communist theories of social organization and economic development. Even finding sufficient food would be a problem; between 1927 and 1930, more than one-quarter of the local population had fallen victim to plague or starvation and died.

Since food production was considered to be everyone's concern, the army played an important role in reclaiming the powdery loess soil around Yan'an. All soldiers helped with the digging, planting, hoeing, and harvesting. By 1944, the Communists claimed that almost 2.5 million acres of land had been opened up and that the production of grain had doubled.

Mao also introduced a large-scale indoctrination program, designed to instill what he called a "firm and correct political orientation." To this end, the politburo established the Kangda military and political institute, which attracted left-wing sympathizers from all over China. In addition, the Communists launched a literacy program; waged campaigns against superstition and unhygienic habits; and set up newspapers, technical colleges, a medical school, and an arts and literature academy.

From the start, economic development was severely disrupted—initially by a Guomindang blockade and later by Japanese bombing. And yet the base survived, becoming a prototype for the kind of self-sufficient society that the Communist party imposed on China after it came to power.

A lecturer instructs his class in the open air. The Communists set great store by oral teaching, for books were in short supply, and most recruits, like the overwhelming majority of Chinese, were illiterate.

Soldiers join the women of Yan'an in spinning. As part of their effort to attain self-sufficiency, the Communists introduced cotton to the region.

Yan'an shows the effects of Japanese bombing. For protection, the Communists dug a gallery of caves into the loess hills surrounding the town.

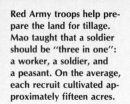

Red Army troops help prepare the land for tillage. Mao taught that a soldier should be "three in one": a worker, a soldier, and a peasant. On the average, each recruit cultivated approximately fifteen acres.

Cavalry troops at Yan'an practice using their horses as shields. The military and political institute was initially headed by Lin Biao, who was the Red Army's leading exponent of guerrilla warfare.

piece of thread from the people; turn in all confiscated property to headquarters. Tactics were governed by rhymed Chinese verses:

When the enemy advances, we retreat.
When he escapes, we harass.
When he retreats, we pursue.
When he is tired, we attack.

When Mao's army grew too large for the local food supply, he led it into an upland region on Jiangxi's southern border, where a succession of corrupt governors had created an area of seething discontent. In this ripe soil, Mao established the largest of the dozen or so Communist base areas scattered in remote areas of China.

But it was not easily done. Jiang, not a man to underestimate the Communist threat, launched the First Annihilation Campaign in 1930, sending 100,000 troops—supplied mainly by warlord allies—against Mao's 30,000-strong Red Army. Adhering to guerrilla tactics, for which Jiangxi's rugged hills and narrow valleys were ideally suited, Mao's commanders lured the Nationalist forces deep into Red territory and then, by hard marching, isolated enemy divisions and dealt with them piecemeal. The result of the first battle exceeded all expectations, the Red Army taking 9,000 prisoners, 8,000 rifles and machine guns, and two radios that greatly improved the Communist army's communications. The capture of the payroll for three Nationalist divisions was a welcome bonus.

At this juncture, the Japanese threw a wrench into the works by seizing several cities in Manchuria. Jiang was placed in an impossible situation. He was indebted to the Japanese for the aid they had given him, and as an accomplished soldier, he knew that the Nationalist Army, with or without its warlord allies, was no match for the Japanese armed forces. He was therefore obliged to make concessions to the invaders, hoping that their ultimate aim was not the conquest of China but a war against the Soviet Union—a policy favored by Japan's influential Strike North faction. In 1932, Japan conquered the rest of Manchuria, setting up the last of the Manchus as puppet emperor of the state of Manchuguo, and the following year, it took the northern province of Jehol. The public was outraged, but Jiang felt that the loss of these territories on the periphery of China was a worthwhile price to pay in return for Japan's continuing support in quelling the Communists. "The Japanese are a disease of the skin," he said later. "The Communists are a disease of the heart."

Mao's tactics against Jiang's first campaign proved a model for the next three. The Communists used their superior knowledge of the terrain, greater mobility, and ruses such as wearing enemy uniforms to confuse the opposing, mainly warlord, forces and pick them off one at a time. Their greatest advantage was the support of the peasants. As a Guomindang general ruefully confessed: "Wherever we go we are in darkness; wherever the Reds go they are in light." Another disadvantage that Jiang was never able to surmount was the reluctance of his warlord commanders to go to one another's assistance. They believed, with justice, that their forces were being used as cannon fodder while the generalissimo kept the Nationalist Army intact, the better to coerce them.

After the Red Army's success against the first three Guomindang expeditions, the Jiangxi base area had been declared a soviet—a region governed by a Communist committee. Covering several thousand square miles, it had a population of between eight and nine million and was the largest in the world outside the Soviet Union. Mao was elected its first chairman, but soon his position was seriously weakened by an influx of Comintern-dominated officials fleeing intense Nationalist repression in the cities. Among them was Zhou Enlai, at that period a follower of the Moscow party line. By the time Jiang launched his Fifth Annihilation Campaign in 1933, Mao no longer had a voice in Communist military operations or political decisions.

For the fifth campaign, Jiang's strategy was different. His plans, drawn up with a large team of German advisers, aimed at the slow strangulation of the Jiangxi soviet. Lines of blockhouses connected with barbed wire were built around the Red Army's base area, and Communist strongholds were isolated by a "fiery wall"—areas where crops and villages were burned. Nearly one million Nationalist troops, including Jiang's best divisions, were thrown into action against the 180,000-strong Red Army. For the first time, the Jiangxi army found itself facing a well-trained and mobile enemy, backed up with armor, artillery, and aircraft, and directed by a purposeful central command with good communications.

As the ring tightened, Mao and Zhu De advocated that the Red Army break through the circle and then split into small guerrilla units. But the party leadership, mainly city-bred and Comintern-dominated, seemed, in the words of one observer, "to be

In December 1937, five months after the outbreak of the Sino-Japanese War, a Japanese tank joins the assault on Nanjing, the Nationalist capital. When the city fell, the invaders engaged in an orgy of rape and massacre that claimed the lives of an estimated 200,000 civilians. The Rape of Nanjing was calculated to destroy the Chinese armies' will to resist, but it achieved the opposite effect and aroused worldwide revulsion.

seized with paralysis." Having been forced out of Shanghai, they could not bear to give up their peasant soviet. Instead, they sought the illusory security of fixed positions, ordering the building of fortifications and exhorting their troops with the slogan: "Don't give up an inch of soviet territory."

All through the winter, the Red Army battered itself against Jiang's ring of steel and concrete. As the blockade intensified, the soviet grew desperately short of salt, cloth, kerosene, and other goods. A shattering military defeat in April 1934 cost the defenders 4,000 dead and 20,000 wounded. Men began to slip away; desertion, said the party newspaper, was "an enemy more fearful than Jiang Jieshi."

As the Communists' situation worsened, the arguments in favor of a complete evacuation gained consideration. On the night of October 2, plans for the abandonment of the Jiangxi base were contracted by a military council that included Mao and Zhou Enlai. More than a decade later, when asked about the Communists' goal, Mao replied: "If you mean, did we have any exact plans, the answer is that we had none. We intended to break out of the encirclement and join up with the other soviets. Beyond that, there was only a very deliberate desire to put ourselves in a position where we could fight the Japanese."

Nationalist soldiers—apparently younger than the official conscription age of eighteen—take a break from training. Conditions for Guomindang conscripts were generally appalling; on the average, ordinary soldiers had meat only once or twice a month, and the poverty of their diet left them anemic and susceptible to eye and skin diseases and parasites. This, combined with a shortage of doctors and medicine, meant that less than one-third of the men were, by U.S. standards, fit to fight.

Toward evening on October 18, 1934, the main body of the Red Army left the town of Yudu, heading south where, they thought, they would find the weakest link in the chain of forces surrounding them. This was the beginning of the Long March—the forge of hardship and heroism that was the making of the Chinese Communist party. About 85,000 men and 35 women—senior party leaders—set out on the epic journey, carrying food, weapons, and printing presses; 20,000 noncombatants and 6,000 soldiers were left behind. Among them were many of Mao's supporters, reflecting his poor standing in the party hierarchy. Subsequently, most were executed by the Guomindang. Mao left three of his children behind; he never saw them again.

The Communists' guess about the weakness of the southern perimeter proved correct. After heavy skirmishing, they forced their way through the lines of blockhouses and moved southwest in the mountains that marked the provincial boundaries. The warlord generals in the region cherished dreams of an autonomous, non-Mandarin-speaking south. They decided not to risk their forces on behalf of the Guomindang.

When the Red Army reached the Xiang River farther west, however, it found that Jiang had anticipated it and assembled far larger forces than the Communists had expected. The battle to cross the Xiang lasted a week and cost 30,000 casualties. Once across the river, the Communists had the choice of heading for either of two Red base areas: Sichuan, on the Tibetan border, or Hunan, Mao's home province.

Jiang had taken steps to close both options, and the Communists ran into new lines of fortifications. For weeks they marched and countermarched through the mountains of Guizhou province, unable to break through the Guomindang lines. Once again, Jiang's generals claimed that they had the Red forces bottled up. But the low cloud that covers the province for much of the year hid the fugitives from the Nationalists' spotter planes, and by ruse and clever maneuvering, the Communists eluded their pursuers. Then the Red Army captured the provincial center of Zunyi, and the party's political and military leaders debated their next move.

This was to be a turning point for the Chinese Communist party. Before the conference at Zunyi, the ruling politburo had been controlled by the Soviet-sponsored faction, and military strategy had been largely determined by foreign Comintern agents. But after an exhaustive review of policy and tactics, it was recognized that Moscow's doctrinaire approach to China was unproductive, and that the Comintern ideologists' reliance on positional warfare was impractical. With the support of Red Army commanders such as the young Lin Biao, who favored unorthodox mobile warfare, Mao was elected chairman of the politburo and Zhu De was made commander of the Red Army, with Zhou Enlai—now and henceforth a firm ally of the chairman—as his chief political officer.

To escape Jiang's armies, Mao determined to head south and then begin a large flanking movement—first west, then north—to link with other Red Army forces in Sichuan. He reasoned that the mountainous terrain of China's western border regions would prevent Jiang from massing troops in force; but he was also aware that even small Guomindang garrisons could hold his men up in the many gorges and valleys they would have to cross.

By the time the Red Army emerged from the highlands of Guizhou, it had shed its printing presses and other heavy equipment and was traveling light, with only food, ammunition, and weapons. Each soldier carried a rice ration of about four and one-half pounds, plus a load of ammunition or grenades or tools and machinery slung from a shoulder pole. In addition, each man started out with a pack containing a blanket, a quilted winter uniform, and three pairs of cloth shoes. Alfred Bosshardt, a Swiss missionary captured by the Communists and later released, recalled the shoes. They were bound onto the feet with string or straw, and in wet weather they would disintegrate in a day. After a long stage, the footsore soldiers would weep with pain. Troops unable to continue were left behind with their rifles, ammunition, and some money; their task was to organize and lead the local peasants in partisan warfare.

Although there was rarely enough food for the marchers, Mao's injunctions about respecting peasants' property were usually obeyed. Bosshardt remembered resting in a fruit grove at a time when everyone was desperate with hunger. But the troops would not touch the ripe fruit because no one could be sure whether it belonged to a peasant or a landlord. The property of landlords and officials could be confiscated only on party orders; the property of the peasants could be purchased only with the owner's consent. In this case, a woman finally came out and offered to sell the fruit.

Despite constant hardship, there were moments of beauty. The chief engineer of the force recalled later that "Night marching is wonderful if there is a moon and a gentle wind blowing. When no enemy troops were near, whole companies would sing and others would answer. If it was a black night and the enemy was far away, we made torches from pine branches or frayed bamboo, and then it was truly beautiful. When at the foot of a mountain, we could look up and see a long column of lights coiling like a fiery dragon up the mountainside."

Such moments were rare. Ten years after the event, Peng Dehuai, an army corps commander, claimed that there were so many battles, he could not accurately recall the sequence of events. "Now when I look back, it seems to be one enormous battle going on all the time."

Among the many incidents that passed into Chinese legend, a few stood out with crystal clarity. At the crossing of the Dadu River in the borderlands of Sichuan, the fate of the Long March hung in the balance. It was the Guomindang's last chance to destroy Mao's army before it joined up with the Communist force in Sichuan, and the local warlord, goaded by Jiang, was moving troops to prevent the crossing and surround the army. On the face of it, he and the Guomindang had an easy task. Here, high in the mountains close to Tibet, the river falls through steep gorges. Within a stretch of 100 miles, there were only two bridges and a single ferry.

The Sichuanese commander had garrisoned the northernmost bridge, at Luding, with two regiments. Another regiment held the north bank of the ferry crossing fifty miles downriver, while two more waited for government reinforcements at the southern bridge. Zhu De made a feint to tie down the forces advancing from the south, and he sent one regiment on a forced march to take the south bank of the ferry. The regiment crossed fifty miles of rugged country in twenty-four hours, surprising the Sichuanese commander and his officers playing mahjongg at a relative's feast. A native of the region, he had not believed that troops could cover the distance in such a short time.

Contrary to Jiang's orders, the local troops had left one of the ferry boats moored on the south side of the river. Using this boat and supported by light artillery and machine guns, a volunteer squad of sixteen Long Marchers crossed the river under fire. The toehold they secured was maintained and enlarged until most of a division had crossed. But by this time, Jiang's air force was bombing the crossing and his reinforcements were getting closer. With the river flooding and the rest of the army

In 1944, during the last major Japanese offensive in China, Nationalist troops retreat through a southern Chinese village. The extent of Japanese-occupied China had not grown much since the massive campaigns of 1937 and 1938, but as the war in the Pacific intensified, the invaders became increasingly concerned about U.S. air attacks delivered by warplanes flying from Chinese bases. Fearing the arrival of American bombers with sufficient range to launch raids on Japan itself, the Japanese directed fifteen divisions to capture strategic targets in south and east China, including the airfields. The Nationalist Army was unable to hold back the advance, and as city after city fell, millions of Chinese troops and civilians alike fled for their lives.

piling up on the south bank, it became obvious that it would take weeks to get all the Long Marchers across. The commanders decided to try to capture the Luding bridge.

In two days, the leading regiment made a march of almost 100 miles, taking two passes by assault and repairing a bridge on the way. During the last twenty-four hours, they had only ten-minute rests every two hours and were falling asleep as they marched. They found the bridge intact. Famed throughout the province, it had been built at enormous expense in 1701 by the emperor Kang Xi, and the Sichuanese troops in the walled town of Luding could not bring themselves to destroy it. Swaying high above the tumbling river, it consisted of thirteen iron chains, each link "as thick

as a rice bowl,'' with two chains as guardrails and the rest carrying wooden planks. The warlord's troops had removed the planks from the Communist side of the bridge.

A force of twenty-two soldiers attempted to fight their way across. An eyewitness later described the assault to Agnes Smedley, a radical American writer:

> The army watched breathlessly as the men swung along the bridge chains. Ma Dajiu was the first to be shot into the wild torrent below. Then another man and another. The others pushed along, but just before they reached the flooring at the north bridgehead, they saw enemy soldiers dumping cans of kerosene on the planks and setting them on fire. Watching the sheet of flame spread, some men hesitated, but the platoon political leader at last sprang down on the flooring before the flames reached his feet, calling the men to follow. They ran through the flames and threw their hand grenades in the midst of the enemy. More and more men followed, the flames lapping at their clothing.

Within two hours the town was carried by assault and the way for the army was clear.

Other well-remembered incidents were triumphs of endurance. After the capture of the Luding bridge, the Long Marchers were only 100 miles as the crow flies from

At their first meeting in eighteen years, Mao Zedong and Jiang Jieshi toast each other during conciliatory talks in 1945. The talks were arranged by an American emissary, General Patrick J. Hurley, who had been dispatched by President Roosevelt to help bring about a coalition government of Nationalists and Communists. Although each side was determined to create a one-party state, both found it advantageous to briefly feign support for the initiative. Jiang pretended that he was willing to work toward a peaceful accommodation with the Communists in order not to jeopardize the U.S. aid on which his regime depended. For his part, Mao reckoned that it would take ten years to defeat the Nationalists, and he felt that even a short-lived treaty would give the Communists time to build their strength.

their comrades in the Sichuan Red Army base, but between them lay seven distinct ranges of high mountains. The first and most formidable obstacle was the Jiajin Shan (Great Snow Mountains). Crossing it took the marchers to heights of almost 16,500 feet, and since most of them were from low-lying provinces, they suffered terribly from altitude sickness. They also endured the agonies of cold, for their clothing was quite inadequate. One marcher recalled: "All along the route we kept reaching down to pull men to their feet only to find that they were already dead."

After the two Red Army forces met, their leaders argued about goals and eventually split, with the Sichuan contingent moving farther west into Tibet, and Mao's force marching north to the Shaanxi base area in the shadow of the Great Wall, close to possible Russian aid. The Long Marchers moved off to tackle the last great obstacle, the grasslands, a trackless wilderness stretching for hundreds of miles. No trees grew there, only clumps of grass that often disguised treacherous bogs. Sometimes the soldiers had to sleep kneeling back to back because there was nowhere to lie down. In the mists that blanketed the area, many marchers lost their way and perished. Because it was impossible to carry stretchers, the sick had to be abandoned. As many as one-third of the force died on the crossing.

Finally, in October 1935, the surviving 20,000 men straggled into the Shaanxi base area. Even this figure does not truly reflect the losses that were suffered en route, for most of the survivors had been recruited during the march. Two months later, Mao summarized what he and his force had endured:

> For twelve months we were under daily reconnaissance and bombing from the air by scores of planes; we were encircled, pursued, obstructed, and intercepted on the ground by a force of several hundred thousand men; we encountered untold difficulties and great obstacles on the way, but by keeping our two feet going, we swept across a distance of 20,000 li (6,000 miles). . . . Has there ever been a long march like ours?

Mao's claim to have won a great victory was less easy to believe. Membership in the Chinese Communist party had fallen and the party's armed force had shrunk to less than 50,000. But the Communists had acquired intangible assets more valuable in the long term than battle honors. Within the party, the marchers' discipline, self-sacrifice, and military skills were to provide an inspiration and a pattern for the future. Among the populace, the legend of the indestructible army dedicated to repelling the Japanese was to grow (with the help of Communist propaganda) through the years. The peasants were to remember the army that did not loot, and whose officers and men, sharing the same uniforms and rations and dangers, preached an end to the iniquities of high taxation and rent.

Jiang's determination to crush the Communists remained unabated, but he had badly misjudged the temper of his military allies, who were more anxious to fight the Japanese than to kill their compatriots. In December 1936, when the generalissimo flew to Xi'an, capital of Shaanxi province, to announce a new anti-Communist campaign, he was arrested by Manchurian warlords who demanded the formation of a united national army to liberate their homeland. The Communists, represented by Zhou Enlai, were invited to join the negotiations that followed. Many of Zhou's colleagues favored putting Jiang on trial, but under pressure from Stalin, who believed that Jiang was the only leader capable of uniting China against the Japanese, Zhou was obliged to recommend the release of his party's sworn enemy. In return, Jiang agreed to abandon his blockade of the Shaanxi soviet. The following year, the Russians pressed Jiang into a formal alliance with the CCP. His reward was a considerable amount of military aid, including 1,000 planes and 2,000 pilots.

For some time, Jiang's Strike North allies in Japan had been losing the struggle for influence with the Strike South faction, which advocated war with China as a means of opening up a path to the oil and rubber resources of Southeast Asia. Now, alarmed by the prospect of a united Nationalist and Communist front, Japan's imperialists decided to strike the first blow while there was still time. On July 7, 1937, Japanese troops apparently provoked a clash with Chinese troops at the Marco Polo bridge, near Beijing. When Jiang made it plain that he intended to resist aggression, the Japanese began inundating north China with their forces. Beijing fell at the end of July, and by the close of the year, both Shanghai and Nanjing, the Nationalist capital, were in Japanese hands.

The invaders wanted a short war and decided that terror tactics were the way to achieve it. When the Imperial Army entered Nanjing, it was ordered to make an example of the city to break the Nationalists' morale. For two months, under the eyes of Nanjing's foreign community, the occupying troops indulged in an orgy of rape and murder. An international tribunal later found that 20,000 women had been raped and more than 200,000 men killed.

Before Nanjing fell, Jiang had transferred his government to Wuhan, cutting the dikes along the Yellow River as he retreated, thereby causing floods. The Japanese advance was temporarily halted, but at the cost of hundreds of thousands of Chinese peasants, who were drowned or died in the ensuing famine. In March of 1938, the Nationalist Army achieved one major military success, inflicting 16,000 Japanese casualties at Taierzhuang, Shandong province. But the setback was only temporary. In late October 1938, the Japanese took Wuhan, forcing Jiang to flee west to Sichuan; as one of his commanders put it, he was trading space for time. Behind the mountain barrier of Sichuan, the Nationalists established a temporary capital at Chongqing, the most important town in the province. Thereafter, they made little effort to recapture lost territory. By the end of the year, the Japanese occupied most of China's major cities, including all its ports, all the principal industrial areas, and most of the main lines of communications.

In the huge areas of north China that the Japanese had overrun but not fully occupied, the Communists began organizing resistance. The railway system, secured by blockhouses every few miles, made an ideal target for the guerrilla tactics of the Red Army, which shredded the Japanese defenders in a week of battle. The Japanese responded by bringing in more troops and launching what they called the Three Alls campaign: Kill all, loot all, burn all. The Communist army then avoided pitched battles, restricting itself to harassment behind enemy lines. "The people are the sea," declared Zhu De's deputy, "while the guerrillas are the fish swimming in it." As well as mobilizing the populace against the Japanese, Mao carried on the social revolution, winning local support by introducing reductions in rent and tax that significantly improved living conditions for the peasantry. Yan'an, the small, dreary town in Shaanxi where the Communists established their capital, became a magnet for tens of thousands of active young people from all over the country. This influx helped swell the ranks of the party to 400,000 by 1940.

While the Communist movement grew and spread in north China, Jiang sat in his fortress at Chongqing, biding his time. He was convinced that Japan's expansionist policies in the Pacific would eventually bring it into conflict with the United States, and that the United States would win. Until then, he would fight the Japanese only as much as he must, keeping his government and army intact so that he would be in a position to take over the whole country at war's end.

Guomindang soldiers bombard Communist positions outside Nanjing, the Nationalist capital, in the autumn of 1948. During the latter stages of the civil war, the Nationalists incurred heavy losses of troops and arms by attempting to defend isolated city strongholds. By 1948, casualties and desertions had reduced their army to a fraction of its former size, but its commanders refused to relinquish their capital without a fight. After Communist troops encircled the defensive forces massed outside the city, severing all lines of supply and communication, Nanjing was lost, and with it all hope of a Guomindang government in mainland China.

The inevitable result of this enforced idleness was a slow corrosion of morale among the Guomindang establishment and an increasing sense of disillusionment among the many patriots who had joined the government-in-exile. Deprived of trade and customs revenues, the Nationalists financed their administration and lined their own pockets by printing money, producing an inflationary surge that caused prices to rise 250-fold between 1942 and 1944. Local governors also introduced a range of special taxes, including such imaginatively named levies as the "contribute-straw-sandals-to-recruits" tax, a "comfort-recruits'-families" tax, and the "train-antiaircraft-cadres" tax. Relations between the Nationalists and the local population deteriorated steadily: "Downriver gangsters" was the term the Sichuanese people

In December 1948, with inflation raging out of control, a crowd rushes a Shanghai bank to exchange devalued currency for gold. Inflation in Guomindang-controlled China meant that city dwellers had difficulty maintaining even a minimal standard of living. On receiving their wages, workers hurried to exchange sackfuls of notes for food or fuel, knowing that only a few hours later prices would double. In a desperate attempt to halt inflation, Jiang Jieshi replaced the Chinese dollar with a new currency, the yuan; nevertheless, prices rose 85,000-fold over the next six months.

used for Guomindang officials. Dissent was crushed by the strong-arm tactics of Jiang's secret police. Because of the fear that the populace would turn against them in armed revolt, the Guomindang made no effort to mobilize the peasantry as the Communists were doing.

In 1939, the United States started providing Jiang's government with financial assistance, which was increased when the Guomindang threatened to make an accommodation with the Japanese. Although Jiang had no intention of following through with the threat, it was given substance by the defection of his deputy and chief political rival, who was installed by the Japanese as head of a puppet government in Nanjing. Elsewhere, warlords and provincial commanders made alliances

with the Japanese, in a few cases fighting with them against the Communists.

When the United States entered the war, the government appointed the abrasive General Joseph Stilwell as Jiang's chief of staff—a position he held in addition to his role as commander of the U.S. China-Burma-India theater. At one of their first strategy meetings, Jiang stunned Stilwell by telling him that Chinese divisions should not be deployed even in defensive positions unless they outnumbered the Japanese by five to one. In fact, the generalissimo continued, Chinese forces should never be massed, because they would simply be destroyed wholesale. "What a directive," Stilwell wrote in his diary. "What a mess."

Given the generally poor state of the Nationalist forces, Jiang was probably right. He did have some good troops, who served with distinction in Burma, but after 1941, when the shaky alliance between the Guomindang and the Communists broke down, many of his best divisions were used to contain the Red Army in the north. The bulk of his army was made up of male conscripts between the ages of eighteen and forty-five. In theory, conscription was by ballot, but the process was warped by corruption, which spared the rich and filled the ranks with disaffected, illiterate peasants, who were often treated as coolies rather than soldiers. Many conscripts had to walk hundreds of miles to their units. Stilwell found in 1943 that only 56 percent of all recruits reached their assigned destinations; the rest deserted or died of disease or malnutrition on the way. Food was scarce anyway, and what little was available was often withheld by officers who sold it on the black market.

During the eight years of what the Chinese call the War of Resistance, the Nationalists mobilized some 14 million troops. An estimated three million of these became combat casualties, many dying of infection from relatively minor wounds that went untreated. About half a million men, including 700 generals, went over to the Japanese puppet forces. Most of the other 10-million-plus men are simply unaccounted for; many must have deserted, but even more probably died of starvation. One U.S. officer reported seeing famished Nationalist soldiers toppling over and dying after marching little more than one mile; the Nationalist army's lines of march could be followed simply by the trail of dead soldiers. Some recruits fell victim to their own countrymen, enraged by the excesses of the soldiery. In Hunan province, suffering under a long-predicted famine that no one tried to alleviate, the peasants disarmed retreating Nationalist troops, shot them, and welcomed the Japanese.

When the United States made its first official contact with Mao's Soviet government in July 1944, it found a striking contrast to conditions in the Guomindang-occupied areas. "We have come into a different country," one of the American delegation reported, "and are meeting a different people." In north and central China, the Communists exerted military and political control over 95 million people in a total area of almost 310,000 square miles. Their administration enjoyed widespread popular support, and their troops were loyal, well-disciplined, respectful of civilian rights, and highly motivated.

Many Americans questioned the Guomindang's fitness to govern a liberated China, but their warnings were drowned out by the voice of Patrick Hurley, President Roosevelt's flamboyant representative, whom Mao regarded—with justification—as little more than the generalissimo's mouthpiece. When Hurley's clumsy efforts to arrange a democratic coalition of Nationalists and Communists broke down, the ambassador urged Washington to give full and unequivocal support to the Chongqing government. In fairness, the United States had little room for maneuver; having recognized its ally Jiang as the rightful head of China, it was legally obliged to support his regime. In this respect, American policy on China differed little from the stance adopted by Stalin, who also regarded Jiang as the legitimate head of state, and who was increasingly displeased by the Chinese style of communism—"two peasants wearing the same pair of pants," as Soviet wags put it. On a stopover in Moscow, Hurley was told by Stalin that Mao's supporters were nothing more than "radish Communists—red on the outside, white inside."

Jiang, however, did not underestimate the task that lay before him when the Japanese were finally driven out. Aware of the weaknesses of his own military, he hoped to take over China on the coattails of an American invasion force. But the dropping of the atom bomb—a weapon that neither the Chinese nor the Soviets were told about in advance—meant that there was no large-scale U.S. invasion. Instead, it was the Soviet Red Army that entered Chinese territory, occupying Manchuria in a lightning advance. The United States diverted 53,000 marines to Beijing in case the Russians advanced too enthusiastically, but Stalin honored his pledge to restore China to Jiang, who asked the Soviet Union to extend its occupation of Manchuria until his own troops could take control. Now that the United States no longer needed its enormous war arsenal, it handed over much of its surplus to the Nationalist Army, and American pilots flew Jiang's representatives to take surrenders from the Japanese, even where the CCP was closest to the former enemy. As both sides raced to take over liberated territory, Jiang ordered Japanese commanders and their troops to resist the Red Army.

Even before the Japanese surrender, Jiang had announced his next goal. "Now at last the time has come to destroy the Communists root and branch," he told his army commanders in August 1945. Unprepared for this struggle for the heart of its ally, the United States tried every expedient to bring the two sides together. It patched up local and national truces between the two sides and even induced Jiang and Mao to meet. General George Marshall, U.S. wartime chief of staff and shortly to be the author of the Marshall Plan that revitalized war-ravaged Europe, was sent to prevent civil war. Teams of American officers were sent around the country to try to stop outbreaks of fighting between the two sides. But a year later, Marshall returned to the United States, confessing his mission a failure. "The greatest obstacle to peace," he reported, "has been the complete, almost overwhelming suspicion with which the CCP and Guomindang regard each other."

On paper, the Communists were much weaker than the Nationalists in 1945. Jiang had more than three million men in arms, many of them trained and supplied by Britain or the United States. With 1,000 American planes, his air force was the unchallenged master of the skies. Most of the major population centers were under his control, and he commanded all the organizational and financial resources of the government. Through eight years of war, he had kept his administration more or less intact, and his forces had made a significant contribution to the Allied campaign in the China-Burma-India theater. Recognized as one of the four main powers in the war against Japan, he enjoyed the security of alliances with the Big Three of Russia, Britain, and the United States.

In contrast, the Red Army—renamed the People's Liberation Army (PLA) after the defeat of Japan—had fewer than one million soldiers, of whom only half were armed. Although the membership of the CCP had grown to approximately 1.2 million, its leader's name was still not well known outside China. The Soviet Union's support was equivocal. It made no attempt to extend Communist influence in Manchuria, returning the cities to the Guomindang and seizing the industrial plants as war booty for itself. Stalin even tried to discourage Mao from engaging in civil war with Jiang, urging him to accept a subordinate role in a coalition government. Mao seems to have been persuaded, for at his meeting with the president, he gave the toast "Long live Jiang Jieshi," and in at least one official document of the period, he accorded Jiang the respectful title of "Uncle."

Jiang, however, was so certain of his strength that no amount of persuasion or coercion would make him pay more than lip service to the truces painfully hammered out by U.S. representatives. In June 1946, he started to move in force against the People's Liberation Army. During this first phase, his armored divisions were every-

Riding on American trucks captured from the Nationalists, Communist soldiers enter Beijing in triumph on February 3, 1949. Demoralized by Jiang Jieshi's failure to send sufficient arms, the city's Nationalist defenders had attempted to negotiate an armistice with the Communists. At the last moment, the long-awaited weapons were dispatched—and were promptly intercepted by the Communists, who then abandoned the negotiations. The Nationalist forces withdrew into Beijing's medieval walled city, and they surrendered six weeks later.

where successful against the lightly armed PLA. Lin Biao, commander of the Communist army in Manchuria, used human-wave tactics to try to neutralize the enemy's advantages in weapons, but after a month of bloody fighting, he was forced to retreat. By late 1947, the Guomindang controlled every provincial capital, most other important cities, and China's major transportation routes. Even Yan'an had fallen into the hands of the Guomindang.

But Jiang's chosen tools of control were unreliable. The Nationalist officials he had brought with him from Sichuan had lived for eight years on a combination of inflation, graft, and American aid. Far from altering their habits, they descended on their nominal posts like robber barons. Loyalty to Jiang rather than competence was the main criterion for office, and indeed it can be said that his subordinates were loyal precisely because they were so incompetent. But their personal allegiance to Jiang was outweighed by their dedication to enriching themselves; corruption at every level of the administration ensured that the generalissimo could never count on getting his orders obeyed. He was also fast losing the support of the middle class, which had hoped for the introduction of a liberal, democratic regime and instead found itself living under an authoritarian military dictatorship that used force to stifle even the mildest demands for reform.

Like the Japanese conquests in China, the Nationalist advances gained little except territory, for in keeping with Communist strategy, the PLA conserved its strength by avoiding disadvantageous actions and by abandoning indefensible positions. In the meantime, Mao set his cadres to winning over the support of the people by replacing the policy of rent reductions with the confiscation and redistribution of the property of the landlords. The implementation of this land-reform program helped consolidate the Communists' support in the countryside and proved to be of considerable value in the struggle.

Jiang, meanwhile, had to confront a serious problem in his main political base—the cities. Inflation, which had been growing throughout the war, was to sweep out of control by 1948, bringing famine in its wake. By the middle of that year, one pound of rice cost almost 250,000 Chinese dollars. Each night, hundreds of people died in the streets, their bodies collected by the municipal garbage trucks in the morning. In the Communist-controlled areas, by contrast, there was little starvation, because the Communists lived, in effect, outside the cash economy. Nor was there any hoarding of food; rations were about the same for all ranks.

Support for Jiang eroded to the point where it could be enforced solely at the point of a bayonet. Demoralized and hungry, Nationalist troops began defecting to the PLA, only too happy to exchange their rifles for a square meal. At the beginning of 1947, an entire division went over to the PLA. Ignoring American warnings that his troops were dangerously overextended, Jiang refused to give ground.

In September 1947, Lin Biao renewed his offensive. By the end of the year, his men had shut down the railway system in Manchuria, isolating 250,000 of Jiang's best troops in the cities and effectively cutting communications with the south, where units of the PLA had reached the Yangtze River, China's great east-west highway. Defections now began in earnest; indeed, of all the Nationalists who fell into Communist hands, three-quarters simply surrendered. By the autumn of 1948, the relative strengths of the two sides had been reversed.

The last great campaign of the civil war was the battle for Nanjing, the Guomindang capital. Half a million troops were committed on each side for sixty-five days.

The PLA cut the Nationalists' communications and picked off Jiang's divisions one by one. Units went over to the Communists with all their military equipment. By the end of the year, the Guomindang regime was on the brink of total collapse. In late January 1949, the PLA entered Beijing, encountering no resistance. The same month, the Nanjing government sued for peace, but when negotiations broke down, Mao ordered his troops to cross the Yangtze and achieve final victory.

After the fall of his capital in April 1949, Jiang retreated, first to Sichuan, then to the island of Taiwan where, vowing that one day he would return to the mainland, he set up the government of the Republic of China in opposition to the Communists.

Wearing the plain cotton uniform that would become one of the symbols of Communist China, Mao announces the establishment of the People's Republic on October 1, 1949. His proclamation was delivered from the Gate of Heavenly Peace in Beijing, a rostrum for the announcement of new dynasties during China's imperial era. Three months after the founding of Communist China, what remained of the Nationalist government left its last base on the mainland and established the Republic of China on the island of Taiwan. Although Jiang Jieshi's Guomindang was still recognized by the United States as the legitimate government of China, the Communists' control of the mainland was unassailable, and within a year, they had extended their power still farther by occupying Tibet.

On October 1, 1949, Mao appeared at the gate of Heavenly Peace in Beijing and proclaimed the People's Republic of China. "Ours will no longer be a nation subject to insult and humiliation," he declared. "We have stood up." But he also had words of warning for his compatriots. "The victory of the Chinese people's democratic revolution, viewed in retrospect, will seem like only a brief prologue to a long drama. A drama begins with a prologue, but the prologue is not the climax."

None of his listeners could have foreseen the nature of the drama that was about to unfold: the Korean War; the economic lunacy of the disastrous Great Leap Forward; the civil turmoil caused by the Cultural Revolution; armed conflict with India and then with the Soviet Union; the Sino-American rapprochement five years before Mao's death in 1976. It had been an arduous journey for the peasant boy from Hunan, and for the Chinese people, it was far from over. "Our past work," Mao had declared, "is only the first step in a long march."

The winter of 1947 was the coldest that most people in Europe could remember, and the freezing weather matched all too closely the Continent's political temperature. The Second World War had been over for a year and a half, but a mounting tide of fear and distrust was eroding the longed-for consolations of peace. To everyone suffering the hardships of that winter, Cold War—a phrase popularized by U.S. commentator Walter Lippmann—was a cruelly apposite description of the deteriorating relations between the Soviet Union on the one side and the United States and Great Britain on the other—nations that had so recently been allies against Nazi Germany. In the summer of 1948, when Soviet occupation forces in Germany suddenly closed the borders of Berlin to all traffic with the West, confrontation teetered on the brink of outright hostilities. An apparently irrevocable split had opened between the Eastern and Western blocs, and the postwar world had taken on the threatening aspect it was to wear for a generation.

The total reversal from victorious alliance to embattled enmity, accomplished within such a short period, had deep roots. The wartime alliance of 1941 between the Soviet Union and the Western powers had masked deep ideological differences that went back at least as far as the Russian Revolution of 1917, when Western governments had actively sought to defeat the rise of bolshevism. Outside the League of Nations until 1934, struggling throughout the interwar years with huge economic and political problems, Soviet leader Joseph Stalin was well aware of the West's hostility—manifested by its reluctance in the 1930s to offer the Soviet Union support against a

hostile Germany. Stalin felt that he had been driven into the nonaggression pact he signed with Hitler in 1939.

Western governments in their turn felt threatened by a Communist government that was still officially committed to exporting revolution—a threat given force by the Soviet Union's growing economic and military strength. In Moscow, the brutal excesses of Stalin toward his own people were observed by U.S. diplomats whose opinions were later to be decisive in molding American policy.

Stalin's alliance with the United States and Great Britain came about only when Hitler betrayed his pact by invading the Soviet Union in 1941, and the strains between the wartime partners began to appear almost immediately. From the start, Stalin was determined to safeguard the postwar security of the Soviet Union by creating a defensive buffer around the nation's borders, whereas President Franklin Roosevelt and, even more so, Prime Minister Winston Churchill were committed to frustrating Communist expansion after the war.

As early as 1943, when Churchill, Stalin, and Roosevelt met for a conference in the Iranian capital, Tehran, Churchill confided to one of his personal staff that he considered Germany already finished and that "the real problem now is Russia." Believing that postwar cooperation with Stalin would be difficult but not impossible, Churchill decided on a pragmatic course designed to determine the political future of Europe. In 1944, during a visit to Moscow, he privately proposed a division of the Continent into spheres of influence. He was prepared to resign eastern Europe to Soviet influence provided that the West retained a control-

ling role in Greece, thereby excluding Stalin from the Mediterranean.

Although Churchill was ready to frame policies that took account of the conflict of interests between East and West, Roosevelt was more reluctant to make hard decisions. He was anxious not to forfeit Stalin's cooperation, both for the final defeat of Japan and for the setting up of the United Nations, which he envisaged as a forum that would resolve international disputes. By his efforts to woo Stalin, he succeeded in postponing the impending split between the Allies. When the Big Three met at Yalta in the Crimea in February 1945, the public appearance of concord was maintained, but the pledge to provide governments responsive to the will of the people of liberated Europe merely disguised Stalin's intention to impose his own brand of government on Poland, Bulgaria, and Rumania—the east European states he regarded as crucial to Soviet security.

By the time Germany surrendered in May, Roosevelt was dead, robbed of his hopes for a new dawn of international reason. In Poland, where elections for a provisional government had been held in March 1945, after the liberation of the country, Stalin's pressure to secure a pro-Soviet government had been quite unconcealed. To the United States, this blatantly contravened the Yalta pledge. It fell to Harry Truman in the first few days of his presidency to point that out to the Soviet foreign minister, Vyacheslav Molotov, whom Stalin had reluctantly sent to the United States for the opening of the United Nations. Molotov protested that he had never been talked to like that in his life. "Carry out your agreements," Truman retorted and you won't get talked to like that.

But American protests about political coercion had little effect on Stalin, who felt that Western scruples about Poland were an attempt to stir up anti-Soviet sentiment on his own doorstep. As he and Churchill had taken ███████ted, the military dispositions at the end of the war were the decisive factor in determining the political map of Europe.

Even in defeat, Germany remained the main source of tension. The country was divided into British, American, Soviet, and French zones prior to an Allied agreement on a peace treaty. At Potsdam in July 1945, a conference to decide the fate of the country ended inconclusively. The Soviet Union insisted on imposing crushing reparations on its former enemy; Britain and the United States, fearing that the reduction of Germany to an industrial desert would promote a Communist revolution, proposed less punitive measures. Such disagreements paved the way for the ultimate division of Germany into two states—one built into the structure of the Western bloc, the other belonging to the East. By April 1946, Stalin had already ███████osed a one-party government in the Soviet zone, and Britain and the United States had merged their zones into a single economic unit.

Until the outbreak of the Korean War in 1950, Europe was the main arena for the Cold War. Between 1945 and 1950, national Communist parties loyal to Moscow installed Soviet-style regimes in Hungary, Poland, Bulgaria, Rumania, Czechoslovakia, and the newly formed German Democratic Republic *(red areas on map)*. But Stalin failed to take over Berlin or impose the Moscow party line on Marshal Tito, Yugoslavia's independent Communist leader. Albania, which had established a Communist regime without outside help, entered into a short-lived alliance with the Soviet Union in 1948.

Discord over the future of Germany soon broadened into a wider confrontation that came to include most aspects of global politics. At first, Great Britain took the lead in trying to counterbalance the Soviet Union, but the country was exhausted—

military as well as economically. With the collapse of war-torn Europe's traditional political structure, the United States and the Soviet Union had emerged as "super powers," and the two rivals had to bear the brunt of the contest.

For both sides in the confrontation, ideology was recruited to provide a rationale for growing hostility and to mobilize the support of their peoples for the efforts required to compete on a global scale. In Marxist-Leninist theory, the march of the revolution was a historical necessity, and the United States was ready to read signs of Stalin's global ambitions in many situations that were perhaps only the results of defensive paranoia—understandable in a nation that had suffered so many casualties in the war. By considering all contact with the West as a threat, the Soviets chose a path of self-isolation and entrenchment that was to lead them into a spiral of repression at home and in Eastern Europe.

In February 1946, George Kennan, a veteran U.S. diplomat in Moscow, sent Washington an influential analysis of Soviet intentions. The Soviet Union, he argued, was committed to the belief that there could be no permanent accommodation with the United States. The Communists could, however, be contained without recourse to war provided that the Americans ensured the "cohesion, firmness, and vigor" of the West. A month later, Churchill—now out of office—added the weight of his rhetoric to Kennan's view. On a visit to Westminster College in Fulton, Missouri—Truman's home state—he evoked for the first time in public the image of an Iron Curtain descending across the Continent. The Soviets did not desire another war, he claimed, but he was convinced that there is nothing they admire so much as strength."

Friction points arose outside Europe, in Turkey and Iran, where the Soviets proposed to establish advance defenses. In the UN pressure forced Stalin to withdraw

from Iran and to stop leaning on Turkey, but many Western diplomats, mindful of Hitler's step-by-step expansion in the 1930s, saw his actions as signs of the Soviet Union's global ambitions. For his part, Stalin saw the West's activities as interference in territories adjacent to the Soviet border.

The rift widened fast, but it was not until 1947 that the point of no return was reached. In February of that year, as blizzards swept Western Europe, the Labour government of Prime Minister Clement Attlee informed Truman that Britain could no longer afford to provide economic support for Greece, where British troops had helped to return a royal government-in-exile to power by overcoming Communist-led resistance forces in 1945. Since then, a new guerrilla movement, supported by the Communist governments of Yugoslavia and Albania, was threatening what it described as Greece's "monarcho-Fascist regime."

That March, Truman responded. In lurid terms designed to accentuate public fear of a Communist terror stalking the world, he persuaded Congress to grant military aid to Greece and Turkey. His administration did not know, or was not prepared to acknowledge, that Stalin had tried and failed to prevent Yugoslavia from giving help to the rebels, precisely because he knew that it would be impossible for the West to allow their only base in the Balkans to be taken.

In the course of his address to Congress, the president enunciated what came to be known as the Truman Doctrine: "that it must be the policy of the United States to support free peoples who are resisting attempted subjugation by armed minorities or by outside pressures."

Believing that the economic chaos crip-

pling Western Europe was giving the Communists an opportunity to advance their cause, Truman's advisers became convinced that massive American aid was the only way to forestall the danger. In March 1947, Secretary of State George Marshall presented the European Recovery Program, better known as the Marshall Plan, as a package of economic aid offered to any state that applied for it. But applicants had to open their doors to outside scrutiny in order to determine the extent of their needs, and Stalin, who condemned the plan as an attack upon national sovereignty, refused to allow any of the Eastern bloc countries to participate. Czechoslovakia was warned not to apply for aid, and when it did, Stalin exploited a Czech Communist coup in February 1948 to put an end to its existing coalition government, which was replaced by a solidly pro-Soviet regime. Pointing to the coup as one more proof of Soviet plans to swallow up the remaining free nations of Europe, Truman persuaded Congress to reintroduce conscription, and moves were undertaken for organizing the collective defense of the West.

Faced with the prospect of a unified Western front, Stalin felt there was nothing to be gained by prolonging any illusion of cooperation between the blocs. In a bid to compel the United States, Britain, and France to abandon their aim to create a prosperous West German state out of their zones of occupation, he decided to block-ade Berlin. The city was divided into four sectors administered by the wartime Allies and France's repatriated government, but it was located at the end of a 110-mile-long road-and-rail corridor deep within the Soviet occupation. In June 1948, fit-days after the Western powers announced currency reforms that would help revive Germany's economy, the Soviets interdicted all traffic in and out of West Berlin.

The city was saved by an eleven-month airlift of supplies, during the course of which U.S. and British aircraft flew in everything from coal to the newest antibiotics. Stalin's efforts to halt the revival of Germany had failed, but the polarization of Europe was now formally acknowledged. In May 1949, the same month that the blockade ended, the Federal Republic of Germany (West Germany) was founded, and in October, the German Democratic Republic (East Germany) came into being. The acute threat of war had already, in April 1949, brought Canada and most of the Western European countries into a common defense policy—the North Atlantic Treaty Organization, NATO—under American leadership. Even before then, during the Berlin crisis, U.S. B-29s reportedly capable of delivering atomic bombs had flown into Britain, and a year later, the United States asked to set up permanent bases of its own in Britain—a request that the British government granted without seeking parliamentary approval.

Throughout his dealings with the Soviet Union, Truman had been emboldened by

the U.S. monopoly of the nuclear bomb, however, on September 23, 1949, he announced that the Soviets had carried out their first nuclear test explosion. In Europe, the Cold War had reached an equilibrium of sorts, but the conflict shifted elsewhere—to China, where the Chinese Communists had ousted the Nationalist government of Jiang Jieshi, and to Korea, where in June 1950, the smoldering animosity between Western democracy and communism finally ignited in open war.

West Berliners watch a C-47 transport coming in to land with supplies for their beleaguered city. In an attempt to drive the Western powers out of the German capital, the Soviets mounted a blockade, cutting off the supplies of two million citizens. Rather than abandon the city, which lay 100 miles inside the Soviet zone, the Western Allies mounted a massive relief operation by air. Starting on June 25, 1948, they had airlifted 2.3 million tons of goods into Berlin by May 12, 1949, when the Soviets, acknowledging the failure of their siege, reopened rail and road links to the West.

	1925-1930	1930-1935	1935-1940

EUROPE

1925-1930

Adolf Hitler reorganizes the German Nazi party and publishes the first volume of *Mein Kampf* (1925).

Nazis win their first seats in the Reichstag, Germany's Parliament (1928).

Joseph Stalin launches the First Five-Year Plan in the Soviet Union and orders the collectivization of Soviet agriculture (1928).

Leon Trotsky, a leader of the Russian Revolution and an opponent of Stalin's policies, is expelled from the Soviet Union (1929).

1930-1935

Unemployment in Germany rises to four million. In elections, Nazis win 107 seats from the center parties (1930).

Field Marshal Paul von Hindenburg beats Hitler in German presidential elections, but in the Reichstag elections, Nazis become the largest party, with 230 seats (1932).

Hitler is appointed German chancellor and is later granted dictatorial powers through the Enabling Law (1933).

Italy's dictator, Benito Mussolini, meets Hitler in Venice (1934).

Stalin uses the assassination of the Leningrad Communist-party chief Sergey Kirov as a pretext to instigate a purge of political rivals (1934).

1935-1940

Hitler defies the Versailles Treaty by reintroducing compulsory military service (1935).

The Nazi government introduces the Nuremberg Laws, depriving German Jews of their citizenship (1935).

Italian troops invade Ethiopia (1935).

German troops occupy the Rhineland (1936).

The Spanish Civil War begins (1936).

Six months after annexing Austria to the German Reich, Hitler occupies Czech border regions (1938).

Hitler and Stalin sign a nonaggression pact (1939).

Britain and France declare war on Germany two days after the German invasion of Poland (1939).

CHINA, JAPAN, AND THE PACIFIC

1925-1930

Sun Zhongshan (Sun Yat-sen), Republican revolutionary and leader of the Guomindang, or Nationalist party, dies (1925).

Jiang Jieshi (Chiang Kai-shek) is named commander in chief of the National Revolutionary Army, a joint Guomindang and Chinese Communist force formed to defeat China's warlords (1925).

Guomindang troops and right-wing sympathizers turn on Communists in Shanghai, beginning a wholesale purge of the Left in China (1927).

Jiang Jieshi is elected president of China (1928).

1930-1935

Jiang Jieshi attacks Communist bases in southern China (1930).

Japanese forces set up a puppet state in Manchuria (1932).

Japan, criticized for its expansionist policies in China, leaves the League of Nations (1933).

Threatened by Jiang Jieshi's Nationalist forces, the main body of Chinese Communists breaks out of its base in southern China, beginning the Long March to the province of Shaanxi. During the year-long trek, Mao Zedong is established as chairman of the party (1934).

1935-1940

A shooting incident near Beijing leads to the Sino-Japanese War. The Japanese seize Beijing, Shanghai, and the Nationalist capital, Nanjing (1937).

Jiang Jieshi establishes a wartime capital at Chongqing, in Sichuan province (1938).

THE UNITED STATES

1925-1930

Herbert Hoover, Republican, is elected U.S. president (1928).

New York's Wall Street stock market crashes, triggering a collapse of confidence in the financial market and an economic slump that gradually deepens into a global depression (1929).

1930-1935

President Hoover approves the imposition of high tariff barriers intended to shield the U.S. economy from foreign competition (1930).

Franklin D. Roosevelt wins the U.S. presidential election in a Democratic landslide (1932).

America protests against Japanese aggression in Manchuria (1932).

With unemployment at 13 million, President Roosevelt approves a program of public works known as the New Deal (1933).

1935-1940

President Roosevelt signs the U.S. Social Security Act (1935).

Roosevelt is reelected president on a "no war" ticket (1936).

Roosevelt boosts the defense budget and demands assurances from Hitler and Mussolini that they will not attack thirty-one named states (1939).

After Britain and France declare war on Germany, Roosevelt declares the United States officially neutral while making it clear that American sympathies are with the Allies (1939).

INDIA, NORTH AFRICA, AND THE MIDDLE EAST

1925-1930

Great Britain appoints an all-British commission to recommend steps toward Indian self-government (1926).

Arabs attack Jews in Palestine following sectarian disputes in Jerusalem (1929).

1930-1935

Mahatma Gandhi, leader of the Indian National Congress, pledges the party to complete Indian independence and launches a campaign of civil disobedience intended to make the country ungovernable (1930).

1935-1940

Muslims in Palestine stage an Arab revolt against the British authorities' refusal to end Jewish immigration (1936).

The British government publishes a White Paper—a policy statement—suggesting an independent Palestine with an Arab majority and proposing limitations on continued Jewish immigration (1939).

TimeFrame AD 1925-1950

1940-1945

In a three-month period, Germany conquers Denmark, Norway, the Low Countries, and France but abandons its planned invasion of Britain after the German Luftwaffe fails to destroy the Royal Air Force (1940).

In contravention of Hitler's pact with Stalin, German troops invade the Soviet Union, approaching Moscow before Soviet counterattacks halt the German advance (1941).

Germany and Italy declare war on the United States (1941).

Regular British bomber raids on Germany begin (1942).

The survivors of the German Sixth Army surrender after a five-month battle for Stalingrad (1943).

The battle for Kursk, the largest armored clash in history, ends with a German withdrawal and a massive Soviet offensive (1943).

An invasion of Sicily is followed by Allied landings in mainland Italy (1943).

Operation Overlord, the Western Allies' campaign for the liberation of Europe, begins with a full-scale invasion of Normandy (1944).

German officers who want to end the war make an unsuccessful attempt on Hitler's life (1944).

Paris and Brussels are liberated (1944).

The Japanese set up a Chinese puppet government at Nanjing (1940).

Japan signs a tripartite pact with Germany and Italy (1940).

Japan attacks the American Pacific naval base at Pearl Harbor, Hawaii, and simultaneously attacks the Philippines, Hong Kong, and Malaya (1941).

In a campaign lasting only 100 days, Japan captures Singapore, the Burmese capital, Rangoon, and the Dutch East Indies (1942).

At the battles of the Coral Sea and Midway, American naval forces break Japan's run of successes (1942).

U.S. landings in the Solomon Islands mark the beginning of an island-hopping offensive against Japan (1942).

Japan renews its offensive in China. The United States launches the first bombing raids on Japan from China (1944).

U.S. landings in the Philippines are followed by the Battle of Leyte Gulf, in which much of the Japanese navy is destroyed (1944).

The United States places an embargo on sales of scrap iron and war materials to Japan (1940).

President Roosevelt, reelected for a third term, signs the Lend-Lease Bill, enabling Great Britain to obtain American war materials in return for a promise of payment after the war (1941).

A day after the Japanese raid on Pearl Harbor, the United States declares war on Japan (1941).

The Manhattan Project of intensive atomic research begins (1941).

As the "arsenal of democracy," the United States produces 40 percent of the world's armaments (1944).

Roosevelt is elected for a fourth term as president of the United States, with Harry Truman as vice president (1944).

At a conference in Washington, D.C., discussions are held on the establishment of the United Nations to replace the League of Nations (1944).

The creation of a separate Muslim state—Pakistan—becomes the official policy of India's Muslim League (1940).

After Italian forces in North Africa are routed by the British, the German Afrika Korps commanded by General Erwin Rommel launches a successful counteroffensive (1941).

Axis forces are defeated at the Battle of El Alamein, and the Allies make landings in Morocco and Algeria (1942).

The Indian National Congress confronts the British government with a "Quit India" policy, and many of its leaders are arrested and imprisoned (1942).

The first authenticated reports of the Nazis' systematic slaughter of European Jews convince many Zionists that only by establishing their own independent state in Palestine can they enjoy peace and security (1942).

Defeat of the Axis forces in North Africa paves the way for an Allied invasion of Italy (1943).

1945-1950

A week after Hitler commits suicide in Berlin, the Germans sign an unconditional surrender (1945).

Winston Churchill makes the first public reference to the Iron Curtain (1946).

General George Marshall, appointed U.S. secretary of state, calls for a European economic recovery program—the Marshall Plan—as a means of countering Soviet influence in Europe (1947).

Stalin lifts a ten-month Soviet blockade of Berlin intended to thwart Western plans for the economic recovery of Germany. The country is then divided into the Federal Republic of Germany (West Germany) and the German Democratic Republic (East Germany) (1949).

The Soviet Union successfully detonates its first atomic weapon (1949).

In the space of four days, the United States drops atomic bombs on Hiroshima and Nagasaki, and the Soviet Union declares war on Japan, which capitulates one week later (1945).

Civil war breaks out between Chinese Nationalists and Communists (1946).

After the Chinese Communist defeat of the Nationalists, Mao Zedong announces the establishment of the People's Republic of China, and the remnants of Jiang Jieshi's Guomindang government retreat to the island of Taiwan (1949).

President Roosevelt dies and is succeeded as U.S. president by Harry Truman (1945).

Scientists of the Manhattan Project carry out a successful atomic test explosion (1945).

The U.S. Congress passes the Marshall Plan, approving $17 billion in aid for Europe (1948).

Harry Truman is elected U.S. President (1948).

The North Atlantic Treaty—a mutual defense pact between North American and Western European countries—is signed in Washington, D.C. (1949).

Rioting and killings follow Muslim League calls for a separate state (1946).

India is proclaimed independent and partitioned into mainly Hindu India and predominantly Muslim Pakistan (1947).

Britain announces that it will hand over its trusteeship of Palestine to the United Nations, which announces plans for the partition of the country into Arab and Jewish areas (1947).

Jewish leaders in Palestine proclaim the state of Israel (1948).

BIBLIOGRAPHY

WORLD WAR II

Bailey, Ronald H., and the Editors of Time-Life Books, *The Air War in Europe* (World War II series). Alexandria, Virginia: Time-Life Books, 1979.

Bauer, Eddy, *The History of World War II.* London: Orbis, 1979.

Bell, P. M. H., *The Origins of the Second World War.* London: Longman, 1986.

Bergamini, David, *Japan's Imperial Conspiracy.* London: Heinemann, 1971.

Bleuel, Hans Peter, *Strength through Joy.* Transl. by J. Maxwell Brownjohn. London: Secker & Warburg, 1973.

Briggs, Susan, *Keep Smiling Through.* London: Weidenfeld and Nicolson, 1975.

Bullock, Alan, *Hitler: A Study in Tyranny.* Harmondsworth, Middlesex, England: Penguin, 1962.

Calvocoressi, Peter, and Guy Wint, *Total War.* London: Allen Lane, 1972.

Carr, Raymond, *Images of the Spanish Civil War.* London: George Allen & Unwin, 1986.

Ciano, G.:
Ciano's Diary: 1937-1938. London: Methuen, 1952.
Ciano's Diary: 1939-1943. London: Heinemann, 1947.

Collier, Basil, *Japan at War.* London: Sidgwick & Jackson, 1975.

Collier, Richard, and the Editors of Time-Life Books, *The War in the Desert* (World War II series). Alexandria, Virginia: Time-Life Books, 1977.

Davidson, Eugene, *The Making of Adolf Hitler.* London: Macdonald and Jane's, 1978.

Deighton, Len, *Blitzkrieg: From the Rise of Hitler to the Fall of Dunkirk.* London: Jonathan Cape, 1979.

Deutscher, Isaac, *The Great Purges.* Oxford: Basil Blackwell, 1984.

Elson, Robert T., and the Editors of Time-Life Books, *Prelude to War* (World War II Series). New York: Time-Life Books, 1977.

Fest, Joachim C., *Hitler.* London: Weidenfeld, 1973.

Goralski, Robert, *World War II Almanac: 1931-1945.* London: Hamish Hamilton, 1981.

Grunberger, Richard, *A Social History of the Third Reich.* Harmondsworth, Middlesex, England: Penguin, 1974.

Grunfeld, Frederic V., *The Hitler File: A Social History of Germany and the Nazis, 1918-45.* London: Weidenfeld and Nicolson, 1974.

Hastings, Max, *Bomber Command.* London: Michael Joseph, 1979.

Hingley, Ronald, *Joseph Stalin: Man and Legend.* London: Hutchinson, 1974.

Hyde, H. Montgomery, *Stalin: The History of a Dictator.* London: Rupert Hart-Davis, 1971.

Irving, David, *The War Path: Hitler's Germany, 1933-1939.* London: Michael Joseph, 1978.

Jackson, W. G. F., *The Battle for Italy.* London: Batsford, 1967.

Jones, R. V., *Most Secret War.* London: Hamish Hamilton, 1978.

Kee, Robert, *We'll Meet Again: Photographs of Daily Life in Britain during World War Two.* London: J. M. Dent & Sons, 1984.

Keegan, John, *Six Armies in Normandy.* London: Cape, 1982.

Kurzman, Dan, *Day of the Bomb.* London: Weidenfeld and Nicolson, 1986.

Lewin, Ronald, *Rommel as Military Commander.* London: Batsford, 1968.

Liddell Hart, B. H., *The Other Side of the Hill.* London: Cassell, 1948.

Lowe, C. J., and F. Marzari, *Italian Foreign Policy: 1870-1940.* London: Roütledge, 1975.

Ludwig, E., *Talks with Mussolini.* London: G. Allen & Unwin, 1932.

Macintyre, Donald, *The Battle of the Atlantic.* London: Batsford, 1961.

Mack Smith, D.:
Mussolini. London: Weidenfeld, 1982.
Mussolini's Roman Empire. London: Longmans, 1976.

Matanle, Ivor, *The Hitler Years: A Photographic Documentary.* Leicester, England: Galley Press, 1984.

Middlebrook, Martin:
Convoy. London: Allen Lane, 1976.
The Nuremberg Raid: 30-31 March 1944. London: Allen Lane, 1973.

Milward, Alan S., *War, Economy and Society: 1939-1945.* London: Allen Lane, 1977.

Mrzkov, Daniela, and Vladimir Remes, eds., *The Russian War: 1941-1945.* London: Jonathan Cape, 1978.

O'Neill, Robert John, *The German Army and the Nazi Party: 1933-1939.* London: Cassell, 1966.

Pryce-Jones, David, *Paris in the Third Reich.* London: Collins, 1981.

Rauschning, Hermann, *Hitler Speaks.* London: Thornton Butterworth, 1939.

Read, Anthony, and David Fisher, *The Deadly Embrace: Hitler, Stalin and the Nazi-Soviet Pact, 1939-1941.* London: Michael Joseph, 1988.

Reynolds, Clark G., *The Fast Carriers: The Forging of an Air Navy.* New York: McGraw-Hill, 1968.

Rutherford, Ward, *Hitler's Propaganda Machine.* London: Bison Books, 1978.

Seaton, Albert, *The Fall of Fortress Europe: 1943-1945.* London: Batsford, 1981.

Shaw, John, and the Editors of Time-Life Books, *Red Army Resurgent* (World War II series). Alexandria, Virginia: Time-Life Books, 1979.

Shirer, William L., *The Rise and Fall of the Third Reich.* London: Secker & Warburg, 1960.

Simons, Gerald, and the Editors of

Time-Life Books, *Victory in Europe* (World War II series). Alexandria, Virginia: Time-Life Books, 1982.

Steinberg, Rafael, and the Editors of Time-Life Books:
Island Fighting (World War II series). Alexandria, Virginia: Time-Life Books, 1978.
Return to the Philippines (World War II series). Alexandria, Virginia: Time-Life Books, 1979.

Taylor, A. J. P., *The War Lords.* London: Hamish Hamilton, 1977.

Toland, John, *Hitler: The Pictorial Documentary of His Life.* London: Hutchinson, 1979.

Trevor-Roper, Hugh, *The Last Days of Hitler.* London: Macmillan, 1947.

Werth, Alexander, *Russia at War.* London: Hamish Hamilton, 1946.

Willmott, H. P., *June 1944.* Poole, Dorset, England: Blandford, 1984.

Wiskemann, Elizabeth, *Fascism in Italy: Its Development and Influence.* London: Macmillan, 1969.

Zhukov, Georgy K., *The Memoirs of Marshal Zhukov.* London: Jonathan Cape, 1971.

Zich, Arthur, and the Editors of Time-Life Books, *The Rising Sun* (World War II series). Alexandria, Virginia: Time-Life Books, 1977.

Ziemke, Earl F., and the Editors of Time-Life Books, *The Soviet Juggernaut* (World War II series). Alexandria, Virginia: Time-Life Books, 1980.

INDIA

Brown, J. M.:
Gandhi and Civil Disobedience: The Mahatma in Indian Politics, 1928-1934. Cambridge: Cambridge University Press, 1977.
Gandhi's Rise to Power: Indian Politics, 1915-1922. Cambridge: Cambridge University Press, 1972.
Modern India: The Origins of an Asian Democracy. Oxford: Oxford University Press, 1985.

Collins, Larry, and Dominique Lapierre, *Freedom at Midnight.* London: Collins, 1975.

Copley, Antony, *Gandhi: Against the Tide.* Oxford: Basil Blackwell, 1987.

Edwardes, Michael, *The Last Years of British India.* London: Cassell, 1963.

Fischer, Louis, *The Life of Mahatma Gandhi.* London: Grafton, 1982.

Golant, William, *The Long Afternoon: British India, 1601-1947.* London: Hamish Hamilton, 1975.

Gopal, Ram, *How India Struggled for Freedom.* Bombay: The Book Centre (Privately published), 1967.

Hardy, Peter, *The Muslims of British India.* Cambridge: Cambridge University Press, 1972.

Nehru, Jawaharlal, *The Discovery of India.* London: Meridian Books, 1946.

Pandey, Bishwa N., *The Break-up of British India.* London: Macmillan, 1969.

Payne, Robert, *The Life and Death of Mahatma Gandhi.* London: The Bodley Head, 1969.

Spear, Percival, *A History of India.* 2 vols. Baltimore, Maryland: Penguin, 1965.

CHINA

Fairbank, John King, *The Great Chinese Revolution: 1800-1985.* New York: Harper & Row, 1986.

Fairbank, John King, and Denis Twitchett, eds., *The Cambridge History of China,* Vols. 12 and 13. Cambridge: Cambridge University Press, 1983 and 1986.

Fitzgerald, Charles P., *The Birth of Communist China.* London: Penguin, 1964.

Griffith, Samuel, *The Chinese People's Liberation Army.* London: Weidenfeld & Nicolson, 1968.

Guillermaz, Jacques, *A History of the Chinese Communist Party: 1921-1949.* Transl. by Anne Destenay. London: Methuen, 1968.

Han Suyin, *The Morning Deluge.* London: Jonathan Cape, 1972.

Harrison, James Pinckney, *The Long March to Power.* London: Macmillan, 1973.

Liu, F. F., *A Military History of Modern China: 1924-1949.* Princeton, New Jersey: Princeton University Press, 1956.

O'Neill, Hugh B., *Companion to Chinese History.* New York: Facts on File, 1987.

Payne, Pierre Stephen Robert, *Mao Tse-tung.* New York: Weybright & Talley, 1969.

Rodzinski, Witold, *The Walled Kingdom.* London: Fontana Press, 1984.

Salisbury, Harrison E.:
China: 100 Years of Revolution. London: Andre Deutsch, 1983.

The Long March: The Untold Story. London: Macmillan, 1985.

Snow, Edgar:
Red Star over China. London: Victor Gollancz, 1968.
Scorched Earth. London: Victor Gollancz, 1941.

Wilson, Dick, *The Long March: 1935.* London: Hamish Hamilton, 1971.

GENERAL

The American Heritage History of the 20's and 30's, by the Editors of *American Heritage* magazine. New York: American Heritage, 1970.

Beales, H. L., and R. S. Lambert, *Memoirs of the Unemployed.* London: Victor Gollancz, 1934.

Bullock, Alan, ed., *The Twentieth Century.* London: Thames & Hudson, 1971.

Byers, Anthony, *Centenary of Service: A History of Electricity in the Home.* London: The Electricity Council, 1981.

Dimbleby, David, and David Reynolds, *An Ocean Apart.* London: Hodder & Stoughton, 1988.

Forty, Adrian, *Objects of Desire: Design and Society 1750-1980.* London: Thames & Hudson, 1986.

Galbraith, John Kenneth, *The Great Crash: 1929.* London: Hamish Hamilton, 1955.

Gordon, Bob, *Early Electrical Appliances.* Aylesbury, Buckinghamshire, England: Shire Publications, 1984.

Mitchell, Broadus, *Depression Decade: From New Era through New Deal, 1929-1941,* Vol. 9 of *The Economic History of the United States.* New York: Holt, Rinehart and Winston, 1966.

Sontag, Raymond J., *A Broken World: 1919-1939.* New York: Harper & Row, 1971.

Sparke, Penny, *Electrical Appliances.* London: Unwin Hyman, 1987.

Taylor, A. J. P., and J. M. Roberts, eds., *History of the 20th Century.* London: Purnell, 1968.

ACKNOWLEDGMENTS

The following materials have been reprinted with the kind permission of the publishers: Page 51: "Hitler always faces me . . .," in *Ciano's Diary, 1939-1943,* by G. Ciano, London: Heinemann, 1947. Page 152 and page 154: "Night marching is wonderful . . ." and "The army watched breathlessly . . .," in *The Great Road: The Life and Times of Chu Teh,* by Agnes Smedley, New York: Monthly Review Press, 1956.

The editors wish to thank the following individuals and institutions for their valuable assistance in the preparation of this volume:
England: Cambridge—Orlando Figes, Trinity College; Mike Kerrigan; David Reynolds, Christ's College. Cumbria—Carolyn Johnson, Holker Hall. Dorking, Surrey—Jon Kimche. London—Diana Condell and Ray Allen, Department of Exhibits and Firearms, Imperial War Museum; Ray Earwicker, Assistant Secretary, Trades Union Congress; Judith Heaton; Kate Poole; Penny Spark, Senior Lecturer, Department of Cultural History, Royal College of Art; Deborah Thompson; Gerald L. Wells, Curator, Vintage Wireless Museum; David Woodcock, Curator, Department of Engineering, Science Museum. Tonbridge, Kent—John Norris, Curator, and Cyril Botterill, Museum Assistant, Milne Museum (South Eastern Electricity Board). Wimborne, Dorset—John Batchelor.
France: Paris—François Avril, Curateur, Département des Manuscrits, Bibliothèque Nationale; Jeannette Chalufour, Archives Tallandier; Michel Fleury, Président de la IV section de l'École Pratique des Hautes Études; Serge-Antoine Legrand, Maisons-Alfort.
Japan: Tokyo—Mieko Ikeda.
U.S.A.: Washington—Larry Sherer.

PICTURE CREDITS

INDEX